RICHARD B. HUGHES
Pioneer Black Hiller

PIONEER YEARS

in the

BLACK HILLS

by

Richard B. Hughes

prospector, miner, cattleman, frontier printer,
surveyor-general, real estate developer,
and pioneer newspaper reporter

edited by

AGNES WRIGHT SPRING
State Historian of Colorado

Third Edition Published by

DAKOTA ALPHA PRESS
Rapid City, South Dakota
2002

COPYRIGHT, 2002, BY

WILLIAM LEWIS HUGHES, DOROTHY HUGHES JOHNSON,
STEVENS H. BURNS BAGWELL, AND HELEN PUTMAN HUGHES

All rights reserved, including the right to reproduce
This volume or parts thereof in any form except for
Short quotations in appropriate context.

**Printed in the USA
Grelind Printing Center**

Dakota Alpha Inc.
6118 Greenleaf Ct.
Rapid City, SD 57702-8845
email: DakAlpha@aol.com

ISBN 0-9673910-0-8

Contents

FOREWORD	v
FOREWORD TO THE SECOND EDITION	vii
FORWARD TO THE THIRD EDITION	x
INTRODUCTION	xi

PART I – TO THE HILLS

Bound for the Hills	1
A Change of Plans and Route	6
The Start	13
Old Red Cloud Agency	22
We Pull Out from the Train	27
The Cheyenne River – A Midnight Alarm	33
A Disobeyed Order	37
First View of Custer and Surroundings	42
From Custer to Deadwood	48
The End of Our Journey	57

PART II – LIFE IN THE BLACK HILLS COUNTRY

My First Prospecting Trip	63
Prospecting in Dry Gulches	73
Deadwood, Biggest Little Town on Earth	78
"Sam's Mine," The Great Homestake, and Stampedes of '76	91
Working and Hoping	103
Strenuous Times	114
A Provisional Government – "Judge" Farnham's Court	128
One of the First Reporters in the Hills	133

BLACK HILLS PIONEER YEARS

General Crook Comes to Deadwood, 1876	143
Hunting Expeditions	157
Camping Companions – End of Our Partnership	178
Father Comes to the Hills	189
Road Agents of the Early Years	199
Home from the Hills	209

PART III – RAPID CITY: HOME FOR MORE THAN FORTY YEARS

Becoming an Editor	221
Mining Swindles	235
Indian Trouble – Battle of Wounded Knee	246
A Pioneer Wins Honors	251

APPENDICES

A. Diary of Richard B. Hughes, 1876-1877, and two letters	265
B. Sam Tull	281
C. Sidney, Nebraska, to Harney's Peak, 1875	283
D. Montana Men in the Hills	285
E. Some Mines in the Hills	289
F. Ancestry of Richard Brown Hughes	291

INDEX 295

Illustrations

RICHARD B. HUGHES, PIONEER BLACK HILLER	Frontispiece
SAM TULL	11
CABIN OF RICHARD B. HUGHES ON SQUAW CREEK	12
CHIEF RED CLOUD	25
GEOLOGICAL MAP OF THE BLACK HILLS	26
Courtesy of South Dakota School of Mines and Technology	
"BUCKSKIN JOHNNIE" SPAULDING	71
SLUICING IN THE BLACK HILLS	72
Courtesy of Minnilusa Pioneer Association	
DEADWOOD IN THE EARLY DAYS	89
Courtesy of Minnilusa Pioneer Association	
LOOKOUT MINE NEAR ROCHFORD	90
JOHN BRENNAN	141
CAPTAIN C. V. GARDNER	142
MICHAEL J. HUGHES	197
MARY HITE HUGHES	197
TOM SWEENEY	198
Courtesy of Minnilusa Pioneer Association	
SCOTT DAVIS	208
ORIGINAL OWNERS OF HOLY TERROR MINE	208
MATTIE LEWIS HUGHES	216
WILLIAM LEWIS	216
LEWIS HALL	217
Courtesy of Minnilusa Pioneer Association	
RAPID CITY IN 1885	218
Courtesy of Minnilusa Pioneer Association	
RICHARD B. HUGHES AS AN EDITOR	233
SAM SCOTT	233

SIGN IN SOUTH DAKOTA FISH HATCHERY, RAPID CITY	234
CLEOPATRA MINE ON SQUAW CREEK	261
FAMILY OF R. B. HUGHES ABOUT 1902	262
PAGES FROM THE 1876 DIARY OF R. B. HUGHES	279

Foreword

Richard B. Hughes, who walked into the Black Hills from Nebraska in the spring of 1876, was described by Dakota's eminent historian, Annie D. Tallent, as "practically the first newspaper reporter in the Black Hills." That was an exact and well-earned title.

Although his original purpose in going to the Hills was to search for gold, young Hughes early sought work on Deadwood's *Weekly Pioneer,* in order to provide funds for his companions and himself to enable them to continue prospecting.

During his trip to the Black Hills and for many succeeding months, Richard B. Hughes kept a daily journal.* More than half a century later he used this as the chronological basis for his reminiscences which are published here. With fingers crippled by arthritis Mr. Hughes picked out his entire manuscript, letter by letter, on a typewriter, by using a tightly gripped pencil.

Though he thus laboriously put into typed form the story of his pioneering years in the Black Hills, these reminiscences bear the enthusiasm of youth and are told with detailed and accurate reporting.

His is not a rocket-like story of a "strike-it-rich" Hiller who scooped up gold nuggets from the waters of Whitewood or Deadwood Creeks. It is, however, a story rich in human experience. It portrays the everyday doings of a young man who joined the gold rush and who so loved the Black Hills that he stayed on and on to become a substantial part of the progress and culture of that land of pine-clad slopes.

I am grateful to Mr. and Mrs. Clarence W. Hughes and to Mrs. Richard L. Hughes for the privilege of editing the manuscript and for their assistance in bringing the manuscript to publication.

---

* *See* Appendix A.

My sincere appreciation is extended to the following who were especially helpful in obtaining data and photographs for me in my research: Miss Helen M. McFarland, Librarian, and Miss Alberta Pantle, now Acting Librarian, Kansas State Historical Society; Mayor T. B. Lewis and Mrs. Barklow, Burden, Kansas; the South Dakota School of Mines and Technology, Rapid City, SD; Miss Ina T. Aulls and her staff of the Western History Department, Denver Public Library; Miss Frances Shea, Librarian, and her staff, State Historical Society of Colorado; James C. Olson, Superintendent, Nebraska State Historical Society; Lucy Lytton Peterson, *Belle Fourche Bee,* Belle Fourche, SD; Lola Homsher and her staff, State Archives and Historical Department of Wyoming; T. B. Werner, Editor of *Gate City Guide,* Rapid City, SD; Boyd Von Seggern, Publisher, *West Point* (NE) *Republican;* Mrs. Orson Wilcox, and Mrs. Web Hill, Rapid City, SD; Archer T. Spring, Denver, CO; and the Editor, *Custer Chronicle,* Custer, SD.

Denver, Colorado, 1957

AGNES WRIGHT SPRING

Foreword to Second Edition

The first edition of this book was issued in 1957 by the Arthur H. Clark Company, then of Glendale, CA, as part of their Western Frontiersmen Series. This first printing was a limited edition, copies of which are now (1999) much in demand. The second edition has been issued in response to numerous requests to us, descendants of the author, that the book be reprinted.

In this second foreword, it seems appropriate to bring the reader up to date on several matters discussed in the original text. Today the Homestake mine operation is only a small fraction of its former size. When the manuscript was written, the price of gold was fixed by the government, but it is now traded on the world metals market as any other commodity. A number of countries produce gold with cheaper mining labor and from richer ore bodies than are available to the Homestake, and the future of the mine is considered to be in significant jeopardy. The parent company is apparently doing well with its worldwide mining operations. See the chapter, *"Sam's Mine." The Great Homestake, and Stampedes of '76*.

Deadwood is also a vastly different community than before. It's only industry of any significance is gambling. Practically every building in the downtown district is full of slot machines and many have poker and black jack tables to accommodate tourists and other outsiders. Some of the returns from the gambling are used for historic preservation, and increasing amounts are siphoned off to state taxes. There is also competition from gaming centers in other states as taxes on that industry become an increasingly popular source of state revenues. See the chapter, *Deadwood, Biggest Little Town on Earth*.

The author commented on the terrible pollution of Whitewood Creek in the chapter *End of Our Journey*. He said, "the tourist who looks upon it now (1927) after it has been polluted for nearly a half century by the refuse of the towns above and the many millions of tons of mill tailings it has carried down its course, cannot imagine it as it appeared on that May day of 1876." Today (1999) Whitewood creek is again a clear running stream supporting trout and other aquatic life. That is so because of a massive multi-year environmental restoration effort, much of which was paid for by the Homestake Mining Company, once its major source of pollution. While some environmental problems do remain in Whitewood creek, it should be considered one of the great success stories instigated by the growing environmental awareness in our country and the cooperative efforts of some responsible industries.

In the chapter, *From Custer to Deadwood,* mention was made of the little town of Pactola on Rapid Creek that was accessible by both road and railroad (The Rapid City, Black Hills, and Western railroad, locally known as the "Crouch Line"). It was noted that many persons had summer cabins there. The "Crouch Line" disappeared several decades ago, and all that area is covered by Pactola Lake, which serves as a primary water source for metropolitan Rapid City and also as a recreational lake for fishing and boating.

The location of Sheridan was also mentioned in the original text. At the time the author wrote the manuscript, Sheridan was a small community of a few families with a post office. That entire location is now under Sheridan Lake which was built as a recreational facility in the late 1930's.

Many other things have changed in the more than forty years that have intervened since the first edition. Writing styles are not the same and various authors in recent years have attempted to re-interpret the historical events of the early Black Hills years. The original manuscript of this book was written in the 1920's depicting events that had happened almost fifty years before. Now, a century and a quarter after those events, it is refreshing to review the writing of a person who lived in close proximity at the time of the battle of the Little Big Horn, the Wounded Knee Massacre, the gold rush in the Black Hills and other events, and who personally knew

FOREWORD TO THE SECOND EDITION ix

many of the major players on the stage at the time. The author described the earlier years in the history of western Dakota Territory and the excitement that accompanied them as both an observer and a participant. He then lived long enough to see the consequences of those early years, and he described both.

The book would never have appeared at all had not the original manuscript, after sitting on a shelf for twenty six years after the author's death, been discovered, magnificently edited, and arranged for publication by Mrs. Agnes Wright Spring, then the state historian for both the states of Colorado and Wyoming. Although Mrs. Spring has been deceased for some years, it must be remembered that she is the one that made it possible for either a first or second edition to exist. She did extensive research (as well as editing) in the 1950's to validate events as can be seen by the footnotes that were created by both her and by the author.

In this second edition, a very few words have been changed to reflect contemporary thought and language interpretation. In the original manuscript, written early in the 20th century, a number of words and some spelling and punctuation conventions were used which are uncommon today (1999). For the most part, those features were left unchanged, but the reader should know they exist. Where copies of some original pictures were unavailable, others of the same era and closely related subjects were substituted. A few new pictures have been added that have turned up in the family archives over the decades or were graciously provided by Robert Preszler, executive director of the Minnilusa Historical Association and curator of the Minnilusa Pioneer section of the wonderful Journey Museum in Rapid City, SD. Other than these small changes, this second edition is a faithful word for word reproduction of the original.

William Lewis Hughes, grandson of the author
Stella Platt Hughes, granddaughter-in-law of the author

Foreword to Third Edition

Only a few hundred copies of the second edition were printed because it was believed that it would be primarily a book of local interest to those few interested in the history of the Black Hills. Much to our surprise, those copies sold out in a very short time, and others have requested that it be reprinted.

Additionally, since the second edition appeared a few relevant events have occurred that may be of interest. The most significant event is that the Homestake Mine, once the world's largest gold mine, and reported to be in jeopardy in the forward to the second edition, has now been permanently closed after a century and a quarter of operation. Since then the parent company, the Homestake Mining Company, has been sold to a Canadian firm and is no longer in existence.

We reported in the second edition that consistent with contemporary social awareness, the gulch once called "Nigger Gulch," was renamed "Negro Gulch." Since that time, it has again been officially renamed "Medicine Gulch," undoubtedly because it runs along the base of a famous landmark in the Black Hills called Medicine Mountain.

Further, the Black Hills historian, Watson Parker, has pointed out that the picture entitled "Lookout Mine" was not really that mine in either the first or second editions. The picture in this edition is indeed the real Lookout Mine.

The printing of this third edition also allowed us to correct a number of typographical and printing software errors that appeared in the second edition. The help of Jan Rathbun in finding many of these errors is gratefully acknowledged.

Wm. L. Hughes, grandson of the author
Stella P. Hughes, granddaughter-in-law of the author

Introduction

In southwestern South Dakota and eastern Wyoming, between the north and south forks of the Cheyenne River, lie the Black Hills – the Pahasapa of the Sioux, once their sacred ground – teeming with bighorn sheep, bear, and elk. The foothills, the feeding grounds of lordly buffalo and graceful antelope, are now the home of the Paleface whose dairy cattle graze where Red Cloud and his warriors celebrated the Sun Dance and taught their youths the lore of the pony and the bow. Where Crazy Horse and his Oglalas cut their tepee poles, is heard the whine of the sawmill or the hum of the tourist's motor along graveled highways; and the roar of the Homestake stamps shakes the hills that echoed to the war whoop.

Black Hills they are called, and black they seem from the Cheyenne River; black they still are to the traveler crossing the fertile plateaus to reach the foothills, but once within the foothills the color changes and the gorgeous beauty becomes apparent. The slow rivers, now changed to mountain torrents, are thickly lined with quaking asp and birch, with pine and spruce and cedar. The hillsides are carpeted with kinnikinic and juniper and, in summertime, with a bewildering variety of multicolored flowers; while luxuriant grass furnishes the finest of summer pastures. The greatest beauty of the Hills is in this verdure and in the great rock exposures showing through it; first, sandstone in variegated colors; then the shales and the limerock walls and ridges; then the majesty of the granite such as crowns Harney's Peak, which marks the highest point reached after leaving the Atlantic seaboard. Everywhere are found little parks and meadows nestling at the foot of lofty peaks, surrounded by mighty forests and watered by beautiful mountain streams – ideal sites for the prosperous farms now everywhere in evidence.

These are the Black Hills of mystery and tradition. "Here," said the Red Man, "lived the Manitou, the sudden thunder storms, the manifestation of this awful presence." Captain Bonneville was shown the black outlines of these mountains by friendly Indians and warned of the terrible spirits as well as the hostile Blackfeet, Crows, and Sioux. Even the early hardy trappers respected the grim superstition and passed them by.

Long ago Father DeSmet was shown gold by the Indians, who pointed to the south where the faint outlines of the Hills appeared and whispered "Pahasapa." That great missionary looked into the future and warned his red brothers to conceal the presence of the gold in their sacred grounds. Perhaps he foresaw the day when Custer's men would wash the yellow sand from the bed of French Creek and take back to civilization the message that would break the spell of mystery and secrecy, the message that would ring up the curtain upon the last great drama of the American frontier.

At first a hardy few heard the call, then dozens, then hundreds; the gray-haired pioneers of many such frontiers, the beardless youth, and the veteran fresh from the fields of the Civil War, all heard and harkened. All endured hardship, some perished by the way, a few turned back. Some prospered, others never attained the Eldorado of their dreams; but into the hearts of many came a love surpassing the love of woman, a love for the beautiful Black Hills. These men stayed and their affection grew with the years. Many have crossed the Great Divide and their dust mingles with that of the Hills. A few remain and their love is even greater than before, as if joined and strengthened by those who have passed beyond.

It is to these men, the true Black Hills Pioneers, we who enjoy their heritage give our respect and affection.

RICHARD L. HUGHES*

INTRODUCTION

When I hear poets sing
Of the beauties of spring
In their own belov'd distant climes,
Sure it's then my heart fills
As I picture the Hills
With the wind sighing soft through its pines.

Burns may sing of the Ayr,
Moore of Erin the Fair,
Kipling writes of his sweet Mandalay;
But to me they bring dreams
Of the rush of the streams
Through the pines on a morning in May.

For the words that they pen
Are the souls of the men
The spot nearest their hearts in the lines;
But where e'er it may be,
It's the Black Hills to me,
Paha-Sapa o' whispering pines.

CLARENCE W. HUGHES [*]

---

[*] Sons of the author.

Part I

To The Hills

Bound for the Hills

On my twentieth birthday, being the fourteenth of April 1876, I completed the teaching of a term of school in a country district.[1] Previous to this I had worked for three years at the printer's trade on the *West Point* (Nebraska) *Republican*. On the seventeenth, I left West Point, bound for the Black Hills, accompanied by William Van Fleet.[2] We expected to be joined at the first station south[3] on the Fremont, Elkhorn & Missouri Valley Railroad by M. D. Rochford,[4] a boyhood friend of my own age.

The winter had seemed a long one, and my thoughts had been busy with the contemplated great adventure, rather than the duties of a pedagogue, so that I fear even the exceedingly meagre salary paid a country school teacher at that time in Nebraska was fully commensurate with my services in the cause of education. On the last day of school I was fortunate enough to find a purchaser for the pony and saddle that had carried me back and forth,[5] thus adding to my savings sufficiently to guarantee payment for necessary supplies of clothing, bedding and provisions, and transportation to our objective point – the last named being by far the most expensive item.

Some time previous I had purchased a "needle gun," as the remodeled Springfield used by the military was generally known, though the term also was applied to some other arms using a similar "firing pin." A friend contributed an old style

---

[1] Near West Point, Nebraska.
[2] William Van Fleet prospected with the party the entire year.
[3] Scribner, Nebraska.
[4] M. D. Rochford was a partner of Richard Hughes during their early mining days. In May 1878, a meeting was held in a cabin built by Richard's father, M. J. Hughes, and a town was organized called Rochford.
[5] According to his Diary, April 1, 1876, he received $40.00 in cash for his pony. *See* Appendix A.

Colt's cap and ball revolver,[6] which was gratefully received and highly prized, though experience with it later proved it somewhat unreliable, as it developed a tendency to fire the entire battery of six shots at once. This was due to the fact that it was loaded with buckshot of more or less irregular shape, which did not completely fill the chambers and thus allowed the fire from a discharge to reach around the lead to the powder. Within a short time the old Colt was retired from service, as of more value as a relic than as an arm of offense or protection.

The report broadcast of the discovery of gold in the Black Hills by the Custer military expedition in 1874 had created great interest throughout the country generally, but more particularly in the states contiguous; and during the year 1875 large numbers of men prepared to start for the district. The party headed by Russell and Gordon from Sioux City had penetrated the Hills as far as French Creek from the south,[7] and spent the winter there with little discomfort and no trouble from Indians. About the time, however, that spring opened, this party was forcibly removed by the military, and orders were issued from Washington[8] forbidding any further trespass by whites on the great Sioux reservation, of which the Hills formed a part. Disregarding this inhibition, a second party, headed by John Gordon, started from Sioux City but was overtaken by the soldiers at a point in Nebraska near the location of the present town of Gordon, and the entire outfit of wagons and equipment destroyed. This drastic treatment convinced the

---

[6] The first and most famous revolver on the western frontier was the Colt. Though invented in the early 1830's, it did not come into prominent use in the West for a decade or so. It was a cap-and-ball weapon, this being before the invention of the metallic cartridge. - Chauncey Thomas, "Frontier Firearms," *The Colorado Magazine*, vol. VII, May, 1930, No. 3, p. 103.

[7] The Gordon party reached French Creek December 23, 1874. There were twenty-six men, a woman and a boy in the party.

[8] From August through the middle of November, 1875, Captain Edwin Pollock and his men of the Second and Third U.S. Cavalry, "scoured the Hills for gold hunters, made a number of arrests, and performed their assigned duties in a creditable manner. In November the troops went into winter quarters at Fort Laramie." Agnes W. Spring, *Cheyenne and Black Hills Stage and Express Routes* (Glendale, CA, The Arthur H. Clark Co., 1949), 70.

great majority that the War Department was in earnest in the determination to prevent any violation of the treaty with the Indians, and for the time there was no general movement toward the new gold field. A few adventurous spirits, however, made their way into the Hills, dodging the soldiers and also the Indians, who by this time were becoming restive and displaying hostility.[9]

When in December of 1875, a party[10] reached as far north as Deadwood Gulch and made a discovery of rich diggings, it was certain that a great stampede would start with the opening of spring, regardless of governmental orders. Realizing that the entire regular army would be insufficient to patrol the district so as to prevent trespass, the attempt to do so practically was abandoned. It was tacitly understood that if "sooners" chose to take their chances with the Sioux they at least were not likely to be molested by the soldiers. After the early spring of 1876 a few demonstrations were made by the military, but they were of the most perfunctory character and were generally so regarded.

Mike Rochford was one of those who had started to the Hills in 1875 and had been turned back by the soldiers. He had then made his way to fort Laramie and on to Cheyenne, where he cached his blanket roll and some mining tools, intending to return for them when conditions for entering the Hills should improve. He spent the winter at home in Nebraska, during which time we had several meetings and agreed to go together as soon as my term of teaching school should expire. Of eight or ten young men who had planned to go with us, Van Fleet

---

[9] By conservative estimate, at least six hundred to eight hundred men had evaded the authorities and were engaged in prospecting and mining in the Hills by July (1875) . . . and when, on July 17, Professor Jenney sent word to Cheyenne that he had "discovered gold in paying quantities in gravelbars on both Spring and Rapid Creeks" . . . the citizens of the town hilariously congratulated themselves upon the good word. *Ibid.*, 66-67.

[10] According to Annie D. Tallent, *The Black Hills, or Last Hunting Ground of the Dakotahs* (St. Louis, Nixon-Jones Pub. Co., 1899), 176-77, the following made first locations in the famous Deadwood Gulch: William Lardner, Alfred Gay, William Gay, Dan Murkle, Ed. McKay, J. B. Pearson, James Hicks, Joe Englesby, _____ Haggard.

was the only one to board the train with me on the morning of April seventeenth.

At the little town of Scribner (Nebraska), Rochford joined us according to agreement. We intended to procure immigrant tickets at Fremont, over the Union Pacific railroad to Cheyenne, where we could leave the railroad and take the wagon trail northward. But upon arriving at Fremont, we found that immigrant tickets could only be procured at terminal points. It was necessary for one of our party to go to Omaha[11] for that purpose.

Leaving my partners at Fremont, I went east to Omaha, secured the necessary tickets and boarded the westbound Union Pacific train the same evening. When the train reached Fremont about ten o'clock that night, I was rejoined by my companions and we felt that we were fairly started on our journey.

As we passed up the valley of the Platte through the town of Columbus, I recalled how in the spring of 1867 – the year of Nebraska's admission to statehood – I had had my first experience in a truly western settlement. Then I was a boy of eleven years and, with my mother and sisters, had come from Illinois to join my father and brother, who had preceded us by a few months – intent on making a new home.[12]

---

[11] The following advertisement of the Union Pacific Railroad appeared in Robert E. Strahorn, *The Hand-Book of Wyoming and Guide to the Black Hills and Big Horn Regions* (Cheyenne, 1877), 270:

SPECIAL NOTICE TO GOLD SEEKERS

In addition to the advantages of quick time and short and comfortable stage journeys via the Union Pacific Route, the following LOW RATES of fare and arrangements for ticketing have been made for your accommodation:
Chicago to Custer City   1st Class $39.00
                          2nd Class $33.00
                          3rd Class $28.00
... Holders of tickets to Sidney, Cheyenne, etc., can exchange them for through tickets to any point in the Black Hills at the Omaha depot.

[12] In June 1867, I walked with my father, an uncle, and my brother directly north from Columbus, a distance of forty miles to the Elkhorn River . . . where Norfolk (Nebraska) is now located. . . Our trip to the Elkhorn had been induced by the representations of the two traders and trappers named "Gassy" Jones and "Ponca" George St. Clair, who had a small store at the junction of the two branches of the

BOUND FOR THE HILLS 5

The immigrant trains on the Union Pacific were not noted for speed, nor was the country traversed interesting to us now. Had our minds not been busy with the possibilities of the near future, we might have found the journey monotonous. With thoughts of the new experiences awaiting us, and with plans for the future, our minds were occupied so that the time did not seem to pass slowly. As the train made its way westward almost every station added a few men bound for the Hills. It was interesting to note the variety of their equipment. Some were well armed and had exercised good judgment in the selection of the supplies for the transportation of which they would have to pay a stiff price. Others, however, lacking experience in camp life, had omitted from their packs many necessary articles and had included as many unnecessary ones. In making our selections the experience of Rochford, in camping, was of great value.

As the town of North Platte was passed I recalled the saying of a witty Irishman regarding this town when it was the temporary terminus of the railroad. It probably was true that North Platte was no worse than other towns on the line, as each in turn became the stopping place of many hard characters; but it certainly was true that the place acquired a most unenviable notoriety. Questioned by an immigrant as to the character of the town, the Irishman replied, "North Platte, is it? Well, Sir, I would say that North Platte is a place where people suffer for a time before going to hell."[13]

---

stream, where they bought hides and furs from the Indians, which they packed on ponies to market in Omaha, distant 120 miles. – [HUGHES].

[13] All this now belongs to the distant past, and today North Platte and all other settlements that underwent the lurid experiences of the Union Pacific extension lack nothing of the refining influences that make life in the average American town desirable. – [HUGHES].

A Change of Plans and Route

On the morning of the second day out from Fremont we reached Sidney. Learning that the train would remain there for a considerable time, we went to call upon some acquaintances in the town. In conversation with them we learned that Sidney had come to rival Cheyenne as a point of departure from the railroad for the new gold field. We were told of various advantages, real or imaginary, that the Sidney route possessed over that from Cheyenne.

Our acquaintances stated that the Sidney road was better watered and the land traversed would furnish better and more abundant forage for teams. It was claimed that the grades were easier, the distance no greater, and, as a most important consideration, it was less liable to Indian attacks. Stories of Indian depredations in the dreaded Red Canyon on the Cheyenne road were numerous, and some of them were true.[14]

Had Cheyenne been the place of narration, no doubt stories equally gruesome, of the perils of Buffalo Gap on the Sidney route, would have been enlarged upon by the narrator. And in those, too, there would have been some truth. Probably, though, to every three tragedies reported only one actually occurred. While there were many deplorable tragedies, the number was greatly exaggerated in the reports broadcast, and they were not a tithe in comparison with those that must have resulted had there been a general Indian uprising. Indeed, under the circumstances existing – the Indians having all the right on their side, and the white invaders not even a shadow of right –

---

[14] Early in April 1876, Mr. and Mrs. Charles Metz of Laramie City, Wyoming, who had been in Custer City engaged in the bakery business, and who were returning home with a small party, were murdered at Red Canyon. Rachel Briggs, a colored woman with them, also was killed. Two of the three men who were wounded died. Only one survived. "Although it was generally accepted that Indians had killed the Metz family, there was some evidence that the crime might have been committed by Persimmon Bill and his gang of renegades." Agnes W. Spring, *op.cit.*, p. 136.

A CHANGE OF PLANS

it is a source of wonder not that so many Black Hillers were killed, as that the number was not infinitely greater. Where here and there a lone prospector or traveler was cut off, it was the act of turbulent young warriors acting in small parties, who could not be held in check by their chiefs or older members of the tribe. Too much credit cannot be given to the restraining influence upon the young men of such noted peace chiefs as Spotted Tail, Old-Man-Afraid-of-His-Horses, Young-Man-Afraid-of-His-Horses, and others of less note.

After some consultation while the train remained at Sidney we determined to leave the railroad at that point for the north, instead of going on to Cheyenne as first intended. Accordingly we unloaded our baggage. When the train pulled out, Rochford went on to Cheyenne to get the tools and bed roll which he had left there the previous fall, while Van Fleet and I awaited his return in Sidney.

We purchased materials for a complete camp and prospecting outfit, in accordance with a list that Rochford had prepared. We also were on the lookout for any wagon train bound for the Hills, in order to obtain transportation for our freight.

As freight rates to the north were certain to be high, we felt that it was important that our outfit, while including everything absolutely necessary, should not be made too heavy or bulky by anything that could be dispensed with without inconvenience. First in importance came the provisions, consisting of flour, bacon, beans, coffee, baking powder, soda, sugar, salt, pepper, and a little of several varieties of dried fruit. These were considered essential. In camp equipment, necessary articles were a Dutch oven for baking bread and roasting game, a galvanized water pail, a sheet iron camp kettle of medium size for cooking or for heating water for washing clothes, a frying pan or two, tin plates, tin cups, knives, forks and spoons, and a grub box, in which the lighter articles could be packed. The grub box was capable of holding prepared food for a day or two's supply. The lid of this box served admirably all the purposes of a table.

Fixed ammunition[15] for our guns and powder, lead, primers and a complete reloading outfit for reloading shells were important, as also were matches. Our purchases in Sidney contained all of the above named articles. As stated previously, I had bought a needle gun before leaving home; Van Fleet had a Spencer carbine, and later, on the road a short distance north of Sidney, Rochford purchased a second needle gun from a returning stampeder.

Our bedding, which we had brought from home, embraced a pair of blankets for each man and a tarpaulin to spread on the ground. This tarpaulin was sufficiently large to cover the bed completely and to confine the bedding in a neat and compact roll when traveling. While desirable, a tent was not considered an absolute necessity, so we omitted it from our outfit because of its weight and bulk.

After having purchased our supplies, and while awaiting our partner's return from Cheyenne, I accepted an invitation from the gentleman at whose house Van Fleet and I were staying to take a ride with him – a distance of twenty-five miles down the Pole Creek valley to a ranch – in search of a stray horse. On our way, at a little station known as Lodge Pole – which consisted mainly of a section house and other accommodations for a crew of section hands – I examined some rifle pits that had been made recently as a protection against Indians. Although there was no general Indian uprising at this time, small bands of Sioux from the northern reservations occasionally made forays as far south as the Union Pacific railroad, or even farther; the usual object being to steal horses from the Pawnees or other tribes. Occasionally on such excursions they had displayed indifference as to the actual ownership of the stock taken, and slight collisions with the whites had occurred. The many disquieting reports brought in by returning stampeders of Indian atrocities on the various trails to the Hills had created, on the part of exposed settlers, apprehensions of more serious trouble. As a precautionary measure

---

[15] Cartridge and shells for breechloaders as distinguished from loose ammunition, the latter being powder and shot. – [HUGHES].

A CHANGE OF PLANS

the people of Lodge Pole had prepared the pits mentioned. These pits were six feet deep and were covered with railroad iron.

After spending the night at our ranch destination, we started on our return to Sidney. Toward the close of the afternoon, when we were about five miles from Sidney, we saw an outfit of three canvas-covered wagons pull out of the road into a bend of Lodge Pole Creek, evidently with the intention of going into camp. Rightly surmising that they were bound for the Hills, we drove over to them, and I accosted one of the men who stepped out to meet us.

MEETING WITH SAM TULL

The party was composed of twelve or fourteen men from Cowley County, Kansas, and seemed to be well-equipped. The wagons were new and were hauled by three splendid teams of mules. The men, so far as I could judge from my brief observation, were fine, upstanding fellows, a majority under thirty-five years of age, though there were several of more mature years.

The man who came out to meet us was Sam Tull,[16] who acted as spokesman of the party, and who had been made captain by common consent. For this position he was well qualified. He was a man of medium height, rather slender, but wiry and active. He had a face that would recommend him anywhere, lighted by a pair of the keenest and yet kindliest gray eyes I ever have seen.

---

[16] *The 1850 Federal Census of Indiana.* Shelby County. Sugar Creek Township, p. 473, shows Samuel Tull, 15, birthplace, Indiana. According to the *History of Shelby County, Indiana,* (Chicago, Brant & Fuller, 1887), 627, Samuel Tull was the seventh in a family of ten children – eight sons and two daughters, "born to Joseph and Hester A. (Pilchard) Tull, both natives of Maryland, of English descent . . . his parents came to Shelby County, and located upon a 160-acre tract of wood land, which the father had entered in Sugar Creek Township . . ."

Tull, Samuel, Tisdale P.O., 2nd Lieut., Company H, 16th Regiment, Indiana Infantry. *Enrollment of Soldiers for the State of Kansas – Cowley County,* 1883. – Kansas State Historical Society, Topeka.

Samuel Tull died March 14, 1919, in Burden, Kansas, *See* Appendix B.

Other members of the Kansas party mentioned later by the author were: Bill Kelley, Jim Sheppard, Jim Moody and John Stevens.

I asked if his party was bound for the gold field, to which he answered in the affirmative. I then told him that I had two partners in Sidney who, with myself, desired to make the trip, and asked if it might be possible to secure transportation for our freight in the wagons of his party.

As I spoke he observed me narrowly, and it did not require an expert mind reader to judge from the half smile on his face and the twinkle of his eyes that he did not hail with enthusiasm the prospect of my joining his party. My four years of indoor occupation had not tended to give me a rugged appearance. It was not strange that if additions to the party were to be made, those of more apparent physical strength should be preferred. Tull was noncommittal, merely saying that we would meet again in Sidney and consider what would be done. With this we drove away.

Frequently in after years, Tull would recall our first meeting and would tell how he had remarked to his partners, "If that young fellow ever reaches the Black Hills he'll not stay very long."

On our arrival at Sidney, we found that Rochford had returned from Cheyenne with his bedding and mining tools. The latter consisted of the regulation prospector's outfit of pick, shovel, and gold pan. These were absolute requirements of the prospector for placers. The quartz prospector needed in addition to these, a mortar and pestle.

On the forenoon of the day following, Tull and his companions pulled into Sidney. Accompanied by my two partners I visited their camp, to learn their decision in the matter of hauling our freight.

After some questions Tull, who acted as spokesman, evidently concluded that we could be depended upon to go to the end of the trail and we were duly accepted as members of the party. In making his decision Tull was influenced to some extent by an examination of our equipment, which convinced him that it had been selected with discretion and a knowledge of what was really important.

SAM TULL

R. B. HUGHES' CABIN ON SQUAW CREEK

The Start

Camped in various places in and about Sidney were small parties all intent upon the same destination – the Black Hills. Meetings of representatives of all of these were held, plans were discussed and a day was decided upon for the start. The date fixed was Monday, April twenty-fourth.

At the appointed time, the teams were hitched and the wagons drawn up in a line. A count was made which disclosed thirty-four men and one woman, a Mrs. Burns, who had accompanied her husband from southwestern Kansas.

The train made a moderate drive the first day, having made a late start. The road was good, and traversed a sparsely grassed section. To many of us it seemed incomprehensible that the light forage could possibly sustain the life of stock in winter, but we were assured by those who had spent some time on the cattle ranges that this "buffalo grass," which cured on the ground with its nutritive qualities preserved, would do this.

Our first camp was made at Water Holes,[17] twelve miles north from Sidney. Here Van Fleet and I were initiated into the art and science of camp cooking, which we took up readily under the coaching of our more experienced partner.

Here we met the first backwash of the stampede. This was a train of ten wagons and fifty men that had made a forced march from the Hills. Not a member of the party had spent a week in the district, and not one had a good word to say for it. There was little or no gold, but vast numbers of Indians, according to their story. They reported many atrocities committed on the Red Canyon and Buffalo Gap trails, and as for the parties that had started north from Custer to the reported new diggings, since they never had been heard from, it was a fair presumption that they had been annihilated. That the returning

---

[17] *See* Appendix C.

pilgrims were overjoyed to find themselves so near to the edge of civilization was made evident by the lusty cheer in which all joined when the sound of a locomotive whistle at the Sidney station reached their ears.

At this camp we purchased another needle gun from a young man named Potts – whose home was in Columbus, Nebraska. To our questions he replied that, while little gold actually had been taken out, favorable reports had reached Custer from various gulches prospected; that fear of Indians had greatly retarded the work of exploration; and that the presence of Indians in considerable numbers constituted a real menace. He added though, "I believe a strong outfit may go through without great danger and that yours should be able to reach Custer all right. If you do, you will find that as many people are leaving the country as are entering. None of the men with me in this train went farther north than Custer. If you make it all right that may not satisfy you, and you may do as I did; go as far north as Hill City and see it all."[18]

At this first camp, after supper had been eaten, a meeting was called for the purpose of electing a captain. In the meantime our numbers had been increased to fifty, by the arrival of three more wagons, which had reached Sidney shortly after our departure, and had hurried on to overtake us. The election was by ballot and resulted in the choice of Burns. We would have preferred Tull for the position, but it was evident some canvassing had been done for Burns before the train pulled out from the railroad. Though close, the result was decisive and there was nothing to urge against Burns' eligibility, the choice was made unanimous.

The newly elected captain made a brief talk, thanking the men for the honor conferred upon him, and asking the assistance and support of all in enforcing compliance with the rules which it would be necessary to make for the camp and road. He then asked that a representative of each wagon prepare a

---

[18] As Hill City is distant from Custer about fifteen miles, young Mr. Potts, intelligent printer though he was, did not have a very comprehensive idea of the Black Hills. – [HUGHES].

THE START

list of names of all in his mess, before going into camp, in order that from the list guards might be chosen for duty in regular order. He stated that until the North Platte River should be crossed, two or three days ahead, none other than stock guards would be considered necessary. On reaching the north bank of the river we would be at the entrance of the Indian country; thereafter a strong camp guard would be placed every night. With this we settled down to our first night of camp life.

Next morning the wagons fell into line for a reasonably early start, and by noon of this second day the train was pretty well adjusted to the pace of the slowest teams. This, of course, was necessary if the train was not to string out to too great length. Toward noon we reached the top of the divide overlooking Greenwood Valley from the south. From this point we could see, to the north, the castle-like Court House Buttes, and to the west towered aloft Chimney Rock.[19]

So pure and clear was the air that those conspicuous objects seemed to loom up in the immediate foreground. Various were the surmises as to our actual distance from them – encouraged by a member of the party familiar with the district. The highest estimate of the distance to Court House Buttes was a mile and a half, while one old Missourian offered to bet a horse that his rifle would throw a bullet that far and not half try. We learned a lesson as to the illusions of distance in this clear atmosphere when, after camping on Greenwood Creek for dinner, we drove the entire afternoon toward the buttes, and at dusk went into camp for the night, not yet within two miles of their base.

At this camp the train captain issued a few orders to be observed on the trail and in camp, and made assignments of guards from the various messes, to go into effect after crossing the North Platte River.

On the evening of the next day, April twenty-sixth, we reached the North Platte, which we found to be at flood stage. A crossing would be impossible until the water should subside. Here we were joined by several other teams and twelve

---

[19] Court House Buttes and Chimney Rock were two of the outstanding landmarks of the old Oregon Trail.

men, who had been waiting for reinforcements before attempting to cross into what they considered the beginning of the Indian country. Now they, like ourselves, were held back from crossing by the flood.

In this new group were three men with whom we later were closely associated. They were from the buffalo range in southwestern Nebraska and Kansas, where they had spent several years hunting buffalo and freighting them to market. The hunter of the party was John Spaulding,[20] the most expert rifleman I ever have met. His companions were Bill Tomlins, usually known as "Spike," because he drove a spike[21] team of two horses and a mule; and Jesse Hall. Hall and Tomlins had acted as skinners and freighters for Spaulding on the Range.

---

[20] In an article written in later years for the Belle Fourche (South Dakota) Civic League, J. T. Spaulding said:
March 12, 1976: W. C. Tomlins (Buffalo Bill of the Black Hills), Jesse Hall and myself joined forces and left the buffalo range for the Black Hills with a supply of grub to last us a year in case the gold excitement proved to be a hoax—as most everyone predicted.
March 21: Pulled to old Fort Sedgwick.
March 22: We laid over and jerked the meat of several antelope we had killed along the way.
March 27: We came to North Platte. "Dick" Hughes and his outfit were camped waiting for the wind to go down so they could ford the river. (He was *then* only a boy and it was on this trip that we formed a lifelong friendship. R. B. Hughes became one of the leading journalists of the West.)
A big wagon train was camped on the other side and when the wind went down in the evening they came with teams and helped us across. They were from Wichita, Kan., and had learned from pony express riders that some buffalo hunters were coming behind. None of them had ever had experience with hostile Indians and they concluded to lay over for us and give their stock a couple days rest. I was engaged to act as scout and guide for the train.
There were 65 men with the usual percentage of "Johns" and to designate me from the others they called me "Buckskin Johnnie" or just "Buckskin," as I was dressed in buckskin from my wolfskin cap to the soles of my feet and the name clung to me as long as I remained in the Black Hills. From boyhood I had killed deer and elk, tanned the skins and made my own clothing. My moccasins I made from the heaviest part of the elk hide. – *Belle Fourche Bee*, Belle Fourche, SD, February 10, 1955.
Note: It is evident from the rest of Mr. Spaulding's account of the trip into the Hills and from Mr. Hughes' diary that the month was April instead of March. *See* footnote page 69.

[21] Hitched in tandem style; one in front of the other in single file.

THE START

Camped on the bank of the river we found Pratt & Ferris'[22] Bull train, comprised of many teams of seven yokes each and a lead and trail wagon to each team. This train, too, was waiting – and had been for two days – for the water to reach a stage when it would be possible to make a ford. We went into camp on the south bank, hoping that by the next morning or some time the next day the water would have receded sufficiently to allow us to cross; but in this we were disappointed. When morning came the water was still high, though going down slowly; and we agreed that if it continued to recede, the attempt would be made on the following day.

The big freight outfit, which was loaded with flour for the Red Cloud Indian agency, however, was preparing to attempt the crossing. At about ten o'clock in the forenoon the first team went down the bank into the river. This team was made up of three ordinary teams of seven yoke each – twenty-one yoke in all. The trail wagon had been unhitched from the lead to make the test of the ford with a comparatively light load, though a part of the flour from the trail wagon had been piled on top of another. When the wagon struck the bottom with a bump, a half dozen or more sacks of flour rolled off into the stream. To a tenderfoot it seemed certain that this flour must be ruined; but not so. Here I learned that flour is not easily spoiled by immersion in water when confined in a tight sack. Comparatively little of it will be damaged unless it remains in the water for a considerable time. The flour next to the sack, to the thickness perhaps of a half-inch, will be penetrated by the water and a paste will be formed that protects the bulk of the sack's contents. Indeed, I have seen good bread made from flour mixed and kneaded in the sack itself when no pan was available. This was accomplished by setting the sack of flour upright and making a bowl-shaped depression in the flour with the hands.[23] Into this flour to be used was placed salt and bak-

---

[22] Pratt & Ferris were contract freighters transporting Indian goods for the government. Later they were owners of extensive livestock interests with Col. J. G. Pratt as manager.

[23] This method of making bread or biscuits was well known to early westerners; also to so-called "sourdough" miners.

ing powder; water was added, and the whole quickly mixed. An expert camper, used to meeting emergencies and accomplishing results with few tools and appliances, would waste very little flour in this process.

The crossing of the river by the big train was a very interesting sight to the spectators upon the bank; one not soon to be forgotten. Into the water on either side of the long team went a half dozen men. When the sacks of flour rolled into the river they were caught, thrown on top of the load, and the men proceeded with their work. They strung the team out, headed for the opposite shore and, armed with their long bull whips, kept the wagon moving to the accompaniment of the pistol-shot-like sound of the "poppers"[24] and such artistic profanity as only the old-time bullwhacker was capable of giving voice. While a less number of cattle would have hauled double the load ordinarily, the fact that at places in the stream there was quicksand bottom made it important that a team of length as well as strength should be used, to the end that at least a number of the animals should at all times have good footing. This insured the continuous movement necessary, because if the wagon stopped it soon would sink in the quicksand to the hubs. The first wagon having made the crossing successfully, and the ford having thus been tested, the others followed more rapidly; by night the big train was safely camped on the north bank.

On the morning of the twenty-eighth, the water having continued to fall, we determined to cross. The passage was effected with no great trouble, by doubling teams. The passengers were allowed to ride across with their baggage; this was the only lift of the kind on the entire journey, every mile of which was made on foot – some of the men walking ahead, some behind, and others alongside of the wagons.

After making the crossing we prepared and ate a late dinner; the train again headed out for the north, reaching Red Willow, where we camped for the night. Here the guards were

---

[24] Whip lashes made of strips of buckskin usually. When the driver "cracked" the whip, the "popper" made a loud report like a gun going off.

THE START

posted, as it was considered that we were now far enough north to warrant precautions against Indian raids on camp or stock.

On the twenty-ninth we camped for dinner at Snake Creek; when we left we filled our casks with water, as we were told we would reach no other stream until the next day. This statement proved to be correct, and we were compelled to make our first dry camp that night. As there was no timber at hand, here we first resorted to "buffalo chips" for fuel to prepare supper. Although at this time no buffalo were on this part of the range, ample evidence showed that they had been there in large numbers at a day not long past, as the chips were everywhere abundant. When these are dry they furnish not by any means a first class substitute for wood, but one not to be despised when no wood can be procured; they will burn with sufficient heat to boil water, bake slapjacks and fry bacon – the three simplest essentials of camp fare.

Our camp, on the thirtieth, was made early in the afternoon. It was on the bank of the Running Water, which at this point is only a small stream. As the day was Sunday we made it in part a day of rest, welcome both to teams and men. Besides this, the weather – which up to this time had been dry and pleasant – now grew chilly, and a drizzle of rain had begun which made travel disagreeable and difficult.

Here we met a second train of returning Black Hillers. In this train there were ten wagons and forty-five men, apparently well provisioned, for they tried to dispose of a surplus to us. All were well armed. They, too, told stories of Indian atrocities calculated to raise the hair of a tenderfoot. They were united in declaring their belief that the whole Black Hills country did not contain enough gold to warrant prospecting. Questioned by Burns, Tull and others, they admitted that not one of the party had been farther north than Spring Creek, and that they had formed their opinions from reports of others. When they, like the first outfit we had met returning, stated that none of the men who had gone north from Custer, bound for the reported new diggings, had returned, they were asked how or from whom they had obtained the assurance that there was no gold in the northern districts. They were at some loss for a reply, but expressed the belief that the northern stampeders had been wiped out by the Indians. The inconsistency of their statements was clearly brought out by Tull, who dryly remarked that the tales they told sounded to him as if they had been agreed upon for the purpose of justifying their precipitate departure from the Hills rather than to furnish correct information to others.

May Day was cold and disagreeable, with a little rain; making travel slow and tedious. We went into camp early at a place that offered wood for fuel but no water. This lack we had provided against by filling our casks at the previous camp. We were now within eight miles of the Red Cloud Indian Agency. At our noon camp that day a party of Oglalas had visited us, showing no signs of hostility, but declining to barter or sell any of their trappings such as bows, arrows, or moccasins – of which they usually had a supply for sale or trade. The adult men were splendidly armed – indeed much better than the average man of our party – their guns being mostly Sharps' or Winchester rifles of late pattern. Several half-grown boys were armed with bows and arrows, with which they were not loath to show their skill in shooting at nickels fixed in a split stick set upright in the ground. While they were quite expert and succeeded in reaping a harvest of nickels, this was done mainly by so "trailing" the arrow that a good line shot would get the money without making a direct hit with the head. One of the men, armed with a Sharps' forty-five – as fine a rifle as was in use at that time – gave us an exhibition of his skill; pointing out small objects at some distance – a stick or stone on an adjacent hillside – he proceeded to center it with a bullet. His marksmanship was good, and he evidently took pleasure in impressing the fact upon us. Accepting the exhibition as in some measure a challenge to a trial of skill, three or four of our best riflemen followed the Indian; using the same targets, they made a very creditable record. Suspecting that the buck who had been so desirous of showing us what he could do was

THE START

the only expert in the party, Tull now challenged others, one after another to a test, but all declined; and as we pulled out from camp they left us.

On this night I was detailed for my first guard duty. In the assignment of guards it was so arranged that Rochford and I would relieve one another – an arrangement very satisfactory to us, and which continued in force on the entire trail to the Hills and in many camps thereafter. As our numbers were considerable, guard duty was not yet onerous, though later on, when our party left the main train, it became a more serious affair. On the night in question a band of Indians, camped a short distance from us, though not within sight, started dancing. All night long the sound of their tom-toms reached our ears. At intervals the dancers would lift their voices in wild cries and yells, and there were not wanting those in our number who imagined that an Indian attack was imminent; and who wished in their hearts that they had turned back with the returning stampeders; or better still, never had started out on the adventure. I confess the sounds that came from the Indian camp did not make the most cheerful music to the ears of a boy on guard – though I had witnessed tribal dances of the Pawnees, Poncas and Omahas, and knew that all were accompanied by a great deal of noise, and were not necessarily indicative of a bad spirit. Of course, as these were Sioux, we had to consider this might be different. When Rochford relieved me in the middle of the night we concluded that no immediate danger was to be feared, and I rolled into my blankets, in reasonable confidence that I still would wear my scalp in the morning.

Old Red Cloud Agency

Our train pulled into Red Cloud Agency on May second. Here we stopped for a time to talk with some of the agency employees, who were not inclined to offer us much information – if indeed they possessed much that would have been of benefit to us. They did, however, tell us that for some time past there had been a notable absence of the usual number of young men from the agency, and they were believed to be going north. They advised us to be careful and keep together, as stragglers from the train would be liable to be cut off.

A few soldiers from a nearby military post[25] loitered about the agency headquarters. A non-commissioned officer among them manifested considerable interest in our venture and said he would like nothing better than to join us if his term of enlistment were at an end. He had been as far north as Custer the preceding fall, with his company, engaged in looking for and escorting prospectors out of the district – a task which he did not enjoy, but which he had to perform as a duty. He, to, called attention to the fact that many of the young Indians had been leaving the agency and he feared it might mean trouble, but he thought that a party as strong as ours could get through without much danger. When asked if he didn't think the War Department might give the whites some protection in case the Indians took to the warpath in large numbers, he said it would not do to rely on any such hope.

"You may consider yourselves fortunate," he remarked, "that you haven't the soldiers to contend with as well as the Indians. A few months ago our orders were to remove all whites excepting government employees from the reservation. I am not even sure that the orders have been rescinded, but activity in that line has ceased, and there seems to be a general understanding that it will not be resumed unless some pressing

---

[25] Probably Camp Robinson, established in 1874.

emergency should arise; such, for instance, as a threat of a general Indian uprising."

While several members of our party were listening to the opinion and advice of the soldiers, others were hearing an old Frenchman who, with his Indian wife, had come into the agency, evidently to do some trading. This old man proved a greater alarmist than any we had yet encountered. He grew quite excited in his admonition to us of the danger we were courting in coming into a country that belonged to the Indians. His words of warning were accompanied by violent gesticulations that were fully as expressive as the words he used, to tell us the probable fate that would overtake us if we foolishly persisted in going north.

"You see," he exclaimed, "here is no young mans; old mans, yes, squaws, papooses. What that mean? Trouble for you – sure. All young mans go nort'; no young mans go sout'; eef white man go nort' Indian keel heem sure; no keel heem eef he go sout'; better you go back to your home; I see some new scalp two day ago. Sure better you go back."

The old fellow seemed to be earnest enough in his warning, but he was so insistent and repeated it with emphasis so often, some suspicion was aroused that he was more interested in frightening a lot of tenderfeet than in imparting information to them. That he succeeded in this to some extent was evident when a number of men suddenly remembered important business that had been neglected or forgotten before they left home. The result was that three wagons of the train, with nine men, remained behind when we moved; their intention being, no doubt, to join the first train for the south. This defection was, however, made up by the addition to our party of several wagons and a dozen men who had been waiting at the agency for a day or two for reinforcements. Among these was a bull team of five yoke, hauling a heavy load of flour. It soon became evident that our captain had come to an understanding with the owner of the flour, under which he agreed to hold back the train to the pace of the bull team for its protection. It was learned that for this service the captain and several others were to receive a certain agreed amount of flour at a greatly reduced price, when they would reach Custer. Much dissatisfaction was expressed regarding this arrangement – the Kansas contingent, which my partners and I had joined, being especially emphatic in protest. For this they had good reason; they had the best and fastest teams in the entire train, and ever since the start from the railroad they had been compelled to accommodate their pace to that of much slower teams. The train, however, moved north with the bull team bringing up the rear.

CHIEF RED CLOUD

EARLY GEOLOGICAL MAP OF THE BLACK HILLS

We Pull Out from the Train

On the night of May second, we camped eight miles north of the agency. After supper a council of our original party was called to discuss a proposition to leave the train and go on ahead. The teams and wagons to which my partners and myself were attached belonged to five men of the Kansas party – Tull, Bill Kelley, Jim Sheppard, Jim Moody and John Stevens – the other members being passengers like ourselves. The owners of the teams wanted to go on, but did not feel that they could do so if the men whose freight they were hauling considered the danger too great.

When the matter was broached to us, we at once agreed that as the team owners had much to risk besides their scalps and were willing to take the chances, we surely would not hold back. Since all of us were of the same mind, it was decided that we would leave camp in the early morning ahead of the rest of the train, and make better time on the road.

Accordingly our wagons lined up while the messes of the others were at breakfast, and started. As we drew into the trail, we were joined by a fourth wagon and several men, who at the eleventh hour had decided to throw in with us. A count of noses at the noon camp disclosed the fact that our party now contained twenty-three men. The only fault to be found was that not all of them were armed as well as could have been desired, for a number had nothing better than Spencer carbines and shotguns. One of the men, who belonged to the wagon that joined us as we left camp, was a tall old Kentuckian, whom we knew by no other name than "the Old Man," from first to last. He was armed with two old-fashioned Colt revolvers, which used loose ammunition. That he considered himself, thus equipped, equal to any emergency that might arise was evident. Those old shooting irons never were out of his hands on the march during the day, and it was a certainty that he slept with them at night. It was refreshing to see him striding along beside the wagon to which he was attached, swinging an old Colt, in either hand, and apparently ready to offer defiance to the entire Sioux nation. Withal he was a perfect guard, and when he was on duty it was a certainty that no danger would approach the camp on the side of his beat without detection and the sounding of an alarm.

At the noon camp we unanimously elected Tull captain of our diminished train. He told us that as our numbers had been decreased, all would have to be called upon for more frequent guard duty. He cautioned us particularly against straggling, and expressed confidence that we would go through all right if we kept together.

While antelope had been seen at intervals from the time we crossed the North Platte, they now appeared in great numbers. It would have been possible to have killed some of them, but the captain gave strict orders against any hunting. We kept a constant outlook for buffalo, but saw none, though even a year or two later bands of considerable size ranged as far south as the district we were now traversing.

Another party of Indians visited us as we prepared and ate dinner, and seemed friendly enough, though desirous of making a closer inspection of our arms and general equipment than we relished. There were a few young men in their party, with some women and children. They offered nothing for sale or trade and rejected any overtures to that end on our part.

When we went into camp for the night we again had Indian visitors. It was apparent that they were scattered in small camps over this part of the reservation, and it was evident that no party of whites could pass to the north without their knowledge. It was noticeable that of all those who came to our camp no one asked for anything – which was unusual, as other Indians with whom we had been familiar were inclined to beg at every opportunity, at least for something to eat.

The moulding of bullets and reloading of needle gun shells by some of our men aroused more interest in the Indians than anything else. This process engaged their attention until it was

WE PULL OUT FROM THE TRAIN

completed, before they departed for their camp. It was apparent that while the Indians had the best of arms, they also were able to procure plenty of fixed ammunition, and did not reload their shells.

On this night a strong guard was posted, the relief going on duty about midnight.

MORE RETURNING PILGRIMS

May fourth was an extremely disagreeable day, with a cold, drizzling rain and occasional spurts of snow. Traveling was exceedingly difficult, made slow and laborious by the gumbo soil that rolled up on the wheels, necessitating frequent stops to remove it. It clung to the boots of those on foot, and its weight seemed as that of lead. Had a suitable camping place offered, we would gladly have unhitched early in the day; but as neither wood nor water was available, we could do nothing better than to keep moving until a desirable spot should be reached.

Our camp finally was made on Horsehead Creek. As we were preparing supper with a very meagre supply of wood available, a train of twelve to fifteen wagons pulled in from the north and went into camp alongside. Several of the men of the outfit at once came over to us and asked if it was possible that we hoped to get through to the Black Hills with an outfit numerically as weak as ours. We told them, of course, that was what we hoped and expected to do. They indicated that they considered themselves exceedingly fortunate to have escaped with their lives, and yet they numbered eighty well-armed men. This was the strongest and best-equipped party of all those we had met, and should have been able to withstand any force of Indians likely to be encountered. The men seemed to have been struck by an unreasoning fear; and the stories they told of the dangers to be encountered at the Cheyenne River, Buffalo Gap and other points on the trail favorable to ambuscades, were awful in character.

To believe them, one must be prepared to find the entire country overrun by Indians and find their dead and mutilated victims all along the way. When questioned as to particulars, however, their stories failed in many details to agree, and not one could be found who would state positively that he had been a witness to a single tragedy.

Finally we learned from them that no member of the party had been farther north in the Hills than Castle Creek, and only two or three had gone so far. All of the others had reached Custer only three days previous, and had attempted to do no prospecting whatever. During their stay two or three men had been killed a short distance from town, on the Red Canyon trail. Three men had been killed farther north, where a party was engaged in building a stockade.

Reports came in of trains attacked and held between Custer and Buffalo Gap, but no casualties had been suffered where men traveled in companies of reasonable strength. The men became so terrified that after only one day's stay in Custer the train had started out of the country. As it left Custer about noon, the intention was to camp at Point of Rocks, ten miles south, that night. Another train left Custer on the Red Canyon trail at about the same time, and went into camp about the same distance from the town. This train was attacked by Indians, and as the two camps were only a few miles apart, the sound of the firing reached the ears of those camped at Point of Rocks. Fearing that they, too, would be attacked, they hurriedly hitched up their teams and made a forced drive through the night, reaching Buffalo Gap in the morning. Here they stopped only long enough to prepare some food and give their stock a short rest, when they again took the trail. Not daring to stop for dinner at the Cheyenne River, they drove hard all day, reaching Horsehead Creek, where we met them as stated.

Though now some distance from the Hills, their fears had not abated. There must have been men among them who did not share the alarm of the majority, or at least of those who talked so volubly to us of the desperate chances we were taking in going on; but if so, we did not hear from them at the time. Later two such men joined us.

WE PULL OUT FROM THE TRAIN

As we were few in numbers, we concluded that the larger outfit could stand guard sufficient for both camps, and we would get an uninterrupted night's sleep. At about dusk, I, with two others of our number, started out to get fuel for our breakfast fire. When some distance from camp we heard a commotion behind us. Looking back we saw men running to and fro with guns in their hands, evidently in a state of great excitement. At the same time we heard Rochford's voice shouting to us to "get down out of sight; these d - - - d fools are going to shoot!" We didn't wait for further explanations before dropping to the ground. We had, in our search for fuel, ascended a little knoll where our heads showed up from the camp against the skyline; still haunted by their fears, the men raised the cry of "Indians!" with a general rush to arms. When we reached the camp – as we did in double quick time – we learned that we would indeed have been fired upon, had not Rochford, Tull, and Moody threatened to shoot the first man who should raise his gun.

This experience taught us that there might be as much danger from frightened individuals in one's own party as from Indians. More than one fatality occurred in this way in the early settlement of the country. As an illustration, one such tragedy took place on our road a few days previously when a guard from a sawmill outfit, between Buffalo Gap and Custer, killed one of his companions through mistake.

Before we rolled into our blankets, two Irishmen came over to our wagons and asked for our captain. They engaged Tull in conversation, asking the number of our men, how we were armed, and if we did not think we were taking undue risk in trying to go through with a weak force. Tull replied that we were confident that any party of our numbers could get through without much danger by traveling carefully and keeping a proper guard at night.

He said, "you must realize that not all the reports of Indian troubles are true, and my experience and observations have taught me that while an Indian will fight desperately when cornered, he is not likely to attack where his chances of killing is not much better than that of being killed."

He expressed the belief that twenty-five determined men, well-armed and exercising proper precautions against ambuscades, could travel through the country at will. To this our visitors gave assent. They told us they were from Sioux City and had gone into the Hills by way of Red Canyon. They had expected to go north to the Deadwood country but had been deterred by the many bad reports they heard; but they were now heartily ashamed of their hurried flight from Custer. They asked if we would not allow them to join us and return. Their proposition having been accepted, they moved their blankets and other belongings to our side of the camp before going to bed; after that time they were with us to the end of the trail. They were good fellows and were welcomed the more heartily because of their possession of two good guns.

The Cheyenne River – A Midnight Alarm

A cold rain again set in during the night and it continued all day on May fifth. We would have remained in camp, instead of moving under the unfavorable conditions, had a good fuel supply been at hand. But the only wood to be found was green and there was not much of that. The road was very difficult and the day was well on into the afternoon when we reached the Cheyenne River tired, wet, and hungry. Wood there was plentiful and a good warm fire and hot supper made the world seem brighter. As we had been warned that this was one of the chief danger points along the trail, extra guards were stationed; all the stock was brought within the guard lines; and all fires extinguished before anyone was allowed to rétire.

I was on guard the first half of the night, and a most disagreeable duty it proved. With nightfall the air grew cold, while a light rain with a little snow continued to fall. My clothing soon was wet and uncomfortable, and as no fire was allowed, it was necessary to keep moving the entire time in order to keep my blood in circulation. I can truly say that in all my previous experience never had I passed a few hours of such discomfort. The thought of danger that might be threatening did not tend to make conditions more cheerful. When Rochford relieved me at midnight I was thoroughly chilled and, even after I rolled into the warm blankets where our bed was made under the wagon, some time elapsed before I attained a degree of warmth and comfort that allowed me to sleep. Finally sleep did come and it was deep and dreamless.

I was suddenly awakened – when it seemed that I had only been in bed a short time – by a hand on my shoulder, and the voice of Rochford saying, "Get up quick, Dick, the Indians are here; the 'Old Man' has just seen them crossing the river about three hundred yards below camp."

Imagine the effect of such a message on a boy thus aroused from his slumbers – exhausted with the day's tramp and the strain of guard duty in the fore part of the night, and trying to realize the full import of the warning while still struggling to overcome the drowsiness that held him. I recall vividly even now, how I strove in vain to keep my teeth from chattering when the chill air struck my now warm body, as I rolled out and pulled on my boots and buckled on my belt of cartridges. (On this night all had gone to bed pretty fully clothed.)

About the time I had awakened sufficiently to get my bearings, two horses that had been picketed in the edge of the camp pulled their picket pins and ran by our wagon snorting in apparent terror. This seemed to dissolve any doubt that might have been entertained as to what the "Old Man" had seen or imagined. In the meantime our captain, to whom the guard had first reported, was up and alert to take charge of the situation. He promptly ordered that every man be awakened and take the post appointed for him when we went into camp in the evening. He then visited the wagons one after another, speaking quietly to all the men. While he advised them to keep cool and not allow themselves to become excited, he himself furnished an example of coolness more assuring than his mere words.

He instructed everyone to make no noise, to remain quietly lying by his guns and by no means to discharge a firearm without orders, unless a most pressing emergency should arise. He was not altogether convinced that the "Old Man" had seen Indians, but had no doubt whatever that he had seen something he fully believed to be Indians. The captain emphasized that we must be prepared for anything that might come, and to this end no man was to go to sleep until full daylight – as the time of greatest danger in Indian country was considered to be the "gray of the morning."

Tull's words and bearing had a wonderfully steadying effect, and I cannot recall that a single man indicated by his manner that he was unduly alarmed. Thus awaiting whatever might come, we passed the rest of the night slowly. It was a welcome relief when daylight appeared without any further startling incident. As the various messes prepared their breakfast there was some badgering of the old guard on account of defective eyesight or too active an imagination. Tull and Rochford were so much impressed with the sincerity with which the "Old Man" reiterated his declaration, that he really had seen a band of Indians crossing the stream, that an investigation was made at the spot he pointed out. It was found that a band of elk had crossed at that exact spot. That the elk were the Indians the scout had seen was considered pretty well established.

For two days past when the clouds would at intervals clear away sufficiently, the Black Hills, the land of our destination, would loom in sight. Our drive from the Cheyenne River, on May sixth, was made slow and disagreeable by rain and mud; but once in a while the sun would appear, shining bright and warm – much to the general relief – and giving apparent promise of better weather not far ahead. At such moments the Hills seemed very near at hand and the view was one that never will be forgotten by those who beheld it. Here we realized why as "Black" instead of "Green" Hills, the country has been designated. So darkly green is the foliage of the pines clothing the landscape that when beheld at a distance and in mass it appears rather black than green.

On May sixth we made no halt at noon, preferring to make the comparatively short drive to Buffalo Gap without a stop, in order to go into camp for the night at an early hour; that all might have a good rest before being detailed on night guard. The serious break in the previous night's sleep, on the part of all, and the laborious travel of the day through the gumbo, made the decision of the captain to halt at the Gap early in the afternoon, a welcome one.

As we went into camp the clouds drifted off and the bright, warm sunshine did much to raise the spirits of the entire party. Only those who have had the experience can understand how great an effect the weather can have upon the temper and general morale of a company of men traveling under our conditions. The utmost cheerfulness pervaded the camp; as the various messes built their camp fires and prepared the evening meal, several voices were heard humming snatches of song or indulging in the usual rough though friendly badinage of camp life, that had been lacking throughout the preceding days of gloomy weather.

Since we were now at the very entrance to the Hills – that dreaded Buffalo Gap, which had been described to us as a place where Indians were always lurking, intent on catching unwary travelers, and which was named as the scene of many tragedies, mostly imaginary, as we afterward learned – our captain delivered a few instructions. He cautioned those who were to act as guards during the two watches of the night that they should exercise the greatest vigilance, and each should so patrol his beat as to meet another guard at either end at short intervals.

"If this order is faithfully observed," Tull said, "a surprise will be almost impossible. Remember that Indians rarely attack a reasonably strong party when found on guard and prepared to resist."

He again admonished us against straggling from the wagons on the next day's march – an admonition that I even now recall with a feeling of shame, as I was the first and only one to disregard it. My dereliction brought me a well-merited reprimand and might easily have cost me my life, as was made clearly evident later.

Our night at Buffalo Gap passed without untoward incident. After a hearty breakfast on the morning of Sunday, May seventh, under a warm sun and bright skies, we strung out into the mouth of the Gap, with head and rear guards and three men acting as guards on either flank. Thus we made our entry into the Black Hills.

A Disobeyed Order

All went well for a distance of a few miles; then we saw one of our forward guards returning to the train in apparent haste. He reported that a short distance ahead he and his companion had found a paper with a written warning that Indians were on all sides. On the paper were directions to the body of a man who had been killed. Arriving at the spot indicated, we found beside the trail the ashes of a small campfire, and a few feet from it a small pile of rocks on which the written warning had been conspicuously placed with a rock to hold it down. The writing had been done with a pencil, on a leaf torn from a memorandum book, and bore the day, May sixth. As memory recalls it, the message was about as follows:

> Boys, for God's sake stay together. The Indians are all around you. We found the body of the man killed here and buried it in the ravine about four rods to the north.

This was signed with a name that I cannot now recall, and with the title of Captain. The writer evidently had been in command of a party that had passed over the trail on the date borne by the warning. Following the direction of the message, we found the place where the body of the murdered man had been deposited; but to say it was buried would not be correct. The men who had discovered it had, no doubt, been hurried and had not wished to remain long at the scene of the tragedy. They had merely wrapped a blanket about the corpse, placed it in the little ravine indicated, and covered it with rocks. As we found it, the head, from which the scalp had been taken, was partially exposed. All that we could do was to arrange the blanket so as completely to cover the remains, pile upon the cairn rocks sufficient for protection against predatory beasts, and continue on our way. Later we learned that the man thus killed and interred was named Wood; that he was from

Omaha; and that he had left Custer alone on horseback against the advice of friends, intending to return to the states. The ashes of the little campfire at the spot where the body was found indicated that Wood[26] had prepared his supper there and that the Indians probably had killed him as he slept.

At a point a few miles farther on we found evidence of wagons captured and looted. For a distance of a hundred yards north of the road, flour and beans were scattered in such quantities as to prove conclusively that it was not through lack of food that the attack had been made. Two days later we encountered a member of the small party that had withstood the Indians at this point. He said his party had succeeded in saving their scalps, guns and ammunition, but had lost their horses and all other parts of their outfit. This party had consisted of eight men with three teams and wagons. The man estimated the number of Indians attacking at about twenty. Contrary to custom the attack was made in daylight, just as the party had hitched up to take the trail after the camp for dinner. It had been necessary for the whites to take to the timber and to leave their wagons to be plundered and their stock driven off, in order to save themselves. The Indians did not attempt to follow them after they reached shelter and were in a position to make a good defense.

At noon we went into camp and prepared and ate a hearty meal. Well it was that we did so, as a considerable interval elapsed before we prepared the next one, though the cold grub, of which all usually kept a supply in the grub boxes, was drawn upon to good effect in the interval.

And now it is my duty as a truthful, if not an accomplished, narrator to tell of an almost unpardonable breach of discipline and disobedience of orders committed by myself, that brought

---

[26] "As we entered the gap we came to where Woods was killed and lightly buried. The coyotes had partly dug him up. We covered him and piled rocks on the grave. A little farther we came to where Pickins and Babbit were ambushed. Babbit was shot through the thigh but they got into the brush and rocks and defended themselves until rescued. They were buffalo hunters and I knew them on the plains and afterwards in the Hills. The Indians took their outfit and burned their wagons." – J. T. Spaulding, *Ibid.*

upon me a severe reprimand from our captain, and might have had far more serious results. At short intervals all day deer were seen, and sometimes so close at hand that they could readily have been killed from the trail. Because orders against discharging weapons were very strict, the men had restrained any desire they had to test their skill as marksmen, though at times the temptation to do so was great.

Shortly after we had passed Point of Rocks, about nine or ten miles below Custer, three beautiful black-tail deer stopped in the edge of the timber close to the road and watched the train as it moved by. Overcome by my desire to kill my first deer, I dismissed all thought of danger or of penalty for disobedience of orders. I stepped to the side of a tree and waited until the wagons had disappeared around a bend, and then entered the timber in pursuit of the deer; they, in the meantime, had moved leisurely away. I soon, however, found that though the deer had seemed to be in no hurry they were making better time than I imagined, and a longer time was required for me to get within shooting distance than I had expected to remain away from the train. I finally risked a shot and missed.

I now began to realize the enormity of my offense in leaving the train in disobedience of the positive order of the Captain. As I started back to the trail my mind recalled vividly the evidence of Indian atrocities which we had witnessed earlier in the day, and in particular the fate of the man whom we had covered with rocks in the lonely canyon – a fate which he brought on himself by his foolhardiness in attempting to travel alone. That we were so watched by a band that hung upon our trail all day was later made certain. I lost no time in my pursuit of the train, which indeed, I reached sooner than expected, owing to the fact that on hearing my shot and discovering my absence, Captain Tull had brought the outfit to a halt. As I appeared in sight, much to the general relief, he was about to send a detail back to find me or at least to learn, if possible, by whom the shot had been fired. It was not considered probable that a member of our party would have done so unless in defense of his life.

During the many years of our acquaintance this was the only occasion on which I saw Sam Tull moved to anger. Certainly this time his indignation was deep and well warranted. I have never forgotten the look he gave me when I shamefacedly approached him, without a reasonable excuse to offer for my conduct and determined to accept without grumbling any penalty that should be imposed. I felt that the anger of the captain must also extend to all members of the party, and that I would be looked upon with distrust thereafter.

Those were my thoughts at the time, but I long have realized since that one experience of the kind would last a lifetime, and that come what might it never would be repeated by me. Tull took a few moments to cool before speaking – evidently realizing that I was undergoing the punishment of remorse, and that any verbal castigation he might deliver could not hurt worse. He, however, considered it his duty to speak distinctly of the manner in which I had endangered not only my own life, but possibly the lives of others; that I certainly had seen enough earlier in the day to convince me that the danger from Indians was real and not imaginary; and that he was grievously disappointed in me. Had he been inclined to be abusive I believe I would have borne it better; but to note the manner in which he struggled to overcome his anger while he addressed his reproaches to me in the presence of the others, and tried to modify his reprimand so as not too deeply to wound the sensibilities of one whom he considered a mere boy, brought tears to my eyes, and served to strengthen the affection with which I had come to regard him. Considerable time, however, was to elapse before I came to believe that I had been fully restored to his regard.

After again getting in motion, our train had not proceeded more that a mile when we met two oxen yoked together. They were traveling south, without wagon or driver, and turned out of the road to allow us to pass. We supposed they were a part of an outfit that would be coming along behind and which we would meet later. When no other teams or wagons appeared we concluded that the oxen had recently been driven into the

Hills and, escaping their owners, had taken the back track for home. While we were discussing this probability we heard two rifle shots fired at a short distance behind us. The reports came so close together as to be almost simultaneous, and it required no great stretch of imagination to conjure up a picture of the cattle we had met lying dead on the road and surrounded by Indians. That the cattle were killed by Indians at a spot not more than a half mile from where we had met them was proven next day, when a party went out from Custer to look for them and found them lying dead in the road. That they could have been killed in a spirit of pure wantonness was clearly manifest, as not a particle of either carcass had been removed.

So convinced was our captain that the Indians were hanging upon our trail, and that there might be danger of an attack at or before morning, that he proposed a forced drive into Custer that night, taking the precaution to keep out a strong guard in front and rear. The plan met with general approval. Although the drive that day had been somewhat longer than usual, the day had been warm and bright, drying the roads completely. Travel had been easier and better time had been made since we had left the gumbo of the foothills behind. After a brief stop to give the teams a feed of grain and the men some time to take a hurried lunch from the grub boxes, the march was resumed; without meeting anything to delay or alarm, we reached Custer at eleven o'clock at night and went into camp at the east side of the town.[27]

---

[27] On August 10, 1875, General George Crook issued a call to the miners to meet at the stockade on French Creek in Custer Park. The next day a townsite company was organized and a townsite a mile square was platted. It was named Custer. Alex Thompson and W. H. Wood were chosen by the miners to remain in the Hills at this site to guard the miners' property, until an agreement could be reached with the Indians. During the winter of 1875-6, Custer became the objective point of many men coming into the Hills to prospect. By the time the big stampede to Deadwood Gulch began in the spring of 1876, Custer had a population of 6,000 to 10,000 persons. Quickly, however, the bulk of its population moved north to seek gold. – [HUGHES].

First View of Custer and Surroundings

The morning of May eighth was one that will linger in my memory while life shall last. The air was balmy, the sun bright, and the skies, I thought, the bluest I ever had seen. The beautiful panorama of the Hills unfolded to our view as we awakened from a night of refreshing sleep, during which it was not deemed necessary to post a guard. Their beauty drew exclamations of delight from every beholder. Wishing to enjoy a view from higher ground, immediately after breakfast – accompanied by Rochford and John Stevens – I walked across from the camp to the south side of French Creek and ascended the hill that overlooks Custer Park from that direction. Here we seated ourselves in the edge of the timber to enjoy the scene spread out before us – the fine, open, grassy park with the picturesque cabins of logs, surrounded by the magnificent dark green forest. The towering granite masses of the Harney Range formed a noble background.

Men could be seen passing to and fro on the one street of the village, and in the immediate foreground a solitary miner was engaged with pick and shovel on work upon a drain ditch to divert the waters of the stream. Even as we watched him, we were startled by a number of rifle shots – perhaps a half dozen – fired almost in volley, from the timber to our left. Judging from the sound, the shots were fired not more than a hundred yards distant.

Simultaneously with the reports the lone miner pitched forward and fell. Several men who had seen him fall ran down from a nearby cabin, picked him up and carried him to its shelter.[28]

---

[28] The injured miner, known as "Smoky" Jones, had long hair which reached well down on his shoulders and he wore a straggly beard, never known to be trimmed. Altogether he was an unattractive and disreputable appearing individual. His figure became a familiar one in the Northern Hills, where he was fortunate enough to

FIRST VIEW OF CUSTER 43

We returned to camp as speedily as our legs could carry us and when we looked towards the spot from which the shots must have been fired, we realized that we must have been nearer to the firing party than its victim, though fortunately hidden from it by the intervening timber. On that morning, so little were we apprehensive of danger, with several hundred white men close at hand, that we had not thought it necessary to carry our guns with us on leaving camp.

At that time there was in existence an organization known as the Custer Minute Men, employed by the people of the town as a lookout for, and protection against, Indians. At the head of this company was Captain Jack Crawford[29] later known as the Poet Scout who was engaged in the Hills as correspondent for the *Omaha Bee*. Crawford wore his hair long, in a manner affected by some other frontiersmen who desired to be considered Indian fighters – but which earned for them generally the appellation of "Bad Haired Long Men," a term of derision. There was nothing of brag or bluster about Crawford either in speech or manner, and later he acquired credit as a

---

discover a valuable mining property and to dispose of it for a considerable sum of money. "Smoky" had one notable accomplishment. He could imitate the howl of the timber wolf to perfection, and when every evening the old mining camp cry of "Oh, Joe!" would resound through the gulches it would at intervals be varied by the wolf's howl to which no one but "Smoky" could give voice. Soon after making his stake Joe disappeared from his accustomed haunts. No one seemed to know where he had gone. Eventually the miners ceased to think of him. But one day there alighted in the Hills, from an incoming Cheyenne stagecoach, a handsome, dapper, and smooth-shaven individual with a fashionable hair cut. He might have been mistaken for a professor from Heidelberg or a New York capitalist in search of mining investments. No one dreamed of identifying him as "Smoky" Jones. And yet, "Smoky" he was. He walked the streets of Deadwood and visited all of his old accustomed haunts without being recognized. Then one night at the Gem Theatre, amid applause given a popular number, there arose from one of the boxes the howl of the lone timber wolf. A dozen voices shouted in unison, " 'Smoky' Jones has come back." – [HUGHES].

According to an item in the *Cheyenne Leader* taken from the *Chicago Times*, in January 1877, "Smoky" Jones got his cognomen from the fact that he was always finding chunks of smoky topaz and lugging them around in his pockets.

[29] About the middle of March, 1876, Custer formed an organization, consisting of 125 men, known as the "Custer Minute Men," to serve as home-guard, with Charles Whitehead as Crawford's first lieutenant. Annie D. Tallent, *The Black Hills; or, Last Hunting Ground of the Dakotahs* (St. Louis, Nixon-Jones Pub. Co., 1899), 291.

carrier of dispatches from the army in the field to various military posts during the Indian troubles of the summer and fall of 1876.

With him in the company of Minute Men were Jimmy Irion, "Buckskin" Frank Smith, and a half dozen others, several of whom were very raw tenderfeet.

The agreed signal to call the company together, in case of emergency, was three pistol shots to be fired in rapid succession. When the alarm was given over the shooting of "Smoky" Jones, one of the scouts endeavored to give the signal for assembly. He had a fine, heavy Smith & Wesson revolver – then coming into vogue. This he produced, and using both hands to cock the weapon, held it out at arms length to discharge it.

"Look out, you d---d fool, you'll shoot that woman," someone in the assembled crowd shouted. And indeed, the weapon was pointed directly at a woman standing in the doorway of a near-by cabin. Then the tenderfoot scout directed the muzzle toward the ground. Someone suggested he fire into the air. While the fellow lacked knowledge of firearms, he evinced a willingness at least to learn, and accepted the advice. Thus he managed to sound the call to arms; in a short time the Minute Men assembled, armed to the teeth, or more so, mounted their horses, and took the direction from which the shots had been fired.

They were gone only a short time. Then they came back and reported that the shooting had been done by a party of Indians – eight or ten in number – as well as could be judged by the tracks of the ponies they had ridden to the top of the hill immediately overlooking the town from the south. At that point the Indians had dismounted and made their way on foot down the hill, through the timber, to the place from which they had fired upon and wounded "Smoky" Jones.

It probably was at this time that the statement was ventured that the reason for dubbing the organization "Minute Men" was that it never went so far from town that it could not get back in a minute. For this, some local humorist – possibly "Doc" Peirce[30] – was responsible.

It was evident that the Indians, immediately after shooting Jones, had regained their ponies and had ridden off to the south. That such a band had followed us the entire previous day, turning out of the trail only when the confines of Custer had been reached, was asserted by Johnnie Spaulding, who arrived the evening of May eighth with the Burns party. Spaulding had acted as scout and lookout for the party from the time we had separated from it at the first camp north of Red Cloud Agency. He, too, placed the number in the party at eight or ten – as well as he could read the pony tracks – and said that the Indians had traveled in the road with no attempt at concealment. Evidently they spent only a short time at the point where they apparently killed the cattle, which Spaulding found lying where they fell and still united by the yoke.

Spaulding did not think a band so small had hung to the trail of our party with the intention of attacking, but probably hoped to pick off some unwary straggler. All of this tended to confirm the belief that had been growing in me that it was perhaps as well that my aim had been defective when I shot at the deer. Had I succeeded in making a kill, I certainly would have been delayed a longer time in rejoining the train, and a few moments more on that occasion might well have been worth more to me than a venison steak.

As stated above, the Burns party reached Custer only a day behind us, having made much better time that expected; and for this difference in time gained by us it really was not worth while to have divided the train. We learned, however, that the expedition made by Burns was partially due to the clamor on

[30] Ellis T. Peirce, who arrived in Custer in March, 1876; "Conspicuous among the residents of Custer in 1876, was the versatile Black Hills humorist . . . familiarly called 'Doc' Peirce, the 'very prince of good fellows' . . . With an acute sense of the ridiculous there was no occurrence so pathetic that 'Doc' could not detect . . . a thread of the comic running through the warp and woof. . . Among the 'boys' he gained for himself the reputation of being very fond and much addicted to practical jokes." Annie D. Tallent, *op. cit.*, 301.

Peirce served Custer County as deputy sheriff; Pennington County as sheriff; and Fall River County as a member of the senate in the early days. – [HUGHES].

the part of some of the men – on learning of the flour deal their captain had made with the owner of the bull team – and the consequent pushing of that team to the full limit of its speed. Even then the owner of the team had been frightened into making concessions, in the way of a reduced price for flour, on a threat of further defections from the train.

Custer, the first town located in the Hills, had an elevation of 5,000 feet above sea level. It was the first objective point for the incoming tide; but we found it true, as foretold by one of the outbound pilgrims whom we had interviewed, that on our arrival we saw as many people leaving for the States as those arriving. The numbers of men we had met on our way all declared the country vastly overrated. Many cursed it utterly. Every man was anxious only to make the best possible speed back to the States; hence we were prepared in a measure to find Custer in a state of gloom.

The population, which a short time previously had numbered more than a thousand souls, had dwindled to a few hundreds; and it seemed that even a majority of those were intent on leaving. Not all, however, were going south. Every day numbers took the trail toward the new diggings in the central and northern Hills. It was noticeable, as pointed out by Tull, that of those leaving the country, with no intention of returning, a large majority were going out by way of the Buffalo Gap trail, over which we had come, while comparatively few left by way of the Red Canyon route. From this, he shrewdly concluded that the outgoing trains embraced chiefly "tenderfeet"[31] from the neighboring states of Iowa and Nebraska; and that the men from the farther West, more accustomed to roughing it – and especially those from other mining districts – were more disposed to give the country a fair trial before abandoning it. Tull was right in his judgment.

---

[31] The word "tenderfoot" has come so generally into use that its significance should be understood by all. In a mining camp it is applied to almost any newcomer from the East, or to any one unaccustomed to the manners of the frontier, in which case it is used in no worse sense that as a term of derision. Applied, however, to any genuine "Old Timer," it became an unpardonable insult.

FIRST VIEW OF CUSTER

We spent two days in Custer and wherever we found a man who had had mining experience elsewhere, we found him disposed to spend some time in exploration and prospecting before condemning the country. Such men were forming parties and going north to Spring and Castle Creeks and their tributaries, but even in greater numbers to the Deadwood country. My partners and I at once decided to take the northern trail. The Kansas contingent, with which we had taken passage at Sidney, to a man voted the same way; and we made a new contract for the hauling of our freight to Deadwood.

From Custer to Deadwood

On the morning of May tenth we started north, our party comprising Tull and his companions; the two Irishmen who had joined us at Horsehead Creek to return to the Hills after their precipitate flight from Custer; my two partners; and myself. A short distance out on the road we overtook Spaulding, Tomlins, and Hall, who had pulled out ahead and were waiting for us.

When we topped the divide between Spring and French Creeks, a few miles out of Custer, the train was halted to look upon the magnificent view unfolded. Within the range of vision were beautiful grassy parks, deep and somber canyons, precipitous gorges, noble forests of spruce and pine, and the whole surmounted by the magnificent mountain range of which majestic Harney Peak was the dominant feature. It reared its towers and pinnacles above the clouds, between seven and eight thousand feet in altitude.

Our first camp was made on Spring Creek, a clear mountain stream. Here we saw several miners who were engaged in prospecting along the sides of the gulch – in miner's parlance known as the "rim."[32] In this and many other gulches of the Hills there was so much water on the bedrock and in the gravel as to preclude prospecting without a drain ditch first having been dug. As that in most cases was an expensive and laborious task, and one requiring much time, such ground as could be tested without such a drain was first carefully tested. Bars which rise above the level of the stream, but on which the auriferous gravel was deposited in ages past, offer the best opportunity for prospecting without trouble from water; and in some cases may be found richer than the gulch itself.

---

[32] The "rim" is what a tenderfoot would probably term the "edge" of the gulch, where the bedrock assumes the slope of the hill on either side, and forms the side line of the placer claim. – [HUGHES]

FROM CUSTER TO DEADWOOD   49

As this was the first time a majority of the men of our party had witnessed the process of "panning,"[33] we spent an hour or more in giving such assistance to the miners as they would accept, and in learning the first steps in the miner's work.

Here, too, we saw a man manipulating a "rocker" – which was a cradle-shaped affair made of lumber, about eight or ten feet long, and provided with riffles in the bottom for catching the gold. It was set on an incline and had a perforated box-shaped receptacle at the upper end, into which was shoveled the pay dirt. To this was added water from a large dipper made of a kerosene can attached to a handle. The whole was kept agitated by a rocking process.[34]

One of the claims on Spring Creek was supplied with a string of three boxes, the lumber for which had been whipsawed. This exceedingly tedious, laborious and slow process of producing boards for the making of the sluice boxes[35] had been resorted to because no sawmill was at hand.

The "sawpit," so called, was not a pit at all, but a heavy frame made of logs, and raised to the height of six or seven feet above the ground, with two logs inclined from bottom to top. Over this inclined plane, the log to be sawed was raised to the top of the frame. By one man on top and one below, the whipsaw was drawn up and down through the length of the log to make a board.

---

[33] The "pan" used in testing the value of mining ground was made of sheet steel. It was about four inches in depth, eighteen inches from rim to rim, with a long flare from bottom to top. Into the pan the gravel to be tested was shoveled. The prospector invariably used the round spring point shovel for that purpose. Immersing the pan in water, he kept the contents agitated by shaking, tilting the pan to wash off the lighter part, and removing the larger pebbles with his fingers. The gold, if any, because of greater gravity, settled at the bottom. An expert panner could make the separation of the gold from the gravel and sand perfectly and without loss. – [HUGHES].

[34] The rocker was used mainly where water was not plentiful and, while much more rapid than the panning method, was not to be compared with the sluice box for efficiency.

[35] The sluice boxes had an average length of twelve feet. Each was made by nailing three boards together. The bottom of each had riffles made with slats or boards perforated with augur holes.

The sluice boxes were set on an incline of four or five inches, and the forty to fifty "miner's inches"[36] of water, necessary for a "sluice head," introduced at the upper end. The dirt to be washed was shoveled in at the upper end of the sluice, and the force of the water was sufficient to carry all but the larger rocks through the entire length of the boxes. The gold settled in the riffles. The rocks were thrown out with a sluice fork, a tool resembling a hay fork, but with more numerous and flattened tines.

The prospectors whom we met on Spring Creek did not speak encouragingly of the district. That gold was to be found there, we had the evidence of our eyes; and bright, beautiful gold it was. But the men had begun to doubt that it would be found in paying quantities. Many already had deserted the diggings and moved north, while others were preparing to go. They had not been molested by Indians and expressed the opinion that there was little danger to be feared from them this far in the interior. They predicted that their depredations would be confined principally to the foothill country. This we found to be true. The Sioux, essentially a horseman, was loath to penetrate to a district where he could not move about freely on horseback.

Before going into camp for the night we encountered Captain Jack Crawford, Jimmy Irion, and "Buckskin" Frank Smith. They had left Custer ahead of us, but we found them with their wagon stuck in the mud, struggling with a balky horse. They, too, were on their way to Deadwood.[37]

---

[36] A miner's inch is an opening one-inch square through a two-inch plank, with a head of water six inches above the opening. One inch will pass ninety-three pounds of water in one minute. – *Ouray* (Colorado) *Times*, November 10, 1877.

[37] During the late summer and fall of 1876, Crawford was engaged in carrying dispatches from the military forces in the field. Later he was appointed Indian Agent. During this time he wrote and published several books of poems, mainly descriptive of western scenes and incidents.

Jimmy Irion, on reaching Deadwood, obtained employment as scout and lookout for a sawmill outfit. While thus engaged, in August, he was ambushed and killed by Indians. He was a printer by trade and came to the Hills from Louisville, Kentucky. He was a boy of fine character and undoubted courage. He had had several encounters with the Indians, and as he had come out of them without injury, had become inclined to think too lightly of the danger.

FROM CUSTER TO DEADWOOD 51

Our camp was made, as stated, on Spring Creek. Guards were posted as usual, though the proximity and bearing of the miners tended to the belief that there was little danger of trouble from Indians. The night was the coldest we had experienced; with a heavy frost. But it passed without discomfort, as pitch pine was abundant, and good fires were kept up until bedtime. The guards had a good bed of live coals to which they resorted at intervals.

HILL CITY NEARLY DESERTED – SLOW PROGRESS

After a short drive on the morning of May eleventh, we reached Hill City – which we found to be mainly a town of abandoned cabins. From the number of the cabins it was evident that there had been quite a population a short time previous, but the majority of the people had moved north in search of better prospects than Spring Creek offered. Here we had reached the spot designated by the young man with whom we had talked on our first camp out of Sidney, as the extreme limit to which it would be necessary to go in order to "see it all." The information thus offered, though given in entire good faith, was now recalled with some amusement, for we realized that here we were little more than entering the most interesting part of the country.

Hill City we found to have a very nice location on Spring Creek, where the gulch widened to a beautiful grassy valley. It was surrounded by a fine forest, with the beautiful mountains of the Harney Range to the east, and apparently close at hand. Here we were joined by three men – "Ad" Geltner, [38] Bill Schafer, and George Lemmon – who had been engaged for

---

Smith, the third member of the Crawford party, fell into bad company during the summer, it was reported, and left the country a short distance ahead of a posse that was intent upon overtaking him to inspect the brand of the horse he was riding. – [HUGHES].

[38] Geltner and I made many prospecting trips together later. A better or more congenial friend and companion could not be desired. He remained in the Hills, finally locating on a ranch near the Wyoming line, where he died thirty-five years later. His companions left the country in the fall of '76. – [HUGHES].

some time in mining on a dry gulch about a mile to the east. They were preparing to quit the district and go north.

As several of our party expressed a wish to visit the dry diggings nearby, we concluded to camp at Hill City until after dinner. General interest was aroused when Lemmon exhibited a beautiful gold nugget, weighing two ounces, and worth forty dollars. We had seen a little fine gold in Custer, but this nugget aroused a desire to start prospecting at once. Under Geltner's instructions we took some lessons in panning, and a few "colors"[39] were obtained. While the diggings here visited had yielded a quantity of gold considerable in the aggregate, when divided among the men employed, it did not constitute miner's wages. Every day the men were leaving for more promising fields. Lack of water in the little gulches mined made it necessary to transport the pay dirt for considerable distances, by wheelbarrows or carts. This was expensive and slow. Had it not been that the bedrock in the little gulches was shallow, requiring no stripping of waste dirt, it would not have been possible to have worked this ground at all.

After dinner we moved on, but such were the difficulties of the road that we made slow progress. Where the road lay through timber, the trees had been cut off, leaving the stumps. In many places rocks of a size too great to be moved without blasting impeded the way, requiring care and skill in getting the wagons over them without breakage. Once in a while a pitch was encountered so steep as to require assistance of men pulling on ropes attached to the tongues of the wagons, to surmount it; while the descent of many such places was accomplished only by using the same man power to act as a holdback or brake. An occasional mudhole, too, tended to delay; on this afternoon we covered very few miles – again camping for the night on the bank of Spring Creek, not far from the present location of Sheridan.

With all the work required to keep the wagons moving at all, and the slow progress made, it might be thought that this

---

[39] The term "color" is applied to any particle of gold visible to the eye. – [HUGHES].

part of our trip would be found tedious; but such was not the truth. The beauty of the country through which we were passing, and the constantly occurring change of scenery as the road wound around the bends of the streams or surmounted the divides, so impressed every beholder that even the hurried and incomplete work of the pioneers who had hewn out the trail we were following, occasioned little or no grumbling.

The experiences of May twelfth were a repetition of those of the previous day, but with more serious delays occasioned by the miring of two of the teams at one of the numerous creek crossings. On this day we made a less number of miles than on any day previous, and again went into camp for the night on Spring Creek, though at a point where we certainly would leave it in the morning. Plenty of good wood and pure water made the camps delightful in contrast with those we had made in the plains country, where in a number of instances neither wood nor water was abundant in quantity nor good in quality.

On this day we saw the only indication of the presence of Indians between Custer and Deadwood. Leaving Spring Creek we crossed a stretch of several miles of high land forming the divide between that stream and Rapid Creek. Part of this divide consisted of high, rolling hills[40] devoid of timber and covered with a fine coat of grass. Leaving the train as we entered this prairie, Rochford and I entered the timber to the west – intent on getting a deer if possible. We traveled for some miles in a course parallel to the road and only a short distance from it, finally descending a high, sparsely timbered hill to the gulch – through the bottom of which ran a small stream. Here we were startled to see, at the point where we crossed, a number of pony tracks so fresh that the water had not yet dried where it had been splashed upon the grass by the hoofs. The tracks led down stream in the direction of the road, and we surmised that the riders were watching the train as it passed, and were at that time very close to us.

Our feelings may be likened to those of Robinson Crusoe when he discovered the print of a man's foot in the sand. In

---

[40] This is now known as the Bald Hills district.

order to leave the gulch it was necessary for us either to retrace our steps, and climb the high hill at our backs – exposed to the sight of any enemies that might be lurking at hand – or to climb the hill, equally high and exposed, to the north – the direction in which we were traveling. We considered the matter for a time while we kept a sharp lookout for danger. We agreed in the opinion that Indians must be very near at hand between us and the road, which they would not cross while the wagons were within a short distance. We indulged the hope that their attention might be so engaged in watching the train as to allow us to climb the hill and get away undiscovered. The conclusion we reached was that our risk would be no greater in keeping on our course to the north, climbing the hill on that side of the gulch, than it would be should we go back the way we came; and in the latter case we would be traveling away from, instead of toward, the train.

In the years that have passed since then I may have been in places of greater danger; indeed, the danger may have been less imminent than I then believed; but I can say with truth that never in the course of my life have I experienced the degree of fear that I felt while climbing that hill. I felt almost certain that we would be fired upon from the gulch as we ascended; and where it was possible we took advantage of the too thin stand of trees, to screen us from the sight of anyone who might be in position to see us from below.

During the short time, though seemingly long, required to reach the summit of the hill, neither of us spoke a word; but I am sure we both breathed a sigh of satisfaction and thankfulness when we attained the shelter of the heavier timber on the other side. When I faced my partner, I knew from the expression on his face that he had fully shared my feelings, and he admitted that he had serious doubts, when we left the gulch, whether we would be allowed to get to the summit alive. We lost no time in striking the road and in a short time overtook the train, having seen nothing more alarming than a lot of tracks of unshod ponies. These, however, were conclusive evi-

FROM CUSTER TO DEADWOOD 55

dence of the presence of Indians, as there were no white men camped in this section.

We learned that the gulch in which we saw the tracks was a tributary of Rapid Creek which, with its larger tributaries of Slate Creek and Castle Creek to the west, winds through much open country, and offers easy ingress from the foothills. This fact, no doubt, accounted for the penetration of the Indians at this time to the center of the Hills. With this single exception we saw no indication of their presence on the entire road from Custer to Deadwood.

On this evening we crossed Rapid Creek where the beautiful valley has a width of a mile or more, and camped for the night on the north bank. This place was known as Camp Crook, from the fact that a camp had once been made there by soldiers of a military expedition under General George Cook.[41]

Rapid Creek at this point was a splendid, clear and swift mountain stream – the largest flowing from the Hills, eastward.[42] It was a matter of some surprise that the waters of this and numerous other streams encountered contained no trout. Suckers, chub and dace there were, but not a single trout.[43]

For the second time on our trip we were reminded that there may be as much danger from excited men of one's own company as from enemies when, in the middle of the night at this camp on Rapid Creek, one of our guards fired twice at his own horse that had broken loose and was running by him. He

---

[41] Later named Pactola by Judge H. N. Maguire, who spent some time there in the fall of '76 and '77. Accessible now by rail and by a fine road from north to south through the Hills, Pactola is visited by many tourists, and residents of the foothills towns have erected summer cabins there. – [HUGHES].

According to the *South Dakota Guide,* (Federal Writers' Project, 1938), 409, Pactolus was the Lydian River whose golden sands were believed to be the source of the wealth of Croesus.

[42] From the head of its longest tributary to the confluence with the Cheyenne River, Rapid Creek has a length of fully eighty miles. – [HUGHES].

[43] Eight or ten years later, Samuel Scott and the author obtained the first consignment of trout brought into the country. These trout from Leadville, Colorado, were planted in the Cleghorn Springs and Rapid Creek at a point four miles west from Rapid City. After that they became wonderfully abundant in all the Black Hills streams. Now (1927), two hatcheries, one at Spearfish, under charge of the United States Fish Commission, and the other at Rapid City, belonging to the state, furnish millions of young fry every year to keep up the supply. – [HUGHES].

imagined the horse was an Indian on horseback, intent on stampeding the stock. This guard was a nervous Swede named John Nelson, who possibly had become frightened by the report of pony tracks seen in the forenoon, and was ready to shoot at anything that he saw moving. He awakened me where I lay under one of the wagons, by running from his beat, dropping on one knee within a few feet of my head, and discharging his rifle. He immediately reloaded and fired the second time. Had he not jammed the shell in the breech of his gun at the second discharge, it is possible that he might have continued firing until he exhausted his ammunition. His gun was what he termed a Sharps navy rifle; the only one of the kind I ever saw. The most distinguishing feature of this firearm was a leather covering that had been shrunken onto the barrel. Poor Nelson and his "leather gun" furnished the butt of many a joke for a good while thereafter.

The End of Our Journey

On the thirteenth of May we crossed the three branches of Boxelder Creek; all fine, clear mountain streams. At the middle and largest of these we found Gilbert Tower – a pioneer of Colorado – engaged in building a ranch house. He had named his ranch the Mountain Meadow, and most appropriately, as the fine, large, grassy meadow surrounded by the mountains naturally suggested the title.[44]

Our noon camp was made at this place, and during our stay the day, which had been bright, brought a change of weather. The sky became overcast, and a light mist obscured the view of the surrounding country as we proceeded northward. Anyone more used to a timbered country would have known better than to have left the road in a strange district, without a compass, under such weather conditions; but the sight of a pair of whitetail deer with their waving flags as they entered a heavy growth of jack pines beside the road, proved too much of a temptation, and I followed them. I fully determined, however, that I would not stray so far from the road that I could not speedily rejoin the wagons. Nor did I go far before, having lost sight of the deer in the pines, I sought to retrace my steps. I had tramped much farther than I thought would have been necessary to regain the road before it dawned upon me that I was hopelessly bewildered as to direction and that it was possible that I had been traveling away from, instead of toward the road.

Only those who have had the same kind of an experience can realize the feeling of utter helplessness that takes posses-

---

[44] For many years thereafter the Mountain Meadow Ranch dispensed a truly western hospitality, and many a weary traveler and prospector had occasion to bless the lucky star that had, in the spring of 1876, influenced Gilbert Tower to settle there and establish a home. Here Tower and his faithful wife lived and reared their family. Here in the beautiful Mountain Meadow they now (1927) lie side by side, their dust mingling with the soil they loved and their memories honored by all who ever were entertained beneath their roof. – [HUGHES].

sion of one under those conditions. After having tired myself pretty thoroughly by the fast pace to which I was urged by my desire to find the road, I finally concluded that I might thus be making a bad situation worse instead of better. I comforted myself as well as I could with the thought that at worst it might but mean a night in the woods for me, and that with clearing weather I should be able to get my bearings. Fortunately the sun broke out for a brief time at its setting and showed me that I had been inclined to look to the west for the road, when it lay to the east.

As I knew that I had left the road on the west side, I immediately turned squarely around and accelerated my pace, in the hope of reaching it before nightfall. When I finally did find myself on the road, it was at the very place I had left. It was then dusk. Though I knew I was in for a pretty stiff tramp before I should overtake the wagons, my feeling of relief was such that for the time I did not feel undue fatigue. I set out in good spirits, and though I tramped six additional miles before I found the outfit in camp, I made the distance in good time; pretty tired and most awfully hungry. My partners had been in some anxiety for my safety, but had not reported my absence to the captain, and seemed no less pleased at my appearance than I was to see them. I found the train camped on Elk Creek – a fine stream similar to the three that we had crossed during the day.

And now it was Sunday, May fourteenth, and we hoped with good fortune to get to the end of our journey before nightfall. Though the road for a part of the distance this day was almost as difficult as any we had encountered, by pushing the teams about to their limit, we made good progress. We crossed the north fork of Bear Butte Creek; thence over a divide heavily timbered – where many stumps impeded – and struck the head of Two Bit Creek. This we followed for several miles over an exceedingly bad road. Leaving it we climbed the divide overlooking Whitewood Creek, and were within three miles of Deadwood – our destination.

END OF OUR JOURNEY

The descent from the divide to the bottom of the little tributary of Whitewood – known as Splittail Gulch – was a more difficult problem than we had encountered on the entire road. The hill was so extremely precipitous that it seemed a dangerous undertaking to attempt the descent with wagons. There was, however, but one way down the hill; and as other wagon tracks could be seen, there was nothing to do but follow them. At the foot of the hill could be seen the broken and twisted remnants of two wagons that had been wrecked in trying to reach the bottom – a significant warning that great care would be necessary if we were to get our wagons down in safety.

On trees at either side of the road at the summit could be seen the marks where they had been girdled by ropes used to ease the wagons down. These indicated to us the method that would be necessary for us to employ. The teams were unhitched from the wagons, the tongues of which were triced up. With a heavy rope attached to the rear axle and paid out gradually from the tree around which a wrap was taken, and with guy ropes held by the men on either side, one at a time the wagons were lowered to the gulch. The work was slow and laborious, but performed without loss or damage. Again the teams were hitched and we proceeded on the last short stage of our journey. We crossed Whitewood Creek at the mouth of the little gulch. At that time Whitewood was one of the finest streams of those we had encountered in the Hills; second only in size to Rapid Creek. Its naturally clear waters only then were beginning to show a little color from the working of the few placer claims opened.[45]

A short drive from the place of crossing brought us to the lower end of Deadwood – named Elizabethtown – in honor of the first white woman in the gulch. Several log cabins were strung along the stream, occupied by miners engaged principally in digging drain ditches and awaiting the time, then near at hand, when it would be possible to procure lumber for

---

[45] The tourist who looks upon it now (1927) after it has been polluted for nearly a half century by the refuse of the towns above and the many millions of tons of mill tailings it has carried down its course, cannot imagine it as it appeared on that May day of 1876. – [HUGHES].

sluice boxes. A sawmill outfit arrived a day or two later and was soon set up and running at its full capacity, to supply the demand. We drew out of the road into the timber before dusk, lighted fires and prepared supper, glad that we had finally reached the end of the road. The humorist of our party, referring to the report we had received from returning stampeders we had met on the road, that none of those who had gone north from Custer toward Deadwood ever had returned, said that with our experience in descending the hill to the Whitewood we could realize the truth of the report; that while it was possible to get down by means of ropes, no one would ever be foolish enough to climb it.

Part II

Life in the Black Hills Country

My First Prospecting Trip

We had been on the road from Sidney a total of twenty-one days, and it had been twenty-eight days since Van Fleet, Rochford and I had left home.

The morning of the fifteenth could not come quickly enough for us to be up and alert to examine our new surroundings. The first thing necessary was to make a permanent camp in a more convenient place. After looking over the embryonic town we pulled up to City Creek, where[1] we built a brush shack of spruce boughs, roofed with bark stripped from the same trees, and finally unloaded our effects from the wagons.

We had brought with us supplies roughly calculated as sufficient for a year. As we were unloading we were approached by a number of men who offered us extravagant prices for anything we had in the way of provisions. Flour especially was lacking in the camp, and for all we had we were offered sixty dollars per hundred. Good judgment would have counselled us to sell at such a price, as in all probability freight trains would arrive before long with abundant supplies, which could be bought for much less. We, however, were inexperienced and feared there might never be any more flour after ours should be exhausted. We did not sell.[2]

The owners of the teams that had hauled our goods, however, wisely took advantage of the high prices offered, sold out completely, and started back to Sidney for another load. On this they realized a good profit also, though much less than for the first. They were more anxious to get out on the road be-

---

[1] Not fifty yards from the site of the Franklin Hotel, still standing in 1927. – [HUGHES].

[2] As the season advanced, flour was brought in in such quantities that it could be bought from the merchants at retail for nine dollars per hundred. During the following winter the price again advanced, and in the early spring of '77, during a time when bad roads made freighting almost impossible, it sold at thirty-two dollars per hundred. This was the price we paid for the first flour that we had to buy. – [HUGHES].

cause in the immediate vicinity of Deadwood there was no forage for their teams.[3] The men who returned to Sidney left Tull behind to put in his time prospecting; and he made his camp with us.

As my partners and myself had determined to devote ourselves to the work of prospecting, we agreed that one or the other of us should represent the party on any stampede to new diggings reported. We lost no time in making a beginning. The fifteenth, we devoted to placing our camp in condition for more or less permanent occupation, and in preparing our outfit for a prospecting trip to the Potato Gulch and Nigger[*] Gulch districts, thirty miles to the west. I was to start with five others on the following morning.

According to program, this party left camp on the morning of May sixteenth. It comprised besides myself, Tull, Spaulding and Sheppard, of our party, and Andy Gough – better known as "Red Cloud," from the fact that we first encountered him at Red Cloud Agency – and Jim Vanderberg, who was camped near us on City Creek. Our route led directly up Deadwood Gulch to the head; thence over the top of Bald Mountain, and down into Spearfish Canyon; thence down the Spearfish past the falls of the Little Spearfish to the mouth of Iron Creek; thence westward up Iron Creek to the head; over a low divide to Beaver Creek; to a point opposite the mouth of Potato Gulch.

We had procured pack saddles and, with our blankets, tools, and provisions securely packed on three mules, the start was made as stated.

We had not gone farther than fifty yards from camp when I found that I had left my jackknife behind and returned to get it. As I was searching for the knife, I heard shooting close at hand. On rejoining the party I found the boys busily engaged in skinning a large silvertip bear. Bruin, who evidently had not been long out of his winter quarters, had made his appearance close to the trail, where Spaulding and one or two others of the

---

[3] When the first hay was later brought into Deadwood it sold at twenty cents per pound. – [HUGHES].

[*] The name of this gulch has now been changed to Negro Gulch.

FIRST PROSPECTING TRIP

party fired upon and killed him.[4] The bear was estimated to weigh from six to seven hundred pounds. As the meat was of a nice pink color and devoid of rank odor, we placed a part of one of the hams on a pack and took it with us. Better meat or more palatable could not be desired. It had little streaks of fat through it, was not tough and, served in steaks with our camp slapjacks and coffee, afforded as good a meal as steaks of beef or venison.[5]

On the night of the sixteenth we went into camp on a mountain not yet named.[6] Its neighbor, that formed a conspicuous landmark for a long distance in every direction, had been known as Bald Mountain almost from the time of the gold discovery in Deadwood Gulch.

The climb from the head of the gulch up over old Baldy was one that taxed the breathing capacity of lungs that had been accustomed to a country of less altitude, but it also furnished an edge to appetite and made bear steak and slapjacks very acceptable. In this camp we made our coffee with water melted from snow of a deep drift nearby; a novel experience to all. The existence of this drift and the sharp air of the night that we spent there reminded us that we not only were pretty well north in latitude, but that we were pretty high up in the air.

On the seventeenth we descended to Spearfish Canyon, over a dim trail that led down from the divide not far from Annie Creek. In its upper reaches, the canyon was heavily timbered with dark pines and lighter green spruce. It was deep cut by the erosion of the swift mountain stream, through ages past. In many places the walls rose from the stream to the level of the divide in sheer precipices of many hundreds of feet in height. As the rock formations were lime and sandstone, laid down horizontally, they naturally broke off vertically, at this

---

[4] The bear was killed not more than fifty yards from the present site of Deadwood's Masonic Temple. – [HUGHES].

[5] This was exceptional. On various occasions since, I have purchased bear steak in the market, hoping to find something equal to that of my first experience, but never have I succeeded. – [HUGHES].

[6] Green Mountain.

part of the canyon, making a climb to the divide very difficult in many places, if not altogether impossible.

As we started down the descent to the canyon, Spaulding left the party and continued along the divide on the east side in a course parallel to the stream. He had decided to devote himself to hunting for market, rather than to prospecting, and wished to explore the country to locate the most promising hunting grounds. Once during the forenoon we heard the report of his rifle, and shortly afterward he came to the top of the canyon wall and called. Understanding that he wanted assistance, Red Cloud and I climbed the wall and found that he had killed a fine bull elk, the first I ever had seen with horns "in the velvet." He had cut off a ham and a shoulder, leaving the legs attached, for us to carry to camp.

Loaded with meat, we found the descent to the creek was little less arduous than the climb. In leaving camp we had gone perhaps a quarter of a mile upstream before crossing on a log. On our return we made the mistake of starting as directly toward camp as the nature of the ground allowed, and when we reached the creek no log was found on which to cross. We did not wish to retrace our steps to the place where we had crossed on going, and finally concluded to try to get over by means of a log that projected a part of the way across the stream.

Red Cloud went first. With the elk's quarter over his shoulder, and holding the shank in his hand, he made his way out upon, and to, the end of the log. Here he balanced himself for a moment and, giving a swing and a heave, threw the meat toward the bank. As the joint was limber, it kicked back when Red Cloud made the throw, and fell midway between him and the bank, into the stream.

As the fall of Spearfish Creek is ninety feet to the mile, the stream is very swift. At that time of year the water was high and almost ice cold. But the meat must be retrieved, and there was but one way to do it – that was by peeling off and going in after it. So lugubrious was the expression of Red Cloud's face as he prepared for his icy bath that "it was to laugh," and laugh I did joyously and without restraint. When the meat had been rescued and Red Cloud, shivering and with teeth chattering, was resuming his clothing, I gingerly stepped out on the log, poised myself carefully for an instant, gave my quarter of meat a swing and a heave, and – repeated the fiasco. Then Red Cloud laughed. I tried, perhaps with indifferent success, to carry off the joke with the good nature of my companion, as I, in my turn, stripped, waded in and recovered my load. As we narrated the experience in camp, all the boys seemed to find it exceedingly funny. Our failure to agree with them did not spoil our appetite for the nice elk steak we enjoyed at supper.

Tramping at this altitude and in this delightful atmosphere made mealtime always welcome, while it also insured dreamless and refreshing sleep.

On the eighteenth, we continued down Spearfish Canyon, through a huge "deadening," where the trail was made difficult by the dead trees encumbering the ground and lying in all positions. Many such deadfalls were found in the Hills, giving rise to various surmises as to their cause. Deadwood derived its name from the fact that the stream for a part of its course flowed through such a deadening.[7]

The falls of the Little Spearfish were passed on this day, and the party stopped for a time to admire the beautiful cascade and its notable setting of deep canyon and lofty precipice.[8] Leaving the canyon, we followed up the course of Iron Creek – a small tributary – to its head, and crossed a low divide to Beaver Creek. There we went into camp at a point where Beaver Creek is joined by the little stream flowing from Potato Gulch. At the mouth of the gulch we found three men engaged in opening a placer claim. They exhibited some gold

---

[7] Later scientific investigation has made it pretty certain that this timber was destroyed by the pine beetle in periodic visits long ago, as within a few years past the timber of the Hills has suffered severely from such a visitation. – [HUGHES].

[8] The waters of this lovely stream are now (1927) diverted through a tunnel several miles in length, as also are the waters of the main stream, at a tremendous expense, to furnish light and power for the Homestake Company and to light the cities of Lead and Spearfish. While many miles of beautiful water, abundantly supplied with trout, remain for the lover of nature on the upper reaches of the Spearfish and its tributaries, it is much to be regretted that a great part of the district's charm thus has been sacrificed. – [HUGHES].

of an extra fine quality, among which were several nice nuggets. One of these had a value of about sixty dollars, estimated, as the miners had no scales for weighing. The men who were working this claim had been subsisting for some time on venison straight, and were grateful for a few pounds of flour we could spare them to make a little bread. Venison is very good meat but, used as an exclusive diet even for a few days, is likely to pall upon the taste. In the early spring, too, it usually is in poor condition. Thus, while deer were everywhere abundant and so tame that even an indifferent hunter could easily procure meat, a little variation in the menu was something to be highly appreciated.

The miners, as well as a party of three others encountered farther up the stream, did not speak encouragingly of the prospect of striking big pay in the district. They had prospected all the neighboring gulches, and the claims on which they were working were the best they had found. Even those they did not consider sufficiently promising to warrant much work. They were contemplating going back to the Deadwood district from which they had come.

While several of our party explored the neighboring gulches, others dug our first prospect hole on Beaver Creek. Working in relays, we soon reached the gravel, but finding not even the finest "color," we abandoned it.

We spent the nineteenth in trying the first of several small dry gulches with shallow bedrock, but finding nothing encouraging, we decided to take the trail for Deadwood on the following morning. Everywhere there were signs of an abundance of big game: bear, deer, elk and mountain sheep; while ruffled grouse frequently were seen so tame that they would not flush, but merely dodged into the timber at the side of the trail and watched us in apparent curiosity as we passed.

On this day we encountered two men as they were skinning an old she bear they had shot. They had captured her two cubs and later took them to Deadwood. Spaulding was well pleased with the game he had seen and the signs of its abundance on every hand, and he realized that he had indeed found a hunter's paradise.[9]

---

[9] During several years succeeding, while he hunted for the markets of Deadwood and other camps, Johnny T. Spaulding took a tremendous toll of the game animals of the Hills and of the buffalo and antelope that were numerous on the plains country to the north. In hauling this game to market Hall and Tomlins, the two men who were with him when we first encountered the party at the North Platte crossing on our way to the Hills, still were his partners. John Spaulding was a fine character, and in some respects, a remarkable one. That he was an expert rifleman, has been mentioned, but this mere statement does not by any means do him justice. It would be more correct to say that he was a phenomenal rifleman – not one of those experts who give exhibitions of marvelous skill in shooting at small targets thrown in the air – but as a hunter. Of his skill with the rifle, no one ever heard him boast. If any attempt was made to draw him out on the subject, he would change it as quickly as possible, or if he talked of shooting at all, it would be to tell of the exploits of some friend or companion of his days on the buffalo range. Though he had spent years among the rough characters of the frontier, he never had adopted their vices. He used neither liquor nor tobacco in any form, and an obscene or profane word I never heard pass his lips. So modest was he in speaking of himself that stories of his skill only became known through others, who had been with him on some of his hunting trips.

Tull, who was no unskilled hunter himself, declared that Spaulding was as certain of killing a deer at four or five hundred yards, as the average marksman would be at half the distance. He told of one instance that occurred when he and Spaulding were hunting together. Tull was somewhat in advance, and on ascending a little knoll saw two deer, but at such a distance that he would not think of risking a shot at them. He stepped back and told Spaulding, adding that by making a detour it would be possible to come within range of the game. To this Spaulding replied, "Let me see where they are." Going to the top of the knoll, he said, "No, Sam, they're not too far," and he killed the first in its tracks. The second had to run but a few yards when it, too, fell, pierced by a bullet from the deadly Maynard rifle. Jesse Hall told of having seen Spaulding kill fifteen antelope on a single "stand" with fifteen shots. That he killed an Indian at a range of five hundred yards, or over, on one of his scouting expeditions on the Belle Fourche was told of him, and as he did not deny the story, it may be considered true. Had it not been true, he never would have allowed it to go without a denial. When range beef began to take the place of wild game in the markets, Spaulding settled down to raising horses in the Bear Lodge country, where I visited him in the eighties, and received a most hearty welcome.

Spaulding finally moved to Washington, and when the Spanish American War broke out, went to the Philippines as one of the volunteers from that state. When he returned home, he moved to California. In 1920 I received a long and interesting letter from him, in which he recalled our first meeting on the banks of the swollen North Platte, alluding to the fact that of the large company I was the youngest member. – [HUGHES].

Johnny Spaulding revisited the Hills and spent many hours with Richard Hughes. These visits, just a few weeks before the end of the trail of the author, gave him what was probably the greatest pleasure of his declining years. – [R. L. H.].

According to program, on the morning of May twentieth our party took the back trail to Deadwood. We camped on Spearfish Canyon again that night. On the morning of the twenty-first, Red Cloud, Vanderberg and I started across the country ahead of the others, intent on saving distance. As a rule the traveler in an unfamiliar country does well to keep to established trails. The truth of this advice we realized before arriving in camp in Deadwood, for we encountered much rough country and had to make our way over much fallen timber; a tiresome process, as any one who has tried it will agree. We reached Deadwood about dusk in the evening, tired as may be supposed, and with appetites that did ample justice to the supper prepared for us by Van Fleet and Rochford.

"BUCKSKIN JOHNNIE" SPAULDING

SLUICING IN THE BLACK HILLS

Prospecting Dry Gulches

On my return from the expedition to Potato Gulch, May twentieth, I found that my partners had not been idle during my absence. They had prospected a number of dry gulches having shallow bedrock, in the neighborhood, and had made plans for testing others; so that our days now were fully occupied. We were somewhat hindered in our operations by the character of the weather. The season was disagreeable, with much rain; and snow fell at intervals as late as June fifth, when it culminated in a fall of five inches.

We took advantage of every dry or partially dry day and frequently reached camp in the evening wet, tired, and uncomfortable. That we always returned hungry goes without saying and a good, warm supper usually made us forget the fatigue and discomfort of the day. The good digestion that waits upon appetite, "and health on both," made life in the open air a pleasure; when one rolled into his blankets at night his sleep was so refreshing as to make him welcome the activities of the next day.

In the life of the prospector there is the constant hope of making a discovery of value, to keep him stimulated; and no matter how often he may have been disappointed he never is utterly discouraged. If he has had long experience in mining districts he can tell you true tales of men whom he has known who were lifted from poverty to affluence by the last lucky stroke of the pick that reached the pay gravel, or the final blast of powder that disclosed rich ore. He can tell, perhaps, of fortunes made and lost by himself, but beyond doubt he can tell of times when wonderful opportunity knocked at his door and he unfortunately failed to recognize it.

Such experiences naturally tend to keep the old prospector buoyed up and hopeful that what has happened may happen again, and his determination to "salt down" his next "stake," he declares, is unalterable. His narrations, too, tend to awaken in the tenderfoot an enthusiasm for the game that rapidly develops, and in a short time he becomes as hopeful and optimistic a prospector as any old-timer.

During our first month we saw much of the northern Hills. If we were not engaged in digging and panning, we put in the time looking over the country, examining such quartz lodes as were in process of development in the various neighboring districts. During this month a number of friends arrived from Nebraska, among them several who originally had intended to join us when we left home. While our prospecting had not resulted in the discovery of anything of apparently great value, we had located ground in Hidden Treasure and Pocket Gulches, about two and a half miles above Deadwood. These were small tributaries of Deadwood and seemed to possess possibilities of value warranting further exploration.

Up to this time we had been camped on City Creek, at what was at that time the upper end of Deadwood, where we had first unloaded our freight from the wagons. Not expecting to camp there permanently, we had not built a cabin, but had occupied a primitive shack made of brush, and covered with bark stripped from spruce trees. This did not make the most comfortable quarters possible for a wet, cold spring, but many of the people now coming in large numbers were not even as well sheltered, and those unaccustomed to roughing it suffered much inconvenience and discomfort.

Now that we had made a definite location of ground, we built a cabin in Pocket Gulch, and on June twenty-second, moved up the gulch and occupied it.

After suppertime every evening, when the night shift would go on duty, at the farthest cabin down the gulch would arise the cry well known in every mining camp of the West since '49, of "Oh, Joe." This cry would be taken up at the next cabin above, and repeated, and on up the gulch would roll the sound, through the camps and towns, gathering volume as it came, and finally dying out in the distance of the cabins farthest up stream. Possibly nothing like it ever was heard outside of mining camps; the tenderfoot who heard it for the first time will still recall the singular sensation it evoked when he listened to the peculiar cry as it woke the echoes through the gulches, and was re-echoed from the surrounding hills, gradually diminishing in volume as it passed him by and finally was lost to his hearing.

Such customs usually grow out of incidents that have occurred in the past, and this was no exception. The story was that a prospector, in attempting to reach his cabin after nightfall in an intoxicated condition, fell into a prospect hole. There he spent the night in calling at the top of his voice, upon his partner, Joe, for assistance.

Discovery of gold on Deadwood Gulch[10] was made in December of 1875, at a point about two miles above its junction

---

[10] "It appears from trustworthy information, that the first exploration of that portion of the northern Hills, bordering on Whitewood Creek, was made by Frank Bryant and party in August, 1875. . . Frank Bryant, with a party of six others, viz: John Pearson, Thomas Moon, Richard Lowe, James Peierman, Samuel Blodgett, and George Hansen, seven in all, arrived in the Hills, from some Missouri River point . . . making the first camp in Spring Valley. . . One of the party, Sam Blodgett, while hunting came upon a gulch and with John Pearson prospected on what was later called 'Deadwood Gulch'." Annie D. Tallent, *op.cit.*, 171-2. Mrs. Tallent later, p. 176-77, listed Ed McKay as one of the early Deadwood prospectors.

John S. McClintock, *Pioneer Days in the Black Hills* (Deadwood, 1939), 33, says, " . . . it can safely be assumed that the Blanchard party (A. S. Blanchard) is the one that came into the gulch from the south . . . and that the Blanchard party from Custer made the first discovery of gold in Deadwood Gulch, September 6th, 1875 . . . a few days later, the same month, the Gay party arrived."

As the first discovery of placer gold on Deadwood was made at a point where later were developed the richest diggings of the district, so, too, was the first discovery of gold-bearing ore made where the premier mine of the Hills is in operation today. This was made in the Hills at the head of Gold Run and crossing the divide to Bobtail and Deadwood Creeks to the west. Many quartz claims were located, our territorial law prescribing that a single claim should embrace no more than a tract three hundred feet in width by fifteen hundred in length, ten acres in all, but placing no restriction upon the number of claims a man might take, provided he complied with the requirements of the law in improving them. He was supposed to do at least one hundred dollars worth of work on each claim per year in order to hold it. In the course of the years that have gone, many men and companies became interested in quartz mines of the district mentioned, but one by one they were absorbed by the giant company that secured the Homestake as a nucleus. The head of this company was the powerful Hearst interest, and the company has developed [at Lead] what is in many respects the world's greatest gold with Whitewood. Within a half mile above and below "discovery" all of the very rich placer claims of the northern Hills were located. Several of these – the best known being the Wheeler and Chisholm claims – were phenomenally rich. While a goodly number of others yielded good pay, none approximated the yield of the gold here obtained.[11] It is doubtful if the owners ever made known the exact amount extracted from their claims, but it was a matter of general understanding that for a considerable time each of those named turned out an average of three to four thousand dollars to the shift.

When the first district was organized[12] the miners established the size of a claim at three hundred feet in length along the path of the gulch, extending, of course, from rim to rim on either side. When later a large number of men drifted in from the mining camps of Montana[13] and other parts of the West and found that all the choice ground had been taken, a strong demand was made that the size of the claims be reduced to one hundred feet each. To this, naturally, there was vigorous protest by the claim owners; and when the controversy became heated, they openly declared that if necessary they would make their protest good by a resort to arms.

For a time the situation was really threatening, but leaders of the newcomers became convinced that due to the character of the ground – deep bedrock in some parts and meagre pay in others – it could not be worked to advantage if divided into

---

mine, employing an average of three thousand men and having a record of approximately six millions of dollars annual gold production for more than forty years past. Such an accomplishment would have been impossible to any but a strong corporation capable of operating on a stupendous scale with the low-grade ores of those mines. – [HUGHES].

[11] Later the finest nuggets ever found in the Hills were taken from Potato and Nigger Gulches, but they were few in number, and on the whole the judgment of the miners mentioned, that the district would not become an important producer, has been justified. – [HUGHES].

[12] At a miners' meeting held in December (1875), a mining district was organized and appropriately named the "Lost Mining District." . . . William Lardner was chosen recorder of the district, and by the rules established to govern the same, was vested with the right to charge a fee of $1.50 per claim for recording locations. – Annie D. Tallent, *op.cit.*, 176.

[13] *See* Appendix D.

smaller holdings; the trouble subsided without a collision. Thus the three hundred foot claim was established; and before the end of the summer there was a miner's cabin on every one – or nearly every one – and a large force of men was employed in opening up the ground and shoveling into the sluices.

Ditches, drains and flumes appeared on every hand; the aggregate of gold taken out was very large, and dust became the well nigh universal medium of exchange. A tramp of four or five miles along Deadwood and Whitewood Creeks and their tributaries of Gold Run, Bobtail and Blacktail – where all the paying placers of the district were located – disclosed scenes of the greatest activity either day or night, as many of the claims were worked in two ten-hour shifts.[14]

---

[14] *See* Appendix E.

Deadwood, Biggest Little Town on Earth

The first part of Deadwood[15] had been laid out twenty days previous to our arrival, in a dense forest of pine and spruce timber; Main Street ran north and south, parallel with Whitewood Gulch, and two or three other streets crossed at right angles. Only Main Street was taking form at this time, as a number of log cabins had been built and others were under way; while for some two or three blocks in length, the trees had been cut. The question of title to lots already was causing trouble. The miners who had located the ground claimed the right to the entire area from surface to bedrock for the whole width of the gulch; while many of those intent on putting up buildings contended that the miners were entitled to no more ground than they found necessary to use in their mining operations. The claim owners had the better of the argument, as they had the undoubted right to enter upon any part of their claims, and a statement that it was intended to sink a shaft in the center of a house being erected by a squatter usually brought the latter to terms.

Where the price demanded for the so-called "bedrock title" was considered exorbitant, sometimes serious trouble arose. More than one shooting affray resulted from such a demand. As a rule, however, the differences were adjusted without great difficulty, and in a short time the squatters came to a general acknowledgment that the miner's right would hold as against any or all others. When controversy over this matter ceased, building went on more rapidly; and as lumber from the sawmills became available it was generally used for the fronts of the buildings designed for business purposes.

Of the structures fronting Main Street, the majority occupied by the last of May were saloons and gambling houses,

---

[15] The site of original Deadwood was located on the 26th day of April, 1876, by Craven Lee, Isaac Brown, J. J. Williams and others below the junction of Deadwood and Whitewood Creeks. – Annie D. Tallent, *op. cit.*, 346.

DEADWOOD 79

where practically every form of gambling known in America was conducted. Such places never closed their doors, day or night; each had a force of men who worked in regular relays in keeping the games running. By the first of June three dance halls offered their allurements to the incoming traveler. Within a short time thereafter two variety shows were giving regular performances, and the legitimate drama was presented at Langrishe's theater. The streets at right angles to Main Street were hewn out through the timber; and building was pushed forward rapidly to supply the demand caused by the rush of people, which now assumed large proportions.

By the middle of June, Deadwood, which had become the objective point of all travel into the Hills, presented a scene of great activity. The placers that had been opened on Deadwood, Whitewood, Gold Run, Bobtail, and Blacktail Gulches were turning out large amounts of dust, which many of the miners were spending in the manner of the proverbial drunken sailor – in drinking, dancing, gambling and every form of carousal offered. Wages to shovelers on bedrock were seven dollars per day or night shift. Such pay, to a lot of young fellows from the States – many of whom probably never had been paid more than fifty dollars per month – made them feel almost rich. They received their wages in gold dust at the rate of twenty dollars per ounce, though this later was reduced to eighteen dollars. It did not seem like paying out real money, to allow a saloon or gamekeeper to help himself to a pinch of the dust from a man's buckskin gold sack, in settling for his entertainment.

Gold scales and a "blower" formed a part of the necessary equipment of anyone who had anything to sell. The blower was a shallow receptacle made of tin or sheet iron, six inches wide at one end and half that width at the other. The edges turned up all around except at the narrow end. Into this the dust to be weighed would be poured from the sack. By shaking it gently and blowing the breath upon it, such sand as accompanied the dust would be separated from it, and the weigher would get nothing but gold for his pay. The fellow who owned the sack, as a rule, was not so well protected, and often found, in payment of a number of small bills, that what he had accepted from his boss as an ounce or two had shrunk several pennyweights.

Sunday was by far the busiest day of the week. On that day work on many of the placer claims was discontinued, and the men employed in them were added to the regular weekday crowd. Prospectors, too, from the many gulches of the surrounding country, on this day visited the town to do their trading and get their mail. On any Sunday it might be said with truth, that nearly the entire population of the northern Hills was concentrated on Main Street, presenting a scene that those who beheld it never can forget. On every side arose the noise of building. On the one hand could be heard the voice of a reverend gentleman preaching to the assembled multitude on the street; within a short distance a street faker could be heard crying his wares; or a gambler with a sure-thing game, trying to convince the unwary tenderfoot that by the investment of a dollar or two he would double the amount ventured. In the throng the buckskin-clad mountaineer jostled the pilgrim from the east, and representatives of every type which the United States produces could be seen.

On such a day the chief interest centered at places where mail from the states had been received during the week previous. No government or other mail service had been established, and the people depended upon incoming wagon trains to gather mail that had accumulated at Sidney, Fort Laramie, or Fort Pierre as the case might be, and bring it through. On several occasions trains with mail were held in camp for a considerable time by Indians. A single train sometimes brought in tons of delayed letters.

The mail distribution was a big thing financially,[16] fifty cents being the price exacted for every letter handed out!

---

[16] Seymour, Utter & Ingalls launched what they called the "Pioneer Pony Express" in July. Their carriers made the trip between Ft. Laramie and Deadwood in forty-eight hours and often carried three thousand to forty-five hundred letters, at a charge of twenty-five cents each. – Agnes Wright Spring, *Cheyenne and Black Hills Stage and Express Routes,* 155.

When the mail was sorted and arranged alphabetically in piles, a man would call out the names of those to whom the letters were addressed. It was not uncommon to see a crowd of from 1,500 to 2,500 men present at such a delivery. Several clerks were kept busy handing out letters, and as many more in weighing in the dust paid for them. When the greatest rush would be past, applicants for mail would line up in front of the delivery window. The lines sometimes stretched for blocks in length. Frequently an individual would be compelled to spend several hours in the line before reaching the window. It was an invariable rule that on reaching it, the man must inquire for mail in no more than one name. To inquire for a second person, it was necessary for the person to take his position at the extreme end of the line and again work his way up. The unsophisticated tenderfoot who promised all his comrades on leaving camp for town, that he would get their mail, never made the promise more than once.

Within two or three months after we built our cabin, Deadwood had spread pretty well across Whitewood Gulch. Down the course of that stream a single long extension of Main Street was made, the lower parts of which were known respectively as Elizabethtown and Fountain City. Where the character of the ground permitted, houses were built on either side. Where the ground was too rough or uneven only one side was built up, principally of log buildings and shanties of rough lumber.

In the upper Deadwood Gulch the same kind of string town was taking shape. Gayville[17] – named for Bill and Al Gay, the discoverers of Deadwood Gulch – was started contemporaneously with Deadwood, and about two miles distant. From this, extensions were made up the gulch; gradually at first.[18]

---

[17] The first cabin in the gulch was built by Alfred Gay in the fall of 1875.- Annie D. Tallent, *op. cit.,* 528.

[18] This string town exceeded Deadwood in length, within a year, though much less in population. Beginning with Gayville, these extensions took in order the names of South Bend, Central, Golden Gate and Anchor. Of the number, Central is the only one that has survived, a post office and some business houses still (1926) being maintained there. A majority of the buildings in the other so-called towns long since have been torn down and the materials used for fuel. – [HUGHES].

As the best of the placers had been located early in the life of the camps, the attention of prospectors naturally turned to the search for valuable quartz; within a short time a great many locations of that kind were made. As a rule the ores discovered were of a grade so low that the miners who had had experience with the ores of California and elsewhere, declared without hesitation that these would not pay for working. Here and there, however, ore running high in values was found, thus stimulating the work of prospecting.

AMUSEMENTS IN DEADWOOD

Vaudeville, or as it was more commonly known, "The Varieties," furnished entertainment which at times was of a high class. Even during the winter there appeared upon the stage artists of more than average ability. A favorite banjo player and vocalist was Dick Brown, known familiarly throughtout the West as "Banjo Dick" or "Handsome Dick." His songs of the mining camps always elicited applause from the old timers of California and Montana, and never was he allowed to retire from the "first" part without rendering the miners' favorite, *The Days of Forty-Nine*.[19] This is the old song, as the writer remembers it:

> Your're looking now on old Tom Moore, a relic of former days,
> And though they call me a bummer sure, I care not for their praise;
> For my heart is filled with the days of yore, and oft I do repine
> For the days of old, the days of gold, the days of forty-nine.
>
> I'd comrades then who loved me well, a jovial, saucy crew,
> Though some were cases I must confess, they were both brave and true.
> They'd never flinch whate'er the pinch, they'd never fret nor whine,
> Like good old bricks they stood the kicks in the days of forty-nine.
>
> There was New York Jake, the butcher boy, so fond of getting tight,
> Whenever Jake was on a spree he was spiling for a fight;
> But he ran against a knife one night in the hand of old Bob Kline,
> And over Jake we made a wake in the days of forty-nine.

---

[19] *See* B. A. Botkin, Ed., *A Treasury of Western Folklore* (New York: Crown Pub., 1951), II, p. 735.

There was Monte Pete, Oh, I'll never forget the luck that he always had,
He'd sit and deal for you all night, or as long as you had a scad;
One night a pistol laid him out, 'twas his last "layout" in fine –
Death caught Pete sure dead in the door, in the days of forty-nine.

There was Rackensack Jim, who could outroar a buffalo bull you bet;
He'd roar all night and he'd roar all day, and I guess he's roaring yet;
One night he fell in a prospect hole – 'twas a roaring bad design,
For in that hole Jim roared out his soul in the days of forty-nine.

Of all the comrades I had then not one is left to boast,
And now I wander 'round the world like some poor traveling ghost;
And as I steer from place to place, they call me a wandering sign –
There goes old Tom Moore, a bummer sure, but a relic of forty-nine.

One night in the winter of '76, Brown had completed his rendition of the old song, to his own accompaniment on the banjo, and was seated in the semicircle of the first part, when a man approached the stage from the front of the house. Picking up an axe, that lay by the big box stove, he threw it on the stage. Brown rose from his seat, drawing a revolver, and stepped to the front of the stage, where he discharged five or six shots into the man's body. He then resumed his seat and the performance was continued. The injured man was carried out and died within the hour. His name was Ed Shaughnessy, and he had been a conductor on the Union Pacific. It developed in the trial of Brown – who was acquitted on the plea of self defense – that Fannie Garretson, a vocalist – who accompanied Brown to the Hills, and who was on the stage at the time of the tragedy – had been living with Shaughnessy, but had forsaken him for Brown. Shaughnessy followed the pair to the Hills and, crazed with jealousy and liquor, had made his way into the Bella Union, where Brown and the woman were performing. Shaughnessy evidently was intent on revenge, though probably in no condition to do injury – as the throwing of the axe on the stage was little more than a drunken gesture and endangered no one. A somewhat remarkable sequel to this tragedy was the publication in *The Pioneer* of a communication from the woman, which stated that her reputation had suffered injury from the circulation of the report that she had been married to Shaughnessy. This report she desired to brand as false; she wanted it distinctly understood that she never had been Shaughnessy's wife; she merely had lived with him. And this statement she had corroborated by several more or less reputable people of Laramie and Cheyenne.

In a rival house across the street from the Belle Union and known as The Gem, a favorite performer was a female dancer named Kitty LeRoy. She was remarkably graceful, and her seeming modesty amid surroundings where not all was modest or refined, always attracted favorable attention. She was unfortunate in arousing the jealousy of an admirer who, after a quarrel, killed the girl and immediately afterward killed himself.

MEN FROM MONTANA COME TO HILLS[20]

Lying in close proximity to the Black Hills, it was natural that the territory of Montana should contribute largely to the numbers of people rushing hither upon the report that gold had been discovered in paying quantities. Especially well represented in this Montana contingent were the mining towns and camps – men who could tell of the palmy days of Last Chance and Alder Gulches; the beginnings of the great quartz mining operations that have made Montana famous; of the struggle between the forces of lawlessness and those of law and order, culminating in the hanging of Joseph Slade and the dispersion of his gang in Virginia City; and of the many interesting incidents that made the name Montana suggest to the tenderfoot a land of romance.

Coming in large numbers, the Montanians were composed of all kinds and classes. It was natural that many turbulent and undesirable characters should welcome the opening of a new gold field with all its possibilities of gain, and where the strings and restrictions of the law would not draw as tightly as they had begun to do in the older territory. Such characteristics, with their hangers-on and camp followers, certainly constituted a considerable percentage of the immigration from

---

[20] *See* Appendix D.

Montana, and helped make conditions in Deadwood such as to stigmatize it as the "wickedest town in America." This, of course, was an exaggeration.

If Montana did thus pour into the Hills many undesirable people, this was far more than counterbalanced by the many fine characters the territory furnished – men who represented to a marked degree all that was best in the life of the frontier. The list of names is a long one, and it would be impossible for the writer to recall more than a small minority worthy of mention. Among them were such men as Seth Bullock (first sheriff of Lawrence County), and his partner, Sol. Star; Ernest May; the Koenigsberg brothers; Aaron Nyswanger; Harry Gregg; A. J. Simmons; J. K. P. Miller; Bart Henderson; John and George Argue; Con Stapleton and John Belding. Pioneers of two – a number of them of three – territories, those men had not only seen history in the making, but they were makers of the history of the northwest. . . Of this Montana contingent Seth Bullock was an outstanding figure.

EARLY NEWSPAPERS

In those early years, during Deadwood's golden days from '76 to '80, there were established in the town six daily newspapers; no less than five struggled for supremacy in the field at the same time. First was *The Pioneer,* the weekly issue of which was established in June of '76. In '77 followed *The Times,* founded by Porter Warner; *The Champion,* founded by that erratic Irishman, Charley Collins who, with Pete O'Sullivan and Cal. Caldwell, had established *The Times* in Sioux City (Iowa), when the town was no more that a frontier hamlet; *The Enterprise,* established by Webster, the big-hearted – always referred to by his employees as "the good, kind jedge;" *The Press,* founded by Charley Moody, who was the peer of any in wit; and *The News,* founded by Miller and Flynn – the former became postmaster at Pierre; the latter, a printer of exceptional ability.

As may well be imagined, in a field so small, there was intense rivalry among the newspapers, and many and bitter were the controversies in which they engaged. The term "Personal Journalism" is one that has long been familiar, but it is doubtful if it ever elsewhere reached the limit to which it was stretched in Deadwood and between the Deadwood papers and the *Central Herald*, published by J. S. Bartholomew at Central. If those who took part were alive today and could look back over the past, the recollections of the vituperative abuse in which they indulged could bring nothing but regret.

With so great a number of newspapers in a limited field it was natural that there should be a concentration here of newspaper talent; many an editorial written and published in the Deadwood papers of that day would have attracted attention in the columns of the most metropolitan publications. The entire United States was drawn upon for able writers, at an expense that could not by any means be warranted by the income possible to papers that could have but a limited circulation at best. Telegraphic tolls over the privately owned lines were exorbitant, but the service was a necessity; altogether the outlay was so great that it was certain so large a number of papers could not long survive. One by one they dropped out of existence or were moved elsewhere – as in the case of the *Enterprise*, which went to Lead; and the *Press* to Sturgis, after the establishment of that town; until there were left but *The Pioneer* and *The Times*. One man who stands out as a prominent figure among the writers for *The Pioneer* was Colonel Pete (though known as "Pat") Donan. He was a man with a wonderful command of the English language, which he delighted in using to demolish everyone who incurred his antagonism. He had been editor of the *Okalona States*, an unreconstructed rebel paper of the most radical type. Coming to this part of the country at a time when the bitterness of feeling engendered by the Civil War had not altogether abated, he found himself in a somewhat uncongenial atmosphere.

One of the very finest editorial writers who ever did duty on a Deadwood paper was Major W. R. Snider. He had a vitriolic pen but socially was a lovable character, and one who held his friends in strong affection. L. F. Whitbeck, whose first newspaper work in the Hills was in the capacity of correspondent of the *New York Tribune,* was one of the brightest writers on *The Times;* followed by the equally competent Dan Scott; and he, by Gene Decker. All of those here named were men whose work would have been considered good in any newspaper field. J. M. Whitton, who served *The Pioneer* well as city editor, and who liked nothing better than a warm newspaper fight with his contemporaries, is deserving of mention as among the best; Colonel Carmack, a New York man who came to the Hills as superintendent of the Cheyenne mine, and who wrote from a wide knowledge of national politics and a love of writing, furnished many editorials for *The News,* of such character as to place him on a par with the ablest men in his field.

As towns grew up about the foothills one or more newspapers were established in them. *The Rapid City Journal* issued its first number in the beginning of '78, grew and prospered, and established a daily.

DEADWOOD'S PIONEER LAWYERS

Before the beginning of '77 an array of legal talent was assembled in Deadwood, that certainly never has been surpassed in ability by the bar of a community of equal population. Men who were qualified to attain high rank in their profession in the highest courts of the country were numerous. When finally the Indian title to the Hills was extinguished, civil government established in legal form and courts provided, it was a constant source of wonder that this out-of-the-way frontier could have allured so great a number of brilliant lawyers. In this list were such men as Corson and Thomas – the former, first Chief Justice of the state; the talented Steel and that compendium of mining law, his partner, Judge McLaughlin; Granville G. Bennett, federal judge for the district embracing the Hills; Claggett of the silver tongue – the same Claggett who was a companion of Mark Twain on the Humboldt Mountain stampede described in Twain's *Roughing It;* Kingsley, Claggett's partner, small in stature but large in intellect; the courtly Van Cise and his no less courtly partner, Wilson; brainy and resourceful Caulfield, and his equally talented partner, Carey; the dignified and able Moody; Eben W. Martin, able member of Congress for four terms; Mason, Gooding, Graham, Parker, Frawley, Plowman, and many others equally worthy of mention as men of outstanding ability, but whose names cannot now be recalled.

DEADWOOD IN 1877

LOOKOUT MINE NEAR ROCHFORD
About 1886

"Sam's Mine," The Great Homestake And Stampedes of '76

While devoting our attention principally to prospecting for placers during the months of May and June, my partners and I did not altogether overlook the opportunity to secure some interests in quartz, which was daily engaging increased attention. The predictions of mining men from other districts that the ores of the Hills would not be profitably worked, because of too low a grade, had ceased to have effect as discoveries were made here and there of ores as rich as known elsewhere.

At the head of Gold Run, two brothers named Fred and Moses Manuel – French Canadians – with a third partner, Alex. Engh, had made the first opening on a location which they named the "Homestake." It was expressive of the hope that the claim would prove of a value sufficient to enable them to retire to their homes in that degree of affluence designated in miners' parlance as a "stake," – a hope in which happily they were not disappointed. While as a whole the ore encountered by the Manuels was of low grade, it is certain that they found some that was sufficiently rich to enable them to meet their expenses for tools, powder and provisions, by pulverizing it in a mortar and panning the gold.

Around the Homestake many other claims were located, and of those, a large number showed good prospects. Among the claims that attained considerable prominence under their original names may be mentioned the Palmetto-American Flag, Golden Star, Giant, and Old Abe.[21]

While the first work was in progress on the Homestake and adjacent claims, others were being located and opened on the opposite side of the mountain, looking toward Deadwood Creek, and on both sides of Bobtail. On the Deadwood side one of the first locations to come into prominence was named

---

[21] Manuel brothers located Old Abe, discovered by Pearson.

the Father DeSmet, in honor of the Jesuit missionary who had spent many years among the Indians. It was told of him that, learning from the Indians of the existence of gold in the Black Hills, he warned them against allowing this to become known, as the whites would surely take their country away from them should they learn the truth.

In the early days of the Hills, the fable that Father DeSmet knew of the location of a veritable "mountain of gold" was repeated around many campfires. The DeSmet lode was located by a party of men named Lardner, O'Neill, Coleman and Flaherty. On one side and parallel to the DeSmet, they claimed additional ground under the names of the Golden Gate and Belcher.

At the same time my partners and I had been prospecting on the Deadwood side of the mountain and had posted our notice, laying claim to the usual amount of ground embraced in a quartz location. Here we came in conflict with the men who had located the claims above mentioned, and we were warned against trespassing on the property. We were not disposed to give up what we considered belonged to us by right of first location and development, but one or two of the men of the opposing party had reputations that guaranteed trouble for those running counter to them, and we took serious counsel as to what course we should pursue. One fact that had greatest weight with us was that neither Rochford nor myself had yet reached his majority; therefore, if the matter should come to a final test, we feared that our right to locate ground at all might be successfully questioned.

The difficulty finally was adjusted by our acceptance of an interest in the Justice fraction,[22] an extension of the Belcher.

---

[22] This proved in later years as valuable as any part of the DeSmet group, of which it formed a part, though the name Justice as applied to this claim and the settlement that gave it the title has ever since been considered by us a misnomer. The owners of the DeSmet group, after some work of development, introduced an arastra or two for crushing ore. By this process the ore was ground between heavy rocks attached to sweeps, carried around in a circular enclosure with a stone floor. While reasonably effective, the process was tedious, the manner of "cleaning up" slow and laborious, and for ores of a low grade it was considered unsatisfactory. With the introduction of stamp mills such tests of the ore were made as enabled

HOMESTAKE MINE—'76 STAMPEDES

Our holdings in the group as a whole being small, our partners not inclined to give us much consideration and, above all, being somewhat pressed for means, in the winter of '76 we sold our interest in the Justice to Captain Nichols for a total of five ounces of gold dust, which had a value approximating one hundred dollars. This we used in equipping Rochford for the great Wolf Mountain stampede.

The first mine on the Bobtail side of the divide to attract favorable notice was known as the Golden Terra. Following its discovery came the location of many other claims adjacent, and the little town of Terraville grew up and soon became a busy center.[23]

One of the early locators in the Bobtail district was our friend, Sam Tull. He had staked his claim – which his partners insisted on naming "Sam's Mine" – immediately after our return from the Potato Creek country. On making his location, Tull immediately built a cabin upon it, wisely concluding that with the interest aroused in quartz it would be well to be in actual possession of the ground at all times. That his judgment was good – as it usually was – is indicated by the fact that while there was much trouble about overlapping and conflicting claims all around him, he never was involved in any such difficulties.

On completion of his cabin he at once moved from our camp and occupied it, and with his accustomed energy de-

---

the owners to dispose of the group at a price then considered large, though much less than that later obtained by the purchaser from the California capitalists, who adopted the name of the DeSmet Company, inaugurated extensive developments and introduced extensive machinery for working it. After a long drawn out contest that involved many issues, and in which the Homestake finally won a complete victory, the DeSmet group passed into the possession of the great rival company, and the names of the original locations that were merged in the group probably are remembered by few persons in the Hills today (1927). Of the locators of the DeSmet claim there is, so far as this writer is aware, no survivor. – [HUGHES]

[23] Located by individuals and small and financially weak companies, it was inevitable that when they reached a stage guaranteeing profit in working, they, too, should be absorbed by a company strong enough to develop and work them on an extensive scale. One by one they fell into the possession of the Homestake, and for many years have been operated as a part of that great company's holdings, all of which are connected by extensive underground workings.

voted himself to its development. In locating the ground he had represented his two partners, who had gone back to Sidney for freight soon after our arrival. While his partners kept Tull supplied with everything necessary for his work, occasionally one of them would spend some time in assisting him.[24]

STAMPEDES OF '76

Up to June 18, 1876, my partners and myself had put in nearly every day when not hindered by bad weather, in prospecting; but without finding anything of value, if the Justice claim be excepted. On the date mentioned there was a stampede to False Bottom Gulch. Though this name has been applied as if given before this date, as a matter of fact, it was on this date it became permanently fixed upon the gulch. Being so near to the populous camps, the gulch had been prospected to such an extent that it was unreasonable to believe that gold could be found there; bedrock had been reached in many prospect holes without finding a color.

Interest in the gulch was now stimulated by a report, generally circulated, that heretofore the true bedrock had not been reached; but that now two miners had sunk a deep shaft, penetrating the formation that had been considered bedrock, and found a bed of pay gravel below. Hence, the name "False Bottom."

This story did not seem probable enough to engage serious attention. But such is the credulity of the average prospector – who, whatever discouragements and disappointments he may have experienced in former stampedes, is ever hopeful of striking rich placer diggings – that hundreds flocked to False

---

[24] By the fall of '77 the development on Sam's Mine was such as to disclose a large body of good ore. Overtures for purchase had been made from time to time by various parties as the work progressed, but those Sam had declined, having determined that he would push the work far enough to prove the property before offering it for sale. When the development had reached the stage he had determined upon, he was not long in finding a buyer at the price he had placed upon it. The amount obtained for the mine was sufficient to enable Sam, with his third share, to buy a tract of fine fruit land in Kansas, and thence he retired and lived out the remainder of his long, active and useful life. *See* Appendix B.

Bottom. The gulch was located in three-hundred-foot claims from the head to the prairie. The excitement died as rapidly as it had arisen, when it was discovered that all was a hoax.

It started with a practical joke played by two young fellows on two of their friends, for whose benefit they "salted" a pan of dirt, not dreaming that the joke would be carried far enough to occasion a stampede.

As my partners were out prospecting in another direction it devolved upon me to "represent" on the False Bottom stampede [June 20] according to our early agreement that one or other of us would go on every such occasion. I was accompanied by a friend who had come in from my old home, and who was anxious to find a mine. We were not long in making up our minds that False Bottom did not offer much encouragement; but having started out, we concluded to spend a few days in exploring the country near the head of the stream, and toward Bald Mountain. This we did without finding a placer prospect, but saw some quartz that attracted my attention; to my uneducated eyes it seemed to resemble samples shown me which were said to be rich. I resolved to visit the spot at a later time with necessary tools to do some work on this quartz.

One matter worthy of notice was the good nature with which the stampeders accepted the disappointment. It was my belief that they had not expected much, and that therefore their feeling of disappointment was not very strong.

I determined to do some work with the above-mentioned quartz but to my cost, as the rock proved absolutely valueless. While prosecuting work upon it we were encouraged by the opinion of a mining man from Utah who said he was familiar with that kind of ore, and that our find was most promising. Whether this man really believed what he told us or not we never knew, but his encouragement induced us to do a great deal of hard work and expend money which we could not well spare. For a period of half a month at least one, and part of the time two or three, of us were thus engaged. In the meantime, our Utah friend had taken samples of our ore to Salt Lake. But he returned with the information that it was of no value. This was one of our early experiences in quartz mining. It did not require many such to prove that the knowledge acquired by men in other and remote mining districts might be of little value here. Soon we learned to prospect the free milling ores; that is, those that would yield color in the pan; while the advent of competent assayers a little later made it possible to have the values of the more refractory ores properly tested.

STAMPEDE TO POLO CREEK

Only a short time after the False Bottom stampede another occurred, very similar in character and altogether similar in results. I was sitting in the cabin one evening, smoking an after-supper pipe, when a friend came up from Deadwood. Calling me outside he imparted to me in strictest confidence that new and rich diggings had been discovered in a nearby gulch. The discoverers were three friends of his from his native town of Polo, Illinois. As a matter of friendship they had decided to guide him to the new diggings, and for this purpose one of the trio had come to town, leaving his partners at the place of discovery.

After much persuasion my friend had succeeded in obtaining permission to pass the information to me, but under implicit confidence, and a pledge on my part that I should not be accompanied by another soul on my trip to the new find. I was directed to be at the mouth of Blacktail Gulch the next morning at daylight. There I would find the track of a sharp-shod mule leading up the gulch a mile and a half, where it would turn to the right along a dim trail and over a low divide to the head of the gulch in which the discovery was made. My informant and his friend would not wait for morning, but were prepared to start at once with a pack mule whose track I was to follow.

Since I only recently had been on the False Bottom stampede, it clearly was the turn of one of my partners to represent on the stampede now on the tapis, but this was made impossible by the pledge I had given my friend that I would go and go alone. Accordingly at daybreak the next morning I was at the mouth of Blacktail, where I found the trail of the sharp-shod mule without difficulty. A light rain had fallen the previous evening, making the tracks plain and easily followed, and I was but a short time in reaching the light trail where they turned from Blacktail to cross the divide. As I climbed the hill, I was wondering what I would see on reaching the summit, and whether this would prove a veritable new gold district or, like the False Bottom, a fraud. The story told me by my friend seemed entirely plausible. He was in entire good faith; I was satisfied; and it was improbable that his friends would attempt to deceive him.

Thus cogitating, I reached the top of the divide, and looked over into the gulch stretching out to the east from the opposite side. But the sight that caused astonishment was that of a tent in the immediate foreground, and clustered about it a crowd of men, probably not less than one hundred in number; while as far as the eye could see along the course of the gulch men were engaged in staking claims, posting notices and digging prospect holes. There was a shorter route to the ground from Deadwood than the one I had followed. The news of the discovery and its location had been imparted to many, as it had been to me, as a secret, and a stampede was assured.

In the tent I found that David G. Tallent[25] had been elected recorder and was prepared to record the ground for claimants at the rate of a dollar and a half per claim. He did not reap a great harvest, however, as the whole affair began to assume the appearance of what would now be termed a "frame up;" and before recording, the majority of the stampeders decided to pan some gravel.

In the crowd I met a number of acquaintances, among them three of the boys with whom I had entered the Hills over the Sidney trail. In company with them, I helped dig two prospect holes, from the gravel of which we tried a number of pans of dirt, without finding color. Each member of the party was

---

[25] David G. Tallent was the husband of Annie D. Tallent. They had first come into the Black Hills in the autumn of 1875, and had helped build the so-called Gordon's Stockade on French Creek. – [HUGHES].

called upon in turn and required to tell just how he had been informed of the new diggings, and there was a surprising similarity in the stories. To every man the news had been imparted as a secret, the informant invariably impressing his hearer as much as possible with a sense of the obligation he was conferring upon him.

Before abandoning the gulch and starting on the return to our several camps, a joke common to such occasions was indulged in at the expense of one of our number. This was the "salting" of a pan of dirt that the victim was washing. It was done by one of the boys standing behind the unobserving panner as he washed, and dribbling a pinch of "dust," taken from his gold sack into the gravel in the pan. Every other member of the party knew of the attempt to have a little fun with the panner, but not one was prepared for the astonishing success of the effort to hoodwink him.

When the gravel was washed from the pan and a "prospect" disclosed that would cause even an old timer to gasp, the man became wildly excited. Swearing his companion to secrecy, he came back to where the other boys were awaiting his report. He assumed an air of nonchalance – reminding me of the manner of Mark Twain's companion when he found the iron pyrites on the Humboldt Mountain stampede – and when one of the boys remarked that, for one, he was ready to quit, the panner agreed that the gulch didn't seem very promising to him; he thought, however, he would not leave without trying a little farther. This brought out an offer from one to dispose of his interest in the common claim for a few dollars. To the apparent general surprise this offer was at once accepted. Others declined to sell their claims at the same figure, when it was offered to each in turn; and the panner finally raised his bid by offering his pack horse for the combined interests.

After carrying the joke as far as was thought proper the victim was enlightened; but was not fully convinced that he had been made the butt of a very common hoax until he had tried a number of pans of gravel without finding another color. The victim of the "salting" joke was the same John Nelson, who fired two shots at his own horse – mistaking it for an Indian on horseback – when our party was camped at Camp Crook. Also, the horse he offered in exchange for the interests of his partners was the identical horse upon which he had made the murderous attempt.

The ravine of the above described stampede was called Polo Gulch, named very properly in honor of the town whence came its discoverers – the friends of my friend.

STAMPEDE TO THE WOLF MOUNTAINS

Numerous and directed to various points of the compass were the stampedes of '76, but in magnitude all were eclipsed by the one known as the stampede to the Wolf Mountains, in the winter of that year. Others originated in various ways; some started, no doubt, in good faith and with no intent to deceive; some, perhaps, as the result of an attempt to perpetrate a comparatively innocent hoax; but not so the wild rush to reach this land of fable.

This stampede was a crime, and a damnable one, growing out of the greed of a few individuals, who had no regard or consideration for the misery and suffering it caused. That the rumors of the discovery of rich placers in the Wolf Mountains were set on foot by men who had, in advance, bought up a large number of ponies suitable for pack animals – expecting to sell them to the stampeders – has been pretty well determined.

Many of those ponies had been stolen from the Indians of the neighboring agencies and driven to the Hills. How the reports grew and were magnified, until every chronic old stampeder was willing to sacrifice his dearest possessions to secure an outfit for the trail, was unbelievable. That the enthusiasm of such men, whose experience should be of value, spread to hundreds of newcomers was not strange; within a short time every town, camp and gulch in the northern Hills was the scene of the greatest activity, while equipment was prepared for the start.

Deadwood, the center of activity, presented a scene never to be forgotten. The streets were crowded for days as the pack animals were offered and sold at auction; the demand was so great that exorbitant prices were ensured. As fast as men secured what they considered outfits adequate for the venture, they left the Hills; not by any means in one direction, but toward almost every point of the compass, for the directions as to route were varied and numerous. Not one in ten of the stampeders could tell anything as to distance; few would venture to speak of direction, unless in a most general way.

The fact was that no one seemed to know whether the so-called Wolf Mountains were a part of the Bear Lodge, the Big Horn, the Wind River Mountains, or the main range of the Rockies. It may seem inconceivable to a reader of this day, who never has witnessed the effect upon human beings of the stampede mania, that men – hundreds of them – yes, whole communities – could become so lost to reason as to start off, in the dead of winter, to an unknown but supposedly distant region, without knowledge of how it might be reached, and with no foundation for their faith in its richness stronger than the most vague rumor.

Yet such is the lure of gold – and has been since the beginning – that men will venture more and endure more of pain and hardship, of hunger and thirst and fatigue, on the slightest possibility of a reward in its search, than any other incentive could spur them to accept. There was much of tragedy in the experience of many of those who took the trail, not knowing whither they were bound; many of them unused to the strenuous life of the outdoors in winter. So little prepared were many to meet the experiences encountered, that they suffered greatly. So little conception had they of their probable destination that they may be said to have started out hoping that by some lucky accident or providential inspiration they would be directed aright. They simply did not know where they were going; but they were on their way.

Now it was Rochford's turn to represent our trio on the stampede; though we, with Van Fleet, agreed that the information was too vague to warrant great risk, he insisted on going – with the reservation that if he could not secure something more definite before crossing the Little Missouri River he would turn back. To this determination he adhered, and he returned to camp in the course of ten days, firmly convinced that none of the stampeders possessed more knowledge as to the locality of the new diggings than himself. Thus he escaped much of the hardship endured by many others, who persisted in going farther. Of those, some were killed by Indians, while many others were seriously threatened but escaped by reason of stronger numbers.

A few reached the mining districts of Montana and wintered there. One party spent the winter on the Crow Reservation; fortunately reaching there after the loss of all their pack animals at the hands of the Sioux, and having subsisted for a considerable time on such game as they could kill on the way. A few arrived in Deadwood, after having endured many dangers and hardships, and in a generally dilapidated condition facetiously described by the actor, Jack Langrishe, in an issue of the Deadwood *Pioneer*:

> This is the man of whom we read
> Who left Deadwood for the big stampede;
> He's now returned all tattered and torn
> From looking for gold on the Big Horn.
>   He has no malt,
>   He has no cat,
>   He has no coat,
>   He has no hat.
> His trousers are patched with an old flour sack
> With "for family use" to be seen on the back.
> His beard is shaggy, his hair is long,
> And this is the burden of his song;
> "If ever I hear or ever I read
> Of another great or big stampede,
> I'll listen but I'll pay no heed,
> But stay in my cabin in Deadwood."

Such was the famous Wolf Mountain stampede. Not one who took part in it escaped suffering and misery.

It was for the purpose of outfitting Rochford on this stampede that we sold our interest in the Justice location of the DeSmet Group.

Often it has been said that the disappointments met by the prospector on his various stampedes never suffice to warn him against the allurements of the next one that gives him an opportunity to pack his burro and strike the trail. His credulity never is exhausted, and though many previous ventures may have resulted in failure he never loses hope that the next may result in the rich strike for which he long has sought. Therefore he looks up his old pack saddle, makes necessary repairs, packs his tools, grub and blankets, and starts out cheerfully, buoyed by the same high hopes that animated him on his first stampede. Illustrating the effect upon an old prospector of a story of new diggings – with little or no foundation – the following old campfire yarn is told:

> An old prospector died and went to Heaven. At the gate he was met by Saint Peter, who inquired as to his occupation while on earth. On being told that it was that of a prospector, the saint sadly shook his head and said, "I'm afraid I can't admit you. We have more of your kind in here now than we can well accommodate; I would much prefer to get rid of some of them if possible, than to allow more to enter." To this the old man replied, "That's all right, Peter; if you let me in I'll soon thin them out for you." On this promise Saint Peter admitted him; whereupon he immediately circulated a report that rich diggings had been struck in the infernal regions. A stampede at once ensued. A day or two later the saint noticed that the old man was uneasy. He wandered about apparently not knowing how to pass the time, and manifestly dissatisfied. The saint accosted him, asking what was troubling him. He replied, "Peter, I guess you'll have to let me out of here; you see on thinking it over there may be something in that report of rich diggings in hell."

Working and Hoping

Returning to consideration of matters more nearly concerning my partners and myself – during the time which elapsed between the dates of the False Bottom stampede, June eighteenth and July thirteenth, 1876 – we were out every day when weather permitted. We either prospected the ground we had located in Hidden Treasure and Pocket Gulches, or were in search of indications of the existence of valuable ore. This work, though laborious, possessed an interest that never flagged; and on leaving a prospect at night, tired and hungry, it was ever with a desire to resume the search the next day. During this time we extended our trips to some length, into the district to the south;[26] and though we located nothing of value we were daily acquiring knowledge of formations, and the probabilities of their carrying ores that were of value – at least in the saving of time and labor; we learned that to prospect in certain of the ores was absolutely futile; that by no possibility could values be found in them.

One short but notable interlude in our work during this time was on July fourth, when mining activities were generally discontinued, and every camp – large or small – and every tributary gulch, yielded up its entire population to swell the crowd on the streets of Deadwood. Here sports of various kinds – such as wrestling, jumping, foot racing and target shooting – were indulged in; prizes being offered for the winners in every event, as was usual in the States on such occasions.

The keynote, however, was patriotism; the participants in the celebration apparently desired to emphasize their patriotism and love for the government upon which they were now to call for aid, and which thus far had given them no recognition. It was the desire to make such a demonstration as should arrest the attention of Congress and compel recognition of the danger

---

[26] Afterward Pennington County, South Dakota.

of the people exposed to the attack of hostile Indians; a danger now manifestly increasing day by day, as indicated by reports from messengers coming in from the settlements in the foothills.

It was desirous that the situation be made clear and Congress be moved to act as soon as possible, to obtain the extinguishment of the Indian title to the Hills. It is probable that little thought was given to the inconsistency of calling upon the government for aid to dispossess the Indians while the petitioners were trespassers upon the Indians' lands, and were there in direct and open violation and disregard of the government's inhibition.

If the thought did intrude that we were not coming into court with clean hands, it was dismissed as unworthy of consideration in view of a really alarming situation. Be that as it may, a memorial to Congress was read immediately following the reading of the Declaration of Independence, and adopted with enthusiasm by the Black Hillers. The language was as follows:

> To the honorable Senate and House of Representatives in Congress Assembled: Your memorialists, citizens of that portion of the Territory of Dakota known as the Black Hills, most respectfully petition your honorable body for speedy and prompt action in extinguishing the Indian title to and the opening for settlement of the country we are now occupying, developing and improving. We have now in the Hills a population of at least seven thousand honest and loyal citizens who have come here with the expectation of remaining and making this their homes. Our country is rich, not only in mineral resources, but is abundantly supplied with timber and a soil rich enough to produce all that will be necessary to sustain a large population. Your memorialists would therefore earnestly request that we be not deprived of the fruits of our labor and driven from the country we now occupy, but that the government for which we have offered our lives at once extend a protecting arm and take us under its care. And as in duty bound your memorialists will ever pray.[27]

---

[27] This memorial prepared and read by Gen. A. R. Z. Dawson, was taken to Washington, DC, by Capt. C. V. Gardner, a native of Ohio, who erected the first frame structure in Deadwood. Captain Gardner brought the first quartz mill to the Hills in September 1876. For a time he was editor of the *Black Hills Weekly Pioneer*,

While enthusiastic crowds were celebrating in Deadwood, two more or less distinct celebrations were held farther down Whitewood Gulch: one, in Elizabethtown; the other, in Mountain City.[28] At these the scenes enacted were similar to those of the main celebration. There were fine orations by able orators; the Declaration of Independence and the Memorial to Congress were read; and the first observance in the Black Hills, of the anniversary of the Nation's birth, passed into history as an undoubted success. It was made more memorable and impressive by the fact that it was celebrated in the Centennial year. Among the prominent figures in the proceedings were: Judge Kuykendall, Judge Miller, A. R. Z. Dawson, H. N. Maguire, A. B. Chapline, A. M. Overman, and Doctor McKinney.

Disquieting rumors about the Indians had been coming to us since the first of June, but we did not fully realize the cause of the increased activity of the Indians in our vicinity until the awful news of the annihilation of Custer's command on the Little Big Horn reached us.[29] Almost a month elapsed after the

---

Deadwood, and established the *Dakota Weekly Register* at Spearfish in 1881. – [HUGHES].

[28] Name later changed to Fountain City.

[29] The so-called Custer massacre occurred on June 25, 1876 on the Little Big Horn in Montana.

The following is the story of a young soldier who died in that battle under an assumed name. It has never before found its way into print. This young man, a year before, had committed a serious crime, had been apprehended, tried, convicted and sentenced to the penitentiary in Nebraska. One night the then acting-governor of the state, on his way from his office to his home, encountered the convict, who by some means had made his escape. He was intent on getting out of the city. The men had been more than mere acquaintances. They had been friends and the recognition was mutual and instantaneous. The escaping prisoner at once abandoned hope of liberty and said, "Governor, if you will have a guard called I'll go back to prison."

The governor considered a moment. He said, "Come with me." And he took the man to his home. There he remained concealed until search for him had been abandoned. The governor furnished him with necessary clothing and a small sum of money and told him to go on his way. The man professed undying gratitude and promised that he would devote the remainder of his life to the work of redeeming the past. A short time afterward the governor received a letter from him, written at Sidney, and conveyed the information that the writer had enlisted in one of the troops of the Seventh Cavalry, then stationed at that place; that his enlistment had been made under an assumed name, which he stated in the letter. He assured the man who helped him to liberty that he would never have cause to repent his act.

disastrous Custer fight in Montana before the news reached Deadwood. When finally the news did come – having first been carried from the command in the field to the military post at Fort Laramie and thence to the Hills by ox train – it was so awful in character as to stagger belief. But every detail necessary to prove it true was at hand. The name of every man who died with Custer was given in the dispatches. It was then that it became known that the increased activity in the Hills was the direct result of the separation of the tremendous force assembled by Sitting Bull and the war chiefs into smaller bands after the Custer fight. Many of those small parties made their rendezvous about the foothills, along the Belle Fourche and Cheyenne and their tributaries, whence they attacked any unwary traveler or small party going in or out of the Hills.

So located, they were within easy reach of the reservations from which they had gone north in the spring and whence, from time to time, they were able to obtain supplies. This was particularly true of the young men of the Oglalas and Brules; during the summer and fall they caused more trouble, killing a greater number of people and stampeded and ran off more stock, than all other tribes.

AN ACCIDENT AT GAYVILLE

While we had our camp in Pocket Gulch an accident occurred on the Scott and Gay claim in Gayville, in which one man lost his life. His companion was also supposed, for a number of hours, to have been killed but, fortunately, was rescued after twenty-four hours of hard work by numbers of miners working in relays. The two men – one of whom was Tommy Carr, the other, whose name I do not remember – were working on bedrock; they were picking down the gravel in the face of a tunnel and wheeling it in a car to the shaft, where it

---

When the acting-governor, then no longer in office, read in the *Omaha Bee* the list of names of those who fell with Custer, he turned to a friend, pointed out the name of the man he had befriended and told his story as I have told it here, adding, "If I ever have a qualm of conscience concerning this, I will not be troubled about it in the future, for I feel that in giving up his life in the service of his country the man has justified my action." – [HUGHES].

was hoisted by means of a windlass to the surface for sluicing. There was much water in the bedrock, and this was drained by a contrivance known as a "wheel and China pump." It consisted of an old-fashioned water wheel, supplied with buckets, which dipped into the sump at the bottom of the shaft as the wheel revolved, and raised the water to the surface. This wheel was revolved by a stream of water carried to it through a flume. At about nine o'clock in the morning there was a "run" of the gravel, commencing at the bottom of the shaft; it knocked down the timbers as it followed the tunnel toward the face. The man who was pushing the car was caught and smashed flat as a flounder – no doubt killed instantly. Fortunately for Carr, some of the timbers caught against the face in such a manner that, though he was thrown on his back on bedrock, where he was held down by a heavy "cap" across his chest, the pressure was not sufficient to prevent his breathing. Here he lay for twenty-four hours before it was possible to reach and rescue him. I saw him taken out without having sustained serious injury.

The work necessary to his rescue found plenty of willing hands – all the miners on near-by claims leaving their work to assist; it was directed by men of experience in handling wet and dangerous ground, or it could not have been accomplished. The shaft could not be used in the rescue, as it was filled from the bottom to the height of the tunnel, and to attempt to make entrance through it to the tunnel would probably make matters worse. A new shaft was at once commenced and the work pushed vigorously. Carr told me afterward that he heard the men at work some time before he could make himself heard, and felt that every possible effort was being made in the hope that he and his companion might be found alive. Just once he lost hope. In the anxiety of the crowd on the surface to be of assistance the flume, that carried the water to the wheel that drained bedrock, was knocked down. At once the bedrock water began to rise. Pinned down with his head on the bedrock it was impossible for Carr to keep from drowning unless the repairs should be made quickly. When the rising water covered his neck and he could barely keep his chin above it, he commended his soul to his Maker and awaited the death that seemed inevitable. But there were wise heads and efficient hands at work on the surface. Quickly was the flume placed in order, the water turned in, and again the big wheel revolved. At once the water began to recede, and hope again took the place of despair.

The imprisoned man had a remarkably clear conception of all that was transpiring at the surface. He could visualize every move that was made. He knew the men at work would not dare to touch the old shaft, but must sink a new one and exercise the greatest care, timbering as they proceeded in order to avoid a further rush of the wet gravel.

When the water rose over his throat he knew that the wheel must have stopped; when the water began to recede he knew that the wheel had again commenced to revolve. So great was the reaction that he went to sleep. He awakened to hear the noise of pick and shovel, and from the sounds he realized that good progress was being made. Now he called, and managed to make himself heard, and in the course of a short time thereafter was able to explain his position so as to make it understood. He instructed the men to proceed with the utmost caution, as the wet gravel surrounding him was likely to be started by a jar; he said that he was in no pain. Finally, several hours before he was taken out, it was found possible to convey a stimulant to him; and with great caution on the part of the workers he was reached and rescued. He was wrapped in blankets and oilskins before being hoisted to the surface and was able to greet his rescuers in a cheery voice. A day or two later he suffered no ill effects from his experience.

The man who was rescued from the shaft, Tommy Carr,[30] was soon thereafter elected recorder of the district and later did a friendly office for my partners and myself.

---

[30] He later proved that a man may survive one danger to perish in another, and the apparent possibility that there is a time and place appointed for the end of all. Rescued from what appeared to be almost certain death in a mine accident, he was killed the following year by Indians. He was a member of a party of twenty men that left the Hills on a stampede. It had forty pack and saddle ponies and was out-

During the time of our possession of the ground in Hidden Treasure Gulch, a belief became general that this ground must be valuable. This belief grew from the discovery of bodies of rich cement ore at the head of the gulch. Therefore our ground aroused the cupidity of a politician named Dietrich. One day as Rochford was at work at the windlass where we were sinking a shaft – with Van Fleet at bottom, filling the bucket, and myself preparing dinner in the cabin – a man stopped at the shaft and accosted Rochford in a loud tone of voice with, "What in hell are you doing here?"

Rochford replied, "We're sinking a shaft."

"Well, this is my ground," said the man, "and I warn you to get off." Rochford naturally replied with some heat and an altercation ensued, which the visitor ended by leaving, saying as he left, "I'll be back tomorrow, and if I find you at work here, I'll put you down that shaft."

That would not have been as small a contract as he might have imagined, as Rochford was a boy of more than average strength and agility; but the man made the threat as confidently as though he had no doubt in his ability to do what he threatened.

When the boys came to dinner we discussed the matter. We had located the ground some time before and had fulfilled all requirements of the miners' laws by doing the necessary amount of work to hold it. But the fact that Rochford and I

---

fitted for a prospecting trip of several months' duration. At a distance of several days' journey from the Hills, the party was attacked by a large body of Indians. A retreat was made to the bank of a stream in order to insure a water supply in case of siege. While a number of men stood the Indians off at long range with their rifles, others proceeded to dig trenches for protection. With these completed they were for the time comparatively safe, but the trenches afforded no protection for the ponies. The Indians kept up an incessant fire upon them, killing all but one. So long as the men kept down in the trenches they could not be reached by the bullets, but incautiously Carr raised his head above the surface for an instant and was killed. His companions buried his body in the trench, and when night came on made their escape. Without horses to pack their provisions, tools and blankets, the men were in a serious situation, and it was necessary to abandon much of their outfit. They, however, escaped with their lives, the Indians for some unknown reason allowing them to go without hindrance. A small number came back to the Hills, among them, Horace Duncklee, with his horse, the only equine survivor. – [HUGHES].

were neither yet twenty-one years of age seemed to make it at least possible that a miners' jury might decide we were not qualified to make a valid location, if the case should be taken to a miners' court for decision.

We concluded to consult Recorder Carr, and accordingly called upon him that evening. After hearing us he said, "Go ahead, boys, and hold possession of the ground. I know your location was made and your work properly done, and I am sure you will be sustained; but it is important that you keep possession of the ground."

We felt relieved and returned to camp determined to hold the claims at all hazards. There was a possibility that the man might have been bluffing, but it would not do for us to rely upon that. Before going to bed we decided upon a course of action. The first thing we did was to build a little lottery, by drawing straws to decide the position and duty of each on the following day. One was necessary in the bottom of the shaft; one must be at the windlass; and the third was to be a reserve force in concealment close by and readily available, so prepared and accoutered as to be ready for any emergency that might arise. The plan was carried out. We were early upon the ground, and each took the place that fate had assigned to him. Thus we awaited whatever might come. Early in the forenoon the windlassman signaled the approach of the enemy. But the demeanor of the man[31] had changed. He muttered a gruff

---

[31] This man was Charles H. Dietrich, who later became governor of Nebraska, and still later, United States Senator, and who was accused of using the influence of his position to the benefit of his private purse, an accusation which retired him from political life. Only once afterward did he come within my personal notice, when I saw him on the Spearfish train with some friends who were viewing the scenery. A Spearfish paper a short time later stated that during the visit to the town he had approached a prominent resident with a plan to attempt the revival of a shadowy claim to a portion of the townsite, and had been advised by the man approached that Spearfish people had a summary way of dealing with attempted blackmail, horse and cattle rustling and other offenses, and that the train was then about due to leave town. Our experience with this man and his subsequent career, indicate the truth of the saying that great events may hinge upon others of trivial character. Had Dietrich attempted to make his threat good to dispossess us of our ground it is possible that a chapter or two of Nebraska's political history would have been differently written, and with no loss to the state's reputation. – [HUGHES].

greeting to the windlassman and passed on up the gulch without stopping. He never again attempted to interfere with us, though he had difficulty with various others before leaving the Hills.

Our prospecting of the ground we had located as placers in Hidden Treasure and Pocket Gulches had left us in doubt as to its value. At times we would obtain a fair showing of gold in the pan, and we would be hopeful that we really had property of value. Again we would be discouraged when the gravel tested showed few colors. To work the ground it would be necessary to dig a long ditch to divert the waters of Deadwood Creek, as our gulches were dry. Flumes of some length would be necessary at the crossing of Sawpit and Hidden Treasure Gulches; and lumber was expensive. The labor of digging a ditch would require considerable time, and the task was one not to be undertaken lightly, but we felt we were able to do it.

As a final test we procured a team and wagon, hauled a number of loads of gravel to the creek, and washed it out by means of a rocker. The result was, on the whole, encouraging; sufficiently so as to decide us in favor of the ditch. After a careful survey the work of digging was commenced on July thirteenth. We employed three men who joined us, paying them in board and interest in our holdings. These men were: Foster Richardson and Ferdinand Westfall, both of whom hailed from Nebraska; and W. W. Wood, from Colorado. With this added force, the work on the ditch progressed fairly well and was completed in just one month from the day it started.

To buy the lumber for the flume strained our meager resources, but in one way or another without resorting to robbery, the necessary money was raised; the flume completed;

Governor Dietrich, usually looked upon as the Burlington's senator, got involved in a nasty difficulty resulting from his removal of the Hastings post office into a building of his own and his collection from the state of the governor's salary for a few weeks while he was also United States Senator. He was hauled into District Court on both accounts, and though acquitted on technicalities, it was clear that Dietrich and railroad influence would do the party no good. His was a short term, and when it ended the Republican state convention endorsed Elmer J. Burkett for his seat over the opposition of the railroads. – James C. Olson, *History of Nebraska*, (Lincoln, University of Nebraska Press, 1955), 251.

and the water turned in. A difficulty arose at once. The heat of summer had so diminished the flow of Deadwood Creek that those having rights secured prior to ours protested strenuously, and with justice, against any diversion of water from the creek channel. This was a serious check; but the difficulty was solved in part by an agreement that we would turn the water into our ditch only after nightfall, when it was not in use by others, and do our work before the day shifts would go on in the morning.

The first night of our operations, a break occurred in our ditch on the hillside, started by the water finding a hole dug by some animal, probably a woodchuck. Before the leak was discovered and "puddled" sufficiently to stop the flow, a garden that it flooded on its way to the creek was entirely ruined. This entailed a bill of expense as well as a good deal of abuse on the part of the gardener, which we endured as well as possible, realizing that he had good cause for complaint. Finally we had our night shifts working, and we looked forward with mingled hope and fear to the time set for the first clean-up.

I do not care to dwell upon our feelings when that clean-up was panned down and the result announced. It was so pitifully small that we realized at once that all our labor and expense, all our hopes and plans, based on belief in the value of the ground, were in vain. In my lifetime I have met with disappointments of various kinds, but I can recall none that hurt as deeply as this. We had told one another that we must not be over sanguine; that we could not expect great returns, and would feel all right about it if our ground should yield reasonable pay for our time and labor; but we really expected something far better. Had our clean-up disclosed big pay, not one of us would have admitted that it was no more than he was prepared to see.

The severe disappointment naturally caused a revision of all our plans. Our new partners, discouraged, talked of leaving the Hills. Our means were exhausted, and if we were to keep up the work of prospecting it was necessary that one of us should find employment that would keep the pot boiling. With

WORKING AND HOPING

this in view, I went down to Deadwood and interviewed A. W. Merrick, proprietor of the *Pioneer,* as to the prospect of a job on "cases." His reply was not wholly discouraging; he told me to keep in touch with the office, and something might offer within a short time.

Strenuous Times

The month of August brought more of excitement to the people than any that had preceded. Homicides were frequent, and at least three notable murder trials were held within the space of a few days: the first, during the last days of July on the streets of Crook City; the second, on August first on the main street of Gayville; and the third, on Main Street in Deadwood, two days later. Added to these and the various activities in this then overflowing camp to make this part of the year especially memorable was the great increase in the number of Indian depredations.

On every trail leading to the Hills men were waylaid and murdered. In some instances women and children were among the victims, and the awful manner in which, in several instances, their bodies had been subjected to mutilation and outrage, caused deep grief and anger, and a general desire for reprisals.

From all the towns, settlements, and isolated ranches in every direction, came reports of the same character of the murder of travelers and stampeding of stock. Almost every day at Rapid City there was an Indian raid. Four bodies of men killed near the town were buried in a single day, and the town of two hundred souls was abandoned by all but nineteen men.[32]

---

[32] In February of '76 a party of men headed by John Brennan had left the diggings in which they had been working on Palmer Gulch in the southern Hills, and striking off in a northeasterly course had struck the foothills at the mammoth springs now known as Cleghorn Springs, where Rapid Creek flows from the Hills into the broad and fertile Rapid Valley. Descending the stream four miles they decided to lay out a townsite at the spot on which Rapid City since has been built. Before doing so they explored the country to the east as far as the confluence of the creek with the Cheyenne River, and found it to be a region well grassed and which could not fail to develop into a rich agricultural district.

Returning on their trail, they at once proceeded to survey the first blocks and streets of Rapid City. Fortunately the little party had been reinforced by several additional men, among whom was Samuel Scott, a surveyor and civil engineer of

STRENUOUS TIMES

Immediately above the town in Rapid Valley several ranches had been located; among the locators were Jim Moody, Bill Kelly, and Jim Sheppard – our companions on the trip to the Hills. They were men not easily frightened, but they finally were compelled to abandon their land, as they could not induce others to settle near them and were worn out by the necessity of keeping constant guard. Within a few miles of Spearfish, several men were killed; Indians were in sight every

---

much experience on the southwestern frontier. Scott made the survey with the pocket compass, which explains why the streets of the original townsite do not have a true north and south course, as the "variation" at that time was unknown. [He was referring to the magnetic declination. – W.L.H. & S.P.H.]

The men who founded Rapid City were of that hardy frontier type that is not easily daunted. Had it not been so the settlement must have died in the year of its birth. The situation made it peculiarly subject to attack by Indians, and no other town of the Hills suffered as severely from their depredations. In August of 1876, the settlement had attained a population of two hundred souls, due largely to the efforts of the founders in going out to the towns of the Missouri River on the east and the Union Pacific on the south and inducing travel in that direction. In a few days' time it had dwindled to the number of nineteen. This was due somewhat to the homesickness of the tenderfoot, but mainly to the alarming frequency of the Indian attacks.

In his memoirs, John Brennan told that a freight train on its way out of the Hills was halted here, and a wagon borrowed to bring in the bodies of four men found killed and scalped a few miles from town. When the return was made with the bodies the train was lined up to start east, and the entire population with the exception of the nineteen mentioned loaded their goods on the wagons and took their departure. Then those remaining took a vote on the question of whether to go or stay. It was decided to stay, and as a means of protection a blockhouse was erected at the center of the town. A guard was maintained at all times, and this with so meager a force was an onerous duty, but the advance post of civilization was held. Finally when it became apparent that Rapid City really was the most advantageous point of entry in the country, and so situated as probably to become the center of a fine agricultural district, immigrants began coming in constantly increasing numbers, the tension was removed, and the future importance of Rapid City assured. – [HUGHES].

According to the *Rapid City Daily Journal,* Feb. 24, 1952:

It was on Feb. 25, 1876 that Sam Scott laid out the original townsite with a pocket compass, a tape line carried by John R. Brennan, J. W. Allen, and James Carney measured out six blocks in a mile square area and Rapid City was born. The foursome, along with eight other men, in the founding party, participated in a raffle for lots. Each man was permitted to draw five lots. . . The new settlement was named "New Denver" but the name was later changed to Rapid City at the suggestion of W. P. Martin. . . Other Black Hills communities envious of Rapid City's ambitious bid for prominence referred to it as "the hay camp."

day and made frequent dashes through the streets of the town itself to stampede and drive off stock.

From Custer, on the south, messengers brought the same report of almost daily trouble, and on the Red Canyon and Buffalo Gap trails many atrocities were committed.

That the Indians were now operating about the Hills in greater numbers than at any previous time was plainly apparent, and with each succeeding day their boldness increased; they now began to penetrate well into the Hills. They even killed several men in the near vicinity of Deadwood. The horse herds on the foothills, especially on Centennial Prairie[33] where many horses were kept on account of scant forage about Deadwood, were subject to almost daily raids. Several herders were killed and as many as one hundred head of horses driven off in a single foray. Finally the attempt to keep the stock at a place so exposed had to be abandoned, and the remnant of the herd was driven into the interior to a point ten miles south of Deadwood.

On the first day of August was held the trial of John R. Carty for the murder of Jack Hinch. The homicide had resulted from a dispute over a game of cards in which Carty and his mining partner, McCarthy, engaged with the victim, a gambler from Nevada. The partners left the country hurriedly, and had made their way as far as Fort Laramie. There Carty was recognized by a friend of Hinch and arrested by Deputy Marshal Jack Davis, who brought him back to the Hills for trial. McCarthy was apprehended later, taken to Yankton, tried, and hanged. It was fortunate for Carty that, when given an option as to his place of trial, he chose to take his chances where the crime was committed rather than in regularly established courts. Had he been tried in Yankton, it is probable that he would have shared the fate of his partner. As there were no legally authorized courts in the Hills, the trial of any important case was by miners' jury, so called; though men of all walks of life took part. When Davis reached Gayville – the scene of the crime – with his prisoner, word was sent out for a mass meet-

---

[33] Named for the Centennial party from Ames, Iowa.

ing; the mining recorder of the district took the initiative in this matter. Mining in the gulch was for the time discontinued, and by nine o'clock on the morning of the day set for the trial the one street of Gayville was a mass of humanity. No building in the camp was large enough to accommodate a tenth of the crowd; therefore the court was organized and proceedings held on the street. A great deal of bitter feeling was manifested. It was plainly apparent that the crowd was divided into two rival factions, one of which evidently had come with the determination to hang the prisoner, while the other – mainly composed of miners – was as fully determined that he should go free. There was much loud talk and an occasional cry of "hang him!" A big bully named Bill Trainor was particularly conspicuous and vehement in denunciation of the prisoner, until Johnny Flaherty – one of the men who had located the DeSmet group of mines – made a break through the crowd, with a big Smith and Wesson revolver in his hand. Reaching over the shoulders of those who intervened between himself and Trainor, Flaherty struck him a terrific blow on the head with the heavy barrel of the weapon, laying open his scalp. Trainor begged like a cur, and on being warned to leave, took his departure.

Before this occurred a space had been cleared in the center of the street for the court, a bench provided for the jury by placing a couple of planks on boxes, and a chair found for the man who should preside as judge. When that big six-shooter appeared above the heads of the crowd there was an attempt to stampede, but the men were packed so closely together that only those on the outskirts found it possible to escape. As stated, when the gun appeared above the heads of the crowd there was a mad rush to get away; the people surged across the space that had been prepared for the trial, and the man who was generally expected to act as prosecuting attorney became entangled in the judge's chair; he was thrown down and trampled somewhat seriously before he could be rescued.

I had quit work on our ditch to attend and report the trial for an eastern paper, to which I had written some letters from the Hills previously. By going early I had secured a seat in a position of advantage on a pile of house logs, where I could see and hear all that should transpire. As I climbed to my lofty perch I was joined by a gentleman, whom I had seen on various Sundays on the streets of Deadwood, engaged in preaching to those who would pause long enough in their occupations to hear him. He was a sincere and kindly man, and was generally esteemed. He was known as "Preacher Smith."[34] As we waited for the completion of the preliminaries of the trial we fell into conversation. Learning that I designed to take a report of the trial for publication, he expressed regret that he did not have either pencil or paper, as he, too, would have liked to be able to report an incident so unique for a paper at his old home in the States. Fortunately I was able to supply his

---

[34] Rev. Henry Watson Smith, fine old man, was killed by Indians a few days later on his way between Deadwood and Crook, to which place he was going on foot to conduct a religious service. His death took place only three or four miles from Deadwood. The Society of Black Hills Pioneers has appropriately placed a fine monument to his memory in the cemetery in Deadwood. Reverend Smith was killed August 20, 1876.

The Rocky Mountain News, Denver, September 15, 1876, p. 2 c. 3, commented on having received a copy of *The Black Hills Pioneer* [Deadwood], printed on manila paper. One of the items quoted follows:

> Early Sunday morning a party arrived in town from Centennial Prairie, and reported seeing a dead man lying by the side of the Deadwood and Centennial road, about three miles from this place. A large party immediately repaired to the spot, and there found the remains of Rev. H. W. Smith. On examination it was found that he had been shot through the heart.
> On the same morning a party of four men who had killed a deer near the same place were in the act of dressing it, and on looking up one of the men saw an Indian riding toward them down the mountain, traveling at a slow pace. One of the party shot and wounded the Indian and killed his horse. The Indian crawled into the brush and in endeavoring to dislodge him, one of the party, Louis Mason, was shot directly through the heart, and instantly killed.

George V. Ayres, pioneer merchant and banker of Deadwood, who went to the Black Hills in the spring of 1876 recorded the following in his Diary:

> May 7, 1876 "Weather cold and stormy. Went to first church held in Custer City this morning. Rev. Smith of the Methodist persuasion preached. He took his text from Psalms 34:7 and preached a very interesting sermon. The congregation consisted of about thirty gentlemen and five ladies, who all paid strict attention to the sermon except when there was a dog fight outside . . ."
> [This Diary was loaned to me for copying in 1937. – EDITOR]

lack and divided with him a new pencil and leaves torn from my notebook for the purpose.

After some discussion as to the manner of procedure between leaders of the two factions, in which disinterested parties were called upon to participate, it was decided that nominations for judge and jurors be offered and the assembled men should vote upon them *viva voce*. Thereupon a man called out from the crowd, "Gentlemen, there is a man here who came in from Fort Pierre yesterday in my train, who I am sure is a good man for judge, as he has had experience in that line in Chicago, where he presided over a municipal court. His name is A. H. Simonton and I offer his name in nomination." No opposition was offered, and no other candidate named; thus Simonton was elected by the unanimous voice. Then proceeded the selection of jurors. Taking into account the feeling that prevailed, it was surprising that the panel was so easily filled; but there was no desire on the part of anyone to delay proceedings or quibble over technicalities, as is usual in proceedings of the regular courts of the country. When one-half the number of jurymen had been chosen, another diversion occurred. Within a few feet of the log pile on which Reverend Smith and I were seated, a log building was in the course of construction; operations on it were impossible while the trial was in progress. The material used in this structure consisted of light, dead spruce poles, which were numerous in the gulch. The ridge pole and parallel rafters were in place; and these were soon covered with men eager to secure so advantageous a place of lookout. Vainly the owner expostulated with those who had taken possession – warning them that the light poles were not strong enough to sustain so great a weight, and begging them to relieve the poles of at least one-half their number.

As he seemed to have no means of enforcing compliance with his request, the crowd simply laughed at him. Finally the request became a demand; this, too, meeting with ridicule, he left, saying, "I'll see if I can't move you." In a moment he appeared with a shotgun, and training it along the roof, exclaimed, "Now, damn you, will you climb down?" This time his invitation was accepted with alacrity. Those who had been compelled to stand in the street vigorously cheered the man who had forced the roof riders down to their own level. This little incident had caused a slight pause in the task of selecting a jury – which now proceeded, without another interruption, to completion.

The most dramatic occurrence of the day was a speech made by the deputy marshal, Davis,[35] who had brought Carty from Fort Laramie for the trial. Davis was a small man. Carty was almost a giant in stature, and much favorable comment on the courage of the deputy in bringing the prisoner into the Hills with every trail infested by Indians, was heard. Therefore everyone gave close attention to what he had to say. He had kept in the background until threats against his prisoner's life were made. Then, standing on a barrel he called for a hearing, and thus addressed the assemblage:

"Boys, I've brought this man from Fort Laramie to the Hills, through a country swarming with hostile Indians, to be tried for his life. When I arrested him I gave him the choice of being brought back here to be tried by miners' jury or to go to Yankton to be tried in the regular courts. He decided to come here, and here we are. I promised him that you would give him a fair trial, and a fair trial he must have. If you give him this and find him guilty, hang him, and I'll help pull the rope. But until you do this, the man who touches a hair of his head will do so over my dead body."

Nothing could be said or done that would have gone farther to secure the prisoner's safety; though as a precautionary measure the court, acting on a motion, made by someone in the crowd, appointed ten men armed with rifles to act as his guard.

A. B. Chapline was chosen to prosecute; Mills and Hollis, two Deadwood lawyers, for defense. The trial proceeded in a wholly decorous manner, lasting through the entire day and until ten o'clock at night. Then the jury brought in a verdict of assault and battery. The evidence tended to prove that the

---

[35] I. C. (Jack) Davis.

knife used in the killing of Hinch had been in the hands of Carty's partner. The verdict was practically one of acquittal, as there was no attempt to impose a penalty for mere assault and battery. Though the court would not assume authority in such case, there would have been no hesitation in the imposition of the death penalty had the jury found Carty guilty of murder. At the solicitation of Carty's friends the court appointed a guard of ten men to escort the liberated man out of the country.[36]

On the day following the Carty trial, J. B. Hickok, known throughout the West as "Wild Bill," was deliberately murdered in a Deadwood gambling house by Jack McCall. In those days Hickok's name was a familiar one from the Rio Grande to the British possessions. It was said of him that he had killed a greater number of men in revolver duels than any other man ever known; and this probably was true. He was so expert with the revolver that it was said that no man living could draw and shoot as quickly and accurately. He had been called upon to act as marshal of Abilene, Kansas, during the times of the great cattle drives from Texas to the North, and thus came into collision with a great many of the most turbulent characters of that wildest part of the Wild West. While marshal of Abilene he had killed several soldiers. It was related of him that he had on one occasion broken all records, made by one man against great odds, in his fight with what was known as the McCanles[37] gang. In it he had killed or seriously crippled ten well-armed men, and lived to tell the tale. In appearance and demeanor Hickok had nothing of the swaggerer or braggart. He

---

[36] He never returned. One day several years later, the Sidney stage brought to Rapid City the body of a man who had taken passage to Sidney for the Hills and had died on the road. I visited the undertaker's rooms where the body was being prepared for burial, and looked down upon the dead face of Jack Davis. My thoughts traveled back to the first day of August of 1876, and again in memory I reviewed the dramatic scenes enacted that day on the street of Gayville. I paid silent tribute to the courage manifested by one whom I considered the bravest man I ever had met. – [HUGHES].

[37] This fight took place in Nebraska. *See* "The McCanles Family. Wild Bill-McCanles Tragedy. True Story of Wild Bill-McCanles Affair in Jefferson County, Nebraska. July 12, 1861" by George W. Hansen. *Nebraska Historical Magazine*, vol. X, No. 2, (April-June, 1927), 71-116.

He was a striking figure; something over six feet tall; with flowing hair and a mustache; rather slender in form; and seldom was known to raise his voice above the ordinary conversational tone. He was a gambler by profession; and while no one would say that he was a man to violate the peculiar code of ethics governing the gambling fraternity, it is not improbable that his reputation as a gun fighter won for him many a stake over the poker table which his cards could not win.

Hickok[38] had made a spectacular entry into Deadwood the month previous, accompanied by four other characters – also of considerable notoriety, but who basked chiefly in the reflected glory of their leader. They were: "Calamity" Jane,[39] Charley and Steve Utter,[40] brothers; and Dick Seymour; the last named being known as "Bloody Dick." Where or how he had earned or acquired the sanguinary title no one seemed to know. Charley Utter was a frontier dandy; he wore his hair in long curls down his shoulders; and his reputation was due chiefly to a story written by E. Z. C. Judson (Ned Buntline) for the *New York Weekly,* in which he was dubbed "Colorado Charlie" – a name he ever afterward affected – and was depicted as a dashing frontiersman and scout. The men who did the really effective and valuable work of scouts in the Indian country were of a different character altogether; usually careless of their appearance, and unlikely to make themselves con-

---

[38] General Custer's "Life on the Plains" in the *Galaxy* of April 1872, speaks of J. B. Hickok (Wild Bill), chief scout of his expedition under General Hancock as follows: "Among the white scouts were numbered some of the most noted of their class. The most prominent man among them was 'Wild Bill'. . . He was a plainsman in every sense of the word . . . whether on foot or on horseback, he was one of the most perfect types of physical manhood . . ." *Rocky Mountain News,* October 7, 1876.

[39] Martha Jane Canary (Burke), clad in complete male habiliments and riding astride, probably attracted more attention than she would today (1926) as such things are common, though buckskin garments have gone out of fashion. – [HUGHES].

[40] The Utter boys did a great deal of hunting of wild game for market in Colorado in 1875 in the North Park and Middle Park areas. Charley Utter ran a pack train in 1869 over Argentine Pass from Central City by way of Georgetown. Both boys owned mining interests in Central City in the 1860s.

spicuous. Such men were California Joe,[41] the Broughiers[42] and "Pony" White.[43]

Steve Utter's chief hold upon fame was as Charley's brother. The female member of the quintet, Calamity Jane, was an Amazonian woman of the frontier, whose name was supposed to be Martha Jane Canary – also given as Canero. She was known as a hanger-on of soldiers' camps, who especially prided herself on her ability to ride and shoot, to guard camp and perform almost any rough duty usually assigned to men. While by no means a credit to her sex, it was said she had a heart quick to respond to the call of distress; many were the tales told of her ministrations in the cause of charity – of injured men helped to recovery, and dying hours soothed by Calamity Jane.

The party above described entered Deadwood and rode the entire length of Main Street, mounted on good horses and clad in complete suits of buckskin, every suit of which carried sufficient fringe to make a considerable buckskin rope.

Hickok naturally fell into the practice of his profession as a poker player, while Charley Utter and Seymour canvassed the situation, with a view to establishing a pony express line between Deadwood and Fort Laramie – the latter being the near-

---

[41] California Joe was "Moses E. Milner, one of the greatest scouts of the West... A halo of mystery has long hovered about the identity of California Joe. Few of the old plainsmen knew his real name... He was chief of scouts for General Custer at one time... California Joe will live in history as one of the most noted scouts of the Old West. He was not of the braggart type, in spite of Buel's statements; but was the direct opposite, always quiet and unassuming, making little of his achievements... He was a Kentukian by birth." Joe E. Milner and Earle R. Forrest, *California Joe,* (Caldwell, Idaho, Caxton Printers Ltd., 1935), 16-17.

[42] The author evidently here refers to the sons of Theophile Bruguier, pioneer of Sioux City, Iowa, who is said to have been endowed with many qualities "necessary to the great man – the man who leads armies, or controls and molds communities." His son Charles, an officer in the Civil War, was promoted for bravery. He was killed at Rapid City, SD, by a competitor in a mail contract. He left a son, Charles, who became an Episcopalian minister as missionary among the Indians. John Bruguier was a scout for General Miles. He was killed at Poplar Creek on the Upper Missouri. Samuel Bruguier for many years was in the employ of the United States as scout and interpreter..." – Albert M. Holman, *Pioneering in the Northwest,* (Sioux City, Iowa, Dietch & Lamar Co., 1924), 104-127.

[43] "Pony" White was a scout with General George Crook. *See* page ... 144, footnote 55.

est point to the Hills to which the United States mails were delivered. In projecting their enterprise Seymour and Utter received much encouragement, for the transportation of mail by bull or mule train was so slow, tedious, and uncertain as seriously to impede business and progress in all lines. Therefore they set diligently to work to inaugurate the service, and had gone far toward perfecting arrangements when they were brought to a halt by the sudden and unexpected death of Hickok.

Hickok was killed in a Deadwood gambling house known as "Number Ten." He was sitting with his back to the door when McCall, who had been in the camp for some time but was little known, entered, stepped quickly behind Hickok, and with a revolver of large calibre shot him through the head, killing him instantly. The bullet passed entirely through his head, and lodged in the wrist of Captain Massey, the player sitting opposite; it was extracted by Dr. A. M. Overman – then a physician in practice in Deadwood.[44]

Many men who played poker with Hickok declared that he never would sit in a game with his back to the door; that invariably he demanded a seat from which he could see everybody who entered the room. As there are said to be exceptions to all rules, so there was to this; and this one lapse cost Hickok his life.

McCall was apprehended and placed in confinement pending preparations for his trial. It is probable that had McCall's victim been a good, reputable citizen, the assassin's tenure of life would have been short and a trial have been made unnec-

---

[44] It would be strange if this bullet was not preserved as an interesting relic of a tragedy the victim of which was so widely known, but I do not know that it ever has appeared on exhibition. – [HUGHES].

According to the (Cheyenne) *Democratic Leader,* July 30, 1885:

> The *Bismarck Tribune* says: The ball that killed Wild Bill arrived in the city yesterday. It is in the wrist of Bill Massey, an old time steamboat pilot, who arrived from below yesterday. Massey is well known to all Bismarckers, and those who have read the history of Wild Bill are familiar with his name. He was playing cards with him in Deadwood when the latter was shot; the ball passed through Wild Bill's head, lodging in Massey's wrist where now it remains.

essary;[45] but the reputation of Hickok was such as to cause little mourning over his fate, and was confined chiefly to those of his own kind. One sincere female mourner he did have. This was Calamity, whose grief for a time seemed uncontrollable.

The trial of McCall was conducted, in all material particulars, under conditions similar to those narrated of the trial of Carty in Gayville. Judge William Kuykendall, formerly of Cheyenne, was called upon to preside as judge; a jury was empanelled; attorneys for prosecution and defense were appointed by the judge; and the trial proceeded. As in the case of the Carty trial, no room in the town would have been large enough for the accommodation of the crowd and Main Street was selected for the purpose. The form of swearing in and examining witnesses was gone through; the prosecution presented the testimony of a number who had witnessed the killing. This number could have been multiplied, had it been considered necessary, as the deed was committed in the sight of many who were in the gambling house at the time. But the evidence given was positive and direct; indeed, the prisoner made no attempt to deny his act. He had no witnesses to introduce and merely asked the privilege of making a statement. This, of course, was granted. It was about as follows:

> Wild Bill killed my brother in Abilene, and swore he would kill me if ever I should cross his path. Here in Deadwood I found myself in the same town with him, and I knew I must either kill him or leave. You all know there is no man on earth that could kill him with a six-shooter face to face, for no man could draw and shoot like him; so I took the only way and killed him.

On this unsupported statement the jury brought in a verdict of acquittal. The judge appointed a guard to give McCall pro-

---

[45] It may be worthy to mention here as a somewhat remarkable fact that with all the crimes committed in Deadwood in the days when everything was wide open and crime rampant, a lynching never occurred in the town. Hangings there have been, but those occurred after the days of the miners' juries, under the jurisdiction of properly and legally constituted courts, and due process of law. – [HUGHES].

tection in leaving the country, and the people of the Hills imagined that was the last they would ever hear of the affair.[46]

Hickok's remains were buried in the cemetery overlooking Deadwood from the east. Charley Utter caused to be placed at the head of the grave a board on which was lettered:

> J. B. Hickok, (Wild Bill) killed by the assassin Jack McCall in Deadwood August second, 1876. Pard we'll meet again in the Happy Hunting Grounds; Good bye.
> C. H. Utter (Colorado Charlie)[47]

At the time of Hickok's death there were camped with us two brothers – whom we had known in Nebraska – named Brant and Dick Street. They had become acquainted with the Utters and Seymour, who had engaged them as pony express riders. The boys had been absent from camp in attendance at the trial and did not return until daylight the next morning. Then I was awakened by Dick, who was searching about for his rifles, ammunition and other effects. I asked what he wanted and where he was going. He replied, "We're going to get that damned murderer, McCall."

As the boys never returned to our camp they no doubt formed part of the posse[48] organized by Hickok's friends, which followed McCall out of the Hills. We never saw the Street brothers again; but we heard of Brant as a daring express rider who had at least one narrow escape from the Indi-

---

[46] There was, however, a sequel. McCall, when he supposed he was safe, foolishly made the boast that he had killed the famous Wild Bill, and had avoided punishment for it by giving the miners a cock-and-bull story that Hickok had killed his brother. This boast proved his undoing, as it caused his arrest, and he was taken to Yankton (Dakota Territory), where he found a court less gullible and he was tried, convicted and hanged. Those looking for a motive in the killing of Wild Bill finally concluded that McCall had been employed and paid for committing the deed by someone who probably cherished an old grudge against him, or possibly by a prominent Deadwood gambler, with whom it was reported he had had some difference causing ill feeling. – [HUGHES].

[47] A sculptor tourist fashioned a lifelike statue which was placed at his grave. This was defaced by souvenir seekers in a short time, but has since been replaced by another, which is protected from spoilation. – [HUGHES].

[48] This posse had no part, however, in McCall's capture. Had it overtaken him it is not probable he would have been tried and executed in Yankton. – [HUGHES].

ans when his horse was shot under him. He crawled into a depression, with his gun and ammunition, and stood the attacking party off until after nightfall. Then he secured the mail sack and carried it on his shoulder into the nearest station, some miles distant.[49]

---

[49] "That the riders had many thrilling experiences with the redskins on their trips, goes without saying; that they sometimes, too, had very narrow escapes is illustrated by the following story from the pen of a young pioneer of 1876, R. B. 'Dick' Hughes, 'Among the riders employed by Seymour and Utter, to carry the mail from Deadwood to Fort Laramie, was Brant Street, now (1899) living the life of a quiet farmer in Dodge County, Nebraska. Street was engaged to ride pony express and for a month or so went through the experiences common in those days to all men in that dangerous occupation. He carried, besides the mail sack tied to his saddle, nothing save a Remington rifle and a bag of cartridges slung across the pommel of the saddle. One afternoon, he was riding along on his down trip about eight miles north of Hat Creek Station, not expecting trouble, for the Indians had been unusually quiet for a week or more, when a volley was fired upon him from the bush, and, in an instant, as he afterward told the story, the world seemed to be full of redskins. His horse fell dead at the first fire. One ball struck the pommel of the saddle and another knocked the heel from his boot.

" 'Extricating himself as quickly as possible, pulling off the gun and cartridges, he ran as fast as he could to a little arroyo close by, into which he threw himself at full length. As he ran the bullets sang and whistled about his ears and kicked up the dust at his feet. The Indians were rapidly closing in on him when he emptied his cartridges on the ground, and, as he expressed it, commenced pumping lead back at them. So warm did he make it for the Indians, that they soon began to look for cover and long range, from which they kept up an intermittent fusillade until night fell, when they withdrew. Street said afterward that the three or four hours he spent hugging the ground seemed longer than so many days at any other time of his life. The nerve of the man is shown in the fact that after darkness had settled down he crawled out to his dead horse, disengaged the pouches of mail, and carried them on his back to the Hat Creek Station.' " – Annie D. Tallent, *op. cit.*, 194.

"Judge" Farnham's Court

A PROVISIONAL GOVERNMENT THAT DIDN'T GOVERN: MINERS' COURTS MORE EFFECTIVE

Early in '76 the people of Deadwood formed a provisional government. As there were no legally qualified courts – no courts, in fact, but those organized by the miners on occasion to settle disputes that arose over conflicting claims to ground, or in cases of homicide – many crimes of less serious nature were unpunished; and it was mainly for the purpose of checking these that the court was established. From the onset it was apparent that the court could be of little avail. It had no standing in law; and there were so many lawless characters in the community who had no sympathy with the movement for better conditions, that it was not possible to accomplish much in the direction desired. The court could not assume authority to act in a case of homicide; for if an examination warranted the holding of the defendant for trial by a higher court, no such court was available. Thus such cases were left to miners' courts, which at least had the prestige arising from long and well established precedent. The miners' court had the strength of all the mining population behind it to enforce its decrees. The decision of the miners' court was final, and there would not have been the least hesitation in carrying out its decree – even to the hanging of a murderer – if the jury found a verdict of guilty. In cases such as horse stealing, which were numerous, the provisional government could not interfere. The reason was that if a man should be convicted, punishment in a penitentiary should follow. The local court could not possibly assume authority to send a man to the territorial prison while neither the territorial nor the federal government recognized any right on the part of miners to be in possession of courts, or even of the land they were occupying. The miners' courts, no

A PROVISIONAL GOVERNMENT 129

doubt, might assume authority to deal with cases of horse stealing if they had been applied to directly for that purpose; but such an instance was absolutely unknown. It seemed tacitly to be agreed that the community in which such crime was committed should attend to the meting out of proper punishment for it; and it may be said with truth that the residents of the foothills, who were the chief sufferers from the depredations of horse thieves, proved themselves equal to the emergency. When certainty of a thief's guilt was established, determined men simply took him out and hanged him. Naturally there has been much indignant protest against the drastic action of the Vigilantes, but those who have been loudest in their criticism know nothing of the conditions that made it seem necessary.

The provisional court could not even assume jurisdiction in any matter of importance; its functions were restricted to dealing with such petty offenses as assault, petty thieving, disturbances of the peace of various kinds – in short, offenses in which action in imposing a fine or imprisonment in the calaboose should be final. No appeal was possible where there was no superior court to which it might be made.

When the provisional court did, on several occasions, assume to hold examinations or – more properly speaking – try cases of some importance, such trials almost invariably resulted in miscarriages of justice. The result was that only matters of little importance to the community occupied the attention of the court and its satellites; the disreputable and vermin-infested jail was filled with the dregs of the town's population, and no good whatever was accomplished.

How such conditions, with the impotence of the court to administer justice, worked shame, hardship, and suffering to one innocent boy, in a case that came to my own personal knowledge, is here told:

The victim was a young German named George Hassler, whom I had known in Nebraska. He came to Deadwood in the fall of '76, with a team of oxen and a wagon load of supplies. Having learned of my whereabouts he came to our camp; and as this was his first experience away from his home and people, he was rejoiced to be greeted by an old acquaintance. He disposed of his load at a satisfactory price, and within a short time afterward found a purchaser for his oxen – which pleased him greatly, as he would now return home by a faster means of conveyance than the oxen could furnish. He made the serious mistake of giving his customer possession of the cattle without receiving their price. The man said he wanted to try them for a few days, and if he found them satisfactory, he would pay for them. While awaiting his money the boy amused himself by watching the miners at work and taking in the sights of Deadwood, all of which he found interesting and new. When the day arrived on which he was to receive the price of his cattle he went to the sawmill at which the purchaser was engaged in hauling logs; but the man put him off, promising payment the next day. When he again asked for payment he was again told to wait. Thus he was met with excuses for non-payment and promises, until he began to fear the man did not intend to pay him at all. He was homesick, and wanted to go home. He kept asking, and finally begging, the man to pay him, that he might go. Finally the fellow became insolent, and told him plainly that he did not intend to pay him, and that he might collect the money if he could. What to do the boy didn't know. He became desperate, and sought me for advice, as I was his only acquaintance in the country; but I was temporarily absent from camp, and the boy did not know how long he might have to wait for my return. He could not submit to so great an injustice as the loss of his cattle, and the man evidently did not intend to pay for them. Surmising, and correctly, that should he have the marshal arrest his debtor it would cause further delay, and probably expense and trouble, he went in the night to where the cattle were kept; he yoked and hitched them to his wagon, and started for home. He was pursued and brought back at the instigation of the man who had swindled him, and haled before Mayor Farnum, head of the provisional government, and ex-officio justice.

A PROVISIONAL GOVERNMENT 131

Here he admitted that he had taken the cattle, but in attempting to establish claim to them his grief, shame and indignation made him absolutely incoherent. The poor fellow imagined himself surrounded by enemies intent on his destruction, and with not a friend in sight. As in the case of Shamus O'Brien's plea of "guilty," the job was made light for the judge, so in Hassler's case the admission that he had taken the cattle from the possession of the plaintiff made it easy for Farnum to order him to jail. Here he found himself in a big log building of a single room, with no furniture but a few benches, and in a crowd of such profane, dirty, unkempt and altogether disreputable men as in all his life before he never had seen.

His entrance was greeted with cries of welcome and a demand for money with which to buy tobacco. He complied and with a wit of which I did not think him possessed, concealed the fact that had more than the dollar that he handed them. They left him to his cogitations, and these were painful in the extreme. All that day and the ensuing night he paced the floor or tried to rest on the hard bench of his prison. As he afterward told me, he formed the resolution that if he should come out of this experience alive he never again would leave his Nebraska farm.

When morning came, bringing some relief of his misery, he caught the attention of the attendant who brought a meagre, ill-cooked and unpalatable breakfast, and induced him to come to my camp and apprise me of his deplorable plight; promising that I surely would reward him for the service. The man was impressed with his promise, and found me without difficulty. I hurried to see what could be done for the boy's relief. After an interview with Hassler – in which I assured him they could not hang him for his offense, and to expect me again in a short time – I proceeded to call upon the "judge," as Farnum was generally known. I explained the entire transaction through which the boy had gotten into trouble, and that he had been swindled shamefully, and asked that he be allowed his liberty at once. I said I would be responsible for his appearance if wanted, or that I would procure other more acceptable sureties.

At first the "judge" adopted a very lofty tone, telling me of the enormity of stealing the cattle in the night and leaving the country, and intimating that the man from whom they were taken was determined to have the culprit severely punished. Seeing that this did not impress me he assumed a milder tone, and finally proposed that he would have the plaintiff withdraw the complaint; and the best thing the boy could do would be to go home.

As for a return of the cattle or exaction of payment for them, that was altogether a different matter; it would be difficult if not impossible; I might consult a lawyer if so disposed, but he would not advise it. I saw Hassler, and gave him the "judge's" proposal, telling him I thought we had better try to recover for him if possible; but he was so overjoyed at the chance to get out of jail and away from the awful company housed in it that he was willing to accept liberty on any terms. The upshot of it was that he started at once for home, having lost his cattle, almost his self-respect because he had been in jail, and glad and happy to escape with his life.

One of the First Reporters in the Hills

On August twenty-ninth I went to work on the *Weekly Pioneer*,[50] in Deadwood, as a compositor; it was more from necessity than choice, for my wages were necessary to sustain us if we were to keep up our prospecting.

When I started to work for the *Pioneer,* Captain C. V. Gardner was the editor. A veteran of the Civil War, a pioneer by nature, and an optimist who never for a moment allowed

---

[50] The date of the first issue of the Deadwood *Pioneer* was June 8, 1876. It had only two pages, a half sheet, due to delay in receiving paper supplies. The *Pioneer* outfit had been brought into the Hills from Denver by Laughlin and Merrick, who had stopped first at Custer, but joined the stampede from that point to Deadwood. With the proprietors was Joe Kubler, who later established the *Custer Chronicle* at Custer, SD, and owned it until 1928. [Kubler continued to work for the new owner until shortly before his death in 1931. His son, Joe Jr., who worked as a printer on the *Chronicle* after his father's death, is now (1955) retired and living at Belle Fourche, SD. Two other sons of Joe, Sr., live in South Dakota: William, in Custer; and Carol, in Deadwood. – EDITOR].

The first and subsequent issues of the *Weekly Pioneer* were in great demand, and were bought at the price of twenty-five cents per copy by representatives of every portion of the United States, who mailed them out to their friends at home, and paid the same amount additional to have them carried out of the Hills to the nearest point reached by the United States mail service. When the first paper was printed on publication day, there were present a dozen customers for it and often Merrick, the proprietor, and Joe Kubler, pressman, an all-round indispensable helper, were kept busy until midnight, handing out copies of the paper and weighing and sacking the gold dust received for them. As far as the writer is aware there are only two copies of the first issue of the *Pioneer* in existence (1926), one belonging to Joseph B. Gossage, of the *Rapid City Journal,* the other owned by the writer himself. The files for the years from 1876 to 1879 were destroyed in the disastrous Deadwood fire in the latter year.

The wide distribution of the *Pioneer,* carrying far and wide the news of the new gold country, its mines, prospects, the growth of various towns, and no less interesting, accounts of the Indian troubles, made the name of the Black Hills a household word throughout the United States, and stimulated the movement from all quarters in this direction, so that by the beginning of fall it may be said to have attained its high tide. On July fourth it was estimated that there were in the Hills altogether seven thousand white people, though as this estimate was made primarily for the purpose of presentation to Congress in an effort to bring about the relinquishment of the Sioux title to the Hills, it may be surmised that the number was not understated. – [HUGHES].

himself to doubt that a great future was in store for his beloved Black Hills, he was interested in everything that tended to build up and improve the country. Gardiner brought to the *Pioneer* a spirit of optimism that enabled him to foresee a great future for this country of his choice, and gave to his writing a sincerity so apparent that it never failed to convince. He was a developer of mining and milling in the Hills.

One of the first communications I set in type on the *Pioneer* was from John R. Brennan,[51] one of the founders of Rapid City. It bore the date of August 28 [1876], and I here reproduce a portion in order to indicate the situation of the exposed settlers immediately before General Crook reached the Hills with his command.

> The redskins have made it hot for the boys for the past two weeks. On the 22nd two of our citizens were engaged in building a cabin on a ranch two miles below town when they were attacked by Indians. They made a running fight for a mile or more, when the Indians gave up the chase without getting either men or horses. One of our citizens mounted a horse and started up the gulch to spread the alarm, but the Indians had been there before him and had murdered two men near the site of the old sawmill about four miles above town. On the same day and about the same time four men on their way here from Deadwood were attacked at Limestone Springs, on the Crook and Deadwood road, and two of them were killed. The party consisted of Sam Scott, G. W. Jones, John Erquot and L. S.

---

[51] John R. Brennan, born in Kilkenny, Ireland, May 22, 1841, reached the Black Hills in October, 1875. He made the trip to the Hills from Denver, accompanied by George W. Stokes, N. H. Hawley and George Ashton. On the Platte his party was joined by a large party including California Joe. In February, 1876, Mr. Brennan helped to locate and establish Rapid City. He was a member of the first Board of Trustees of the City in March, 1876. In 1884 he was the City's postmaster. His daughter, Ruth (Mrs. Web Hill), of Rapid City was the fourth president of the Minnilusa Historical Association, formed several years ago.

This society, organized to preserve data and relics of the early-day West River country and Black Hills area, has in its membership many descendants of pioneers. The first president was John A. Boland, chairman of the Rushmore Mountain Commission. His father and mother kept a changing station on the old Sidney Trail at Buffalo Gap, with Senior Boland's brother. Second president was C. W. Hughes, son of the author. Carl Leedy, third president, a nephew of Mrs. John Brennan, was the son of an early mining man. Mrs. Ralph Gordon, present president [1957], is the daughter of Victor Anderson, a well known pioneer rancher and business man of Rapid City.

Livermore. Jones and Erquot were killed, Scott and Livermore making their escape to the woods a half mile distant, where they lay until after nightfall, when they made their way to town, arriving at about ten o'clock. Livermore had been shot in the arm above the elbow. The next morning fifteen or twenty men went out to bring in the bodies. We went to the Springs first and procured the bodies of Jones and Erquot, and then drove over to the old mill site to get the two others. We found one body lying in the creek, and the other lying a hundred yards or so distant. They were placed in the wagon with the other two bodies and brought to town. Here coffins were made and the bodies consigned to the grave after an appropriate funeral service read by O. Nicholson. The names of the murdered men are J. W. Patterson, George W. Jones, John Erquot and Thomas Pendleton. The bodies were horribly mutilated, almost shot to pieces, their ears were cut off, etc. . . . On the next day a man came in on the Custer road and reported having found the body of a man about eight miles southwest from town. A party went out, found the body and buried it where found. None of the party could identify it. . . . All work has been suspended for six or eight miles along the creek, as the miners do not consider it safe to try to open their claims under present conditions. Men have come down from the Hills to town, and the upper town (so called) is entirely deserted, all the men having moved here. We have a block house in course of erection which will be completed in a few days, when we believe we will be able to stand off any force of Indians that come.

Also connected with the *Pioneer* were George Stokes, Dr. C. W. Meyer, and Jack Langrishe; versatile and interesting writers. Meyer could do justice to a description of a fancy dress ball or a mill in the "bad lands."[*]

It was not as a comedian alone that Langrishe was qualified to shine. He was a printer and a good one. Invariably he put in type on all playbills, and other matter of display, advertising which announced his dramatic productions. A readier pen than his in dishing up current news or in caustic or witty editorial comment was difficult to find. He had the faculty of narrating in rhyme, events of general interest.

One cold blustery day in the winter, Langrishe entered the old log building in which the *Pioneer* was housed – rubbing

---

[*] The lower part of Deadwood, home of Chinatown and the red light district, was referred to as the "Bad Lands." Helen Rezatto, *Mount Moriah: Kill a Man – Start a Cemetery* (Rapid City, SD: Fenwyn Press, 1989), 65.

his very prominent nose which the frosty air had nipped – and after warming himself at the roaring fire in the stove, sat down at his desk and wrote the following:

> Oh the stove, the beautiful stove,
> Heating the room below and above;
> Broiling, roasting, keeping warm –
> Beautiful stove you can do no harm.
>
> Fill her to thaw your freezing toes,
> Fill her to thaw the end of your nose –
> Open the damper and let her go,
> She'll soon knock H - - l out of beautiful snow.

An epitaph for Crazy Horse by Langrishe records with historical accuracy and in the fewest possible words an event of much importance to the people of this frontier. News came that Crazy Horse, a hostile Sioux chief who, with his young men, had given much trouble about the foothills, had been killed by Lame Deer – a member of his band. Langrishe treated the news thus:

> The happy grounds are found at last,
> And Crazy Horse's days are past.
> On earth he struck a poor Lame Deer,
> Who sent him to another sphere.

For a time, after going to work for the *Pioneer,* I made the trip from our camp in Pocket Gulch to Deadwood in the morning and back in the evening, a distance of three miles; but we concluded I should be nearer my work. We moved camp to Deadwood where we secured ground and built a cabin on City Creek.[52] This we made comfortable with a good fireplace; it furnished us very acceptable quarters and was considered "home." One or both of my partners (Rochford and Van Fleet), were absent a good part of the time. Usually they came in to spend Sunday with me, report their doings, and secure

---

[52] A short distance above the present (1926) location of the Gilmore Hotel. – [HUGHES].

A REPORTER IN THE HILLS 137

supplies. On Monday morning as a rule they would start out again for the district in which they were working.

Their prospecting for the principal part of the fall and winter of '76 was confined to Bear Butte district, where the boys located several claims on which they and I did much work later; and from which, for a time, we expected great returns.

Within a few days after going to work on the *Pioneer,* I met Jimmy Irion for the second time. He was employed as scout and lookout for an outfit of haymakers on False Bottom but, being a printer, he usually made the *Pioneer* office his loafing place when in town. On this occasion he told with much glee of a little experience he had had with Indians on the False Bottom trail that day. Indians had fired on a solitary traveler and then started to ride him down. They had not seen Irion, who was coming up the trail on horseback, until he, whooping and yelling and firing his six-shooter was almost upon them. Then, no doubt fearful that they had been caught in a trap, they urged their horses at full speed into the forest and disappeared. Listeners warned Irion that the Indians would ambush him, if he were not careful; but he laughingly said he guessed he could look out for himself. The following or second day afterward, the Indians did ambush and kill him, as he ascended a little knoll from which he was accustomed to examine the surrounding country each day through his field glasses.

SNOOZER – OUR DOG

Thus far in these memoirs I have neglected mention of a member of our party who certainly is worthy of notice. This was a dog whom we called "Snoozer," though this name should not have been applied to him, as he really was very wide awake. He was of medium size and had long, shaggy hair, locks of which hung over his eyes almost concealing them. He joined our train as we were pulling out of Sidney in April, having been attracted by the firing of two or three shots at prairie dogs by members of our party. He became a favorite with all, but attached himself to our wagon. When we reached our destination and the men scattered out into various camps, he made our shack his home. He was accustomed to make the trip two or three times a week to the camps of all his friends, where he always met with a hearty welcome; but invariably he returned to us to spend the night.

He was a splendid camp guard and I believe he would have tackled a lion in defense of any of our property. In camp he would not touch food, however hungry he might be, unless it was given to him; but away from home, shame to say, he was an inveterate thief. On one occasion he brought to camp a fine dressed turkey and on another, a five-pound roll of butter neatly wrapped in muslin cloth; in neither had he left the mark of a tooth.

One day I was on my way from Gayville to Deadwood, accompanied by Snoozer. On the east side of the gulch the trail led over a bar about one hundred feet wide; the ascent and descent were quite abrupt. On this bar was the tent of a solitary camper. As I ascended the bar from the south I saw the occupant of the tent come out with a steak in his hand. In front of the tent was a bright campfire evidently kindled for the purpose of preparing dinner; a frying pan was on the ground beside the fire. In this pan the man placed the steak and turned back into the tent, undoubtedly for salt, as when he emerged again he had a salt shaker in his hand. As he entered the tent the dog passed me on the ascent, trotted over to the fire, lifted the steak from the pan and trotted down the trail to the north. In an instant he had reached the level of the gulch and was as completely out of sight as though the earth had opened and swallowed him. This he did without exhibiting any of the demeanor of a thief. He simply acted as if he were taking something that he knew was his by right. When the man came out with the salt in his hand he started to pick up the frying pan, gave a perceptible start, turned and looked at the stub limb of a bush beside the fire where it was plainly apparent he had been accustomed to hang his meat. He looked again into the pan, and then all around in every direction, shaking his head and muttering something which I could not hear, but which could readily be translated into, "I'll be damned if that don't beat me."

I was then in sight but as I was approaching the tent I could not be guilty. The whole affair transpired in much less time than it has taken in the telling, and the look of bewilderment on that camper's face was simply too comical for any description. It was a case where a man could not believe his eyes. He went again into the tent, came out and again looked at the bush and the frying pan. As I started the descent at the north side of the bar and looked back, he sat down as if to try to think the thing out.

On a hunting trip in the fall, Rochford was accompanied by the dog. He wounded a deer and the animal, in its struggles, hurt one of Snoozer's legs, so that he was left in camp to rest. A party of men on the way out of the Hills camped close by. They took a fancy to the dog, and tried to induce Rochford to part with him; which he declined to do. In his absence, the men and the dog disappeared. We were destined to hear from Snoozer once again. When the party reached Sidney the dog returned to the home from which he had joined us in the spring, and resumed life where he had left off on starting on his Black Hills adventures. His owner was Dennis Carrigan of Sidney.[53]

MY BUCKSKIN SUIT

Boylike, I had a desire for a buckskin suit. They were by no means uncommon. Nearly all hunters wore them, and even the finest suits of cloth frequently were seen to have the principal wearing parts reinforced with buckskin. I could have a tailor make such a suit, but it must be of the skins of deer killed by myself and tanned by my own hand. In my hunting trips at various times I had killed a number of deer and had saved the hides for this purpose. I tanned them, working on them at odd times when I had no other work more pressing. I did this under instruction of Sam Tull who, as I have stated heretofore, was

---
[53] Afterward a well known banker in Custer, SD, for many years.

competent to do or direct any necessary or desirable thing in camp. There is a peculiar saying of hunters that "any deer has brains enough to tan his own hide." This saying is not as foolish as it sounds to a tenderfoot, and is absolutely and literally true. That is, the brains of a deer, thoroughly rubbed into the hide after the "grain" has been removed and the hide thoroughly manipulated and massaged by the hands, imparts the final softening necessary. When this is done the hide is rolled up tightly and laid away for a time; then it is thoroughly washed with soap and water and gradually dried, being stretched and manipulated until completely dry. This plan is used when soap is scarce in camp, but where soap and grease are abundant the brains are seldom used. The commonly used method of tanning hides in camp may be described thus: the hide is thoroughly soaked in water for forty-eight hours; then it is stretched upon a "horse" made by setting legs in one end of a perfectly smoothed pole, and raising that end four feet; the other end of the pole rests on the ground. The hide is laid on the pole horse with the flesh side down, and the hair and grain with it are removed by scraping; the back of a drawknife is a very good tool for the purpose. A graining knife is better, but in the hands of a beginner it is more likely to cut the hide. The grain is a thin membrane on the outside of the hide, in which the hair is rooted. After the removal of the grain a thick application of grease or soap is rubbed on, and the hide is rolled up and laid away for a day or two; then it is thoroughly washed out with warm soapsuds and dried, being constantly stretched and manipulated with the hands during the process of drying. While the process is somewhat tedious, it possessed the interest for me that is attached to novelty. Besides, it was well worth the time and labor to have a suit of clothes, in the making of which I had so much part. This may seem foolish to the average reader, but given the same age, conditions and surrounding, I believe the pride I felt in my first (and last) buckskin suit would be felt by almost any red-blooded boy. The suit did me good service, on hunting and prospecting trips, but was discarded for more conventional garments when in town.

JOHN BRENNAN

CAPTAIN C.V. GARDNER

General Crook Comes to Deadwood, 1876

The sixteenth of September, '76, was a day long to be remembered. On that day General George Crook entered Deadwood with several officers of his staff; he had left his command camped in the foothills near Crook City.[54] The first report of his coming reached Deadwood on the eleventh, and was hailed with pleasure. The scout[55] bringing the news told of

---

[54] Crook City, which was located on or about May 15, 1876, was peculiarly exposed, and during the summer and early fall of that year the settlers were kept constantly on the alert to guard against attack. Horse herds were stampeded and driven off, and several of the men in charge were killed. Though in a state of almost constant preparation against surprise, it was seldom that the whites succeeded in killing any of the marauders. The Indians knew the country so well, took advantage of their opportunities and acted so quickly that to make successful resistance or counter-attack was well nigh impossible. On one occasion a young Indian with more zeal than discretion was overtaken by a posse and killed. The posse passed on, leaving the body lie where it fell. Later a Mexican following their trail, found the body, which he decapitated, and took the head to Deadwood, where he received a reward. For some time a reward of $250 was offered for each Indian killed. On the return to Crook City the Mexican was confronted by the man who had killed the Indian, and who was justly incensed that his reward and more especially his thunder had been stolen. In the altercation that ensued the Mexican was shot, though not fatally.

Though thus harassed, and though Deadwood was attracting the great majority of the immigrants, Crook City made a considerable growth during that and the following year, was made a station on the Pierre stage line when established, and finally designated as the county seat of Lawrence County when organized. This dignity it did not long enjoy, as the people, when allowed to vote on the location, very promptly and emphatically decided in favor of Deadwood. The prospecting of lower Whitewood Creek, on which Crook City was located, disclosed the fact that the ground would not pay for working, and when the fact was established the fate of the camp was sealed. During its brief day of glory a newspaper was established, but it died with the town. Now few are left of those who knew Crook City at its best, when hopes for its future were high, and when it possessed in miniature all the attributes of a town of the wild west. – [HUGHES].

[55] Red Cloud Agency via Ft. Laramie – Sept. 18. Gruard, Crook's chief scout, arrived here last night with dispatches for McKenzie from Crook. He left the command on the afternoon of the 11th. He reports that last Sunday Crook's advance of 150 men struck an Indian camp about fifty miles north of Crook City. That night the remainder of the command arrived, and an attack was made by Crook, the fight lasting until noon Monday, when the Indians were routed, with a loss to the whites of only 3 killed and nine wounded. Fourteen dead Indians were found on

the destruction by the soldiers of a Sioux Village near the Slim Buttes; which also was welcome news.[56] He stated that a num-

---

the battle field, and four persons were known to have been carried off... Among the killed... White, a scout... two privates... 2d Lt. A. H. Von Hutwitz of 3rd Cavalry wounded in knee. He was Captain of 54th New York during the War... *Rocky Mountain News,* Sept. 19, 1876.

[56] From the *Denver Brand Book,* vol. IX 1953, published by the Denver Westerners, 1954, pp. 291-292, we quote part of the "Notebook kept by Dr. V. T. McGillycuddy, M.D., while a member of the Yellowstone and Big Horn Expedition, May 26 – Dec. 13, 1876." The original Notebook is now owned by Fred A. Rosenstock of Denver, Colorado.

 Sept. 2 (1876) Moved camp 19 m. North. Camped at Big Bend of Beaver. 42 Pickets. Firing. Frost at night, in *Dakota.*

 Sept. 3. Moved camp 20 m. E. and camped on Andrews Cr. near Sentinel Butte.

 Sept. 4. Moved camp 18 m. E. Camped on Little Missouri. Rain all day & cold.

 Sept. 5. Moved camp 25 m. N. of E. and camped on Custer's Trail on head of Heart River. Rain all day. Lunar Bow. Command put on *half rations.*

 Sept. 6. Moved camp 30 m. South. Camp on Head of Bear 6 m. S.W. from Rainy Butte. Rations ¼ minus the bacon. No wood to cook the bacon we did not have. Clay water. 150 m. north from Deadwood City. 14 horses abandoned. Burned one saddle.

 Sept. 7. Moved camp 30 m. South. Camp on North Fork of Grand River. rose bushes for food. Good water. ¼ rat. & bacon. Capt. Mills & 150 men left for Deadwood for rations.

 Sept. 8. Moved camp 23 m. S.E. camped on S. Fork Grand River. rain all day. Shooting horses for rations. recent Indian camp signs.

 Sept. 9. Capt. Mills attacked Indian village of the Brule American Horse. 17 m. South of 48. reinforcements of 250 men sent forward at 7 A.M. from 2d & 3d Cav. & whole of 5th Cav. Mills attacked at daylight. Assigned to go with reinforcement. Arrived in field at 12 M. found Lt. Von Leutwitz and 9 men wounded old Village captured & a few Indians trapped in a ravine. In attempting to dislodge them 1 soldier & Buffalo Chips were killed & two soldiers wounded. The Sioux, 3 bucks & 7 squaws surrendered at 3 P.M. We found in ravine 1 buck & 3 squaws dead.

 Chief Am. Horse was mortally wounded. Shot in abdomen. I operated and tried to return intestines. He died that night at 4½ P.M. While amputating Lt. Von Leutwitz's leg Sioux attacked us on all sides but were forced off. They wounded two more of our men, fired more or less all night. Kennedy of the 5th wounded in morning died at midnight. Again next morning wounding one more man.

 Sept. 10. I was assigned in charge of travois train of wounded moved at 7 A.M. to No. 50 25 m. south on S. Fork of Grand River. Wrote to Mother & Fanny telegraphed next day to Fanny via Lt. Bubb who left for Deadwood in Black Hills 75 m. south. Rain all day.

 Sept. 11. Moved 25 m. south and camped on Owl River. rain all day. wood plenty.

 Sept. 13. Moved camp 5 m. South at 12 M. and got rations on Belle Fourche. We traveled from Heart River on two days rations & horse meat.

CROOK COMES TO DEADWOOD

ber of Indians had been killed, and that in the camp had been found a lot of plunder from the Custer battle field. The force attacking had lost four men, one of whom was the widely known scout, "Pony" White. The soldier's report was fully confirmed a day or two later when a small detachment of the soldiers came into town, and procured a large quantity of provisions of all kinds. It was learned that the command, comprising two thousand men, had made a forced march while short of supplies and had endured much hardship.

When, on the sixteenth, General Crook entered the town with a number of his officers, they were accompanied by Robert E. Strahorn, the well known correspondent, who had been with Crook and Terry throughout the campaign of this summer. The complete story of that forced march was written for the *Pioneer* by Strahorn.[57]

Sept. 14. Remained in camp on Belle Fourche. Courier arrd. from Ft. Laramie at 11 P.M. ordering Gen. Crook on to Ft. Laramie.

Sept. 15. Moved camp 5 m. S. camp on Whitewood. wrote to Fanny.

Sept. 16. Gen. Crook left with staff at 5:30 A.M. for Ft. Laramie. Gen. Merritt took command. Men in camp all day, assigned to the 3d. Cav. In addition to 2d. Dr. Stevens detached.

Sept. 17. Moved 5 m. up Cr.

Sept. 18. Moved 10 m. and camped in Centennial Park 2 m. beyond Crook City.

Sept. 19. Moved camp 24 m. south went into camp on Middle Box Elder where I camped in 1875. 7 m. from Custer's Peak. 2 cos. of 4 artillery from Red Cloud with rations.

Sept. 20. In camp. 60 cases of cholera morbus in 2d, 3d. Cav. Sick myself.

[57] Since the files of the *Pioneer* were later destroyed by fire, we are unable here to quote Strahorn's account. The following, however, is an account of the Deadwood visit written by John (Long) Finerty, another one of the correspondents who accompanied General Crook on the campaign. Finerty represented the *Chicago Times*. From the *Rocky Mountain News*, Oct. 12, 1876:

After dark, all Deadwood and the surrounding settlements, over 2,000 people, turned out and gave Crook an "ovation." It was very noisy. The general had to address the crowd from the hotel balcony. He made an off hand speech which showed intimate acquaintance with the habits and sentiments of the mining fraternity. Neither did he hesitate to crack a few rough jokes about the Indian troubles which as the phrase goes, were "well received." Afterward he was ushered to the Deadwood theatre, where he was formally addressed and presented with the "freedom of the city." His sentiments have already been published per telegram.

When that much was disposed of, Crook, who abhors handshaking, was subjected to the pump handle nuisance at the front door of the dramatic temple. He survived it all, not without some wry faces, I imagine. The general appears to be

The officers who accompanied Crook into Deadwood on the sixteenth wore badly tattered uniforms, but were cheerful in the knowledge that the toilsome march was over, and that a square meal was once more a possibility. They one and all agreed that the men of the command had acted the part of heroes, and that there was little grumbling about the hardships endured. All were interested in reaching the Hills, of which they had heard many reports during the summer. With the arrival of the first detachment, wagons were loaded with supplies in Deadwood and Crook City and dispatched to the camp on the Belle Fourche.

---

very much liked by the miners, his long residence on the Pacific Coast having familiarized him with hundreds of the brotherhood.

In the evening I took a stroll around the city and examined everything of interest. Wearing cavalry pants, and looking altogether like one of Uncle Samuel's boys, out of repair, the hardy and hearty miners took it for granted that I was earning $13 per month fighting "Injuns." As I wished to post myself on the country, I did not undeceive them, but was compelled to swallow enough "forty rod" to kill an ordinary alderman. The effects of that accursed "beverage" were apparent a week later, and I was not the only awful example.

But as I am now making my own confession I'll say nothing about other people's follies. As Mickey Free would poetically observe, "Their fallin's nothin' to me."

I visited a half dozen "hells" where I noticed some Chicago "Mugs" all engaged in the noble art of faro or some other thimble-rigging devilment. It must be a strong temptation that keeps such worthless away from Cook county during election times. However, the chances of their getting speedily shot or scalped around Deadwood are infinitely better than if they were here. In the lively season Deadwood "sports" kill off a man or two every night. Between them and the Sioux it is a hard matter to keep the population of the place up to the maximum standard. Women, as in Cheyenne, act as "dealers" at many of the tables, and more resemble incarnate fiends that do their vulturelike male associates. I observe that decided brunettes or decided blondes are more engaged in evil work than are their negative fellow women. Most of the miners would prefer playing "faro" or "monte" with men, for the women are generally old and unscrupulous hands, whose female subtlety makes them paramount in all the vices of cheating and theft...

Nearly every horse-shoer in town happened to be on a spree, and Lieut. Clark, our acting quartermaster, had to go around with a posse of soldiers and sober up sufficient of the gang to get our horses shod. This operation consumed several hours, and it was nearly daylight before we got to bed. We did not start very early the next morning, and at breakfast I read a copy of the *Black Hills Pioneer* – a neat little sheet, which contained a very good account of our recent campaign, and of Crook's oratorical effort on the preceding night. It "blew" a little about the Hills, and advertised the Cheyenne and Sidney routes in sensational style. I did not notice any politics in its pages.

CROOK COMES TO DEADWOOD 147

The detachment of Captain Mills had left the main command on the south fork of Grand River – probably twenty miles within the present state of South Dakota. The departure was made in the night, in a driving rain; the men stopped only for an hour's rest after midnight, when again they pushed on without breakfast; the rain still continued. In the afternoon Frank Gruard – considered one of the best scouts ever known on the frontier – returned from a scouting expedition ahead and reported the discovery of a Sioux village in the foothills of the Slim Buttes. The troops went into camp at a point about three miles from the Indians, and spent the night in a ravine. They pushed out under Gruard's guidance, reached the Indian camp, and attacked at daylight. The camp consisted of thirty-five tepees. The surprise was complete, and the Indians, therefore were not able to offer serious resistance, though when a warrior managed to get his gun he fought bravely. As stated, the loss to the soldiers was four killed, with several wounded. The Indian dead numbered forty, with a number of prisoners taken. The latter were mainly women and children. In the camp were found about 5,000 pounds of buffalo meat, many sacks of dried and drying berries, 2,000 buffalo robes and the usual camp equipment. The main command was communicated with, and reached the spot the same day in time to repel an attack by a large force of Indians that evidently had been encamped nearby. The provisions were very welcome by way of variety to a menu of horse meat that had become distasteful. At this time there were in the command fifty sick and disabled men, who were transported on pack mules; and it is worthy of note that all survived the hard experience.

The feeling of relief occasioned by the coming of the soldiers was great and general, for the Indians had been active all around the foothills in such numbers that it was evident they had been largely reinforced. Crook probably was correct in his surmise that a general attack on the people of the Hills was intended. Reports of the most alarming character came from every exposed point on the fringe of the Hills, and a greater number of whites were killed in the Hills during this and the previous month than in double the length of time before or after.

It was desired that General Crook's influence be secured, if possible, toward the establishment of a permanent camp at some point in the foothills; and a reception for him and his officers was held. The Langrishe theatre was secured for the occasion, and there the citizens of Deadwood met the general and had the privilege of shaking his hand.

Several speeches were made by prominent citizens and replied to by Major Burt on Crook's behalf. Burt told the story of the march and extolled the general under whom, as he stated it, he had "enjoyed the satisfaction of standing in a Sioux village and seeing it burn."

A man in the crowd shouted, "You had better turn over those Sioux prisoners to us. If you take them to the agency, Uncle Sam will feed them up until they want to take the war path again."

To this Burt replied, "No, we can't do that; we won't give you those Indians to kill, and we won't kill them ourselves – provided they show us where there are more to kill."

The general was chary of promises regarding the establishment of a permanent camp, and properly so; for the higher authorities decided that pending the outcome of the efforts of the commission to extinguish the Indian title such action might hinder the work. The reason for refusal, however, given by Crook in answer to a formal petition, was that the War Department believed greater protection would be afforded the Hills people by keeping a force moving in the field than by stationing soldiers in a camp.

After a short stay, and the receipt of supplies of all things necessary, the army marched on its way, and left us in the same situation as before so far as danger from Indians was concerned.

In the meantime the Indian Commission[58] was at work endeavoring to obtain the signatures of the chiefs and "head

---

[58] The Indians. Sioux-thing Syrup for the Winter. Spotted Tail Agency, Neb., September 22, via Sidney, Neb., Sept. 26. – The first council with the Sioux at Spotted

CROOK COMES TO DEADWOOD 149

men" to the cession treaty. But there was no cessation of depredations about the foothills. It was apparent enough that whatever the chiefs and "head men" might agree to do, many of the young warriors did not intend to give up the warpath; and with the removal of the troops from the foothills, these became if possible, bolder than ever before. It was a matter of daily occurrence that stock was raided and driven off; in two or three instances as many as a hundred head of horses were driven away in a single foray.

The people of Deadwood, through their provisional government,[59] kept in touch with General Crook, and probably placed him in a somewhat embarrassing position by their requests for his influence in securing protection for the settlers. No doubt he was in entire sympathy with their desires, but so long as the title remained with the Indians the government could not well interfere in our behalf. We were trespassing and must be so regarded.

I have a distinct recollection of a short but rather significant correspondence in which General Crook, General Sheridan and General Sherman figured, regarding petitions of the Black Hillers for relief. The petitions were forwarded to General Sheridan, and by him transmitted to General Sherman, who interviewed the President regarding them. It is not to be wondered at if the President manifested some impatience. The Indian troubles of that year had been worse than since 1869. The loss of Custer and his command was deplorable. Although the government was doing its utmost to punish the Indians they had led Crook and Terry a fruitless chase over a great part of the northwest, all summer and well into the fall, without those generals having been able to bring them to a decisive engagement.

All this apparently was caused by an invasion of the Indian country by the people who were now interceding with the government to intervene and save them from the results of their own folly and disobedience. Therefore the President was

---

Tail Agency with the full Commission was held this afternoon. Colonel Boone, as Chairman. – *Rocky Mountain News*, Sept. 27, 1876.
[59] *See* pp. 128-132.

not inclined to look with favor on the petitions, and expressed himself somewhat forcibly regarding them. The most significant part of the correspondence was a brief instruction by the President, transmitted by General Sherman to Crook's command, to "give such protection as possible to any whites desirous of leaving the Hills."

While seeking federal aid, without success, the people of the Hills also were trying to get some relief from the territorial government. It was charged that Governor Pennington[60] had little sympathy with the people here, and he became very unpopular. His apparent indifference to our necessities was contrasted with the extremely sympathetic attitude of Governor Thayer of Wyoming, who had enlisted himself warmly in our behalf... The people of the Hills felt somewhat relieved when it was learned that the War Department had determined to keep a force in the field all winter; it was hoped operations might be conducted sufficiently near to afford some measure of protection. Crook, however, made his camp well down on the Belle Fourche, instead of in the foothills as was expected, and the presence of the soldiers there did not prevent small parties of Indians from continuing their depredations. It did, however, have the effect of keeping them from concentrating in force, had such been their intention, and this was given as a reason for the presence of the troops; though when the Indians had acted in large bodies, it usually had been earlier in the year.

Finally, when it was learned that orders had been given Crook to move southwestward, leaving the Hills altogether, the residents could only determine to hold the country by their own efforts until such time as the cession should be completed, and the treaty ratified by Congress. Following this would come not only freedom from the Indian menace, but the establishment of county governments, laws and regulations to check the turbulent element among the inhabitants, and the beginning of a general improvement in conditions of living.

---

[60] Governor John L. Pennington.

CROOK COMES TO DEADWOOD 151

With the year of 1876 drawing to a close, a great many people left the Hills, some intending to return in the spring, but a considerable percentage had had all the frontier experience they desired. With the military withdrawn, and a general movement of the floating element toward the states, those who had determined to spend the winter did have a feeling of isolation not altogether pleasant, as they contemplated the months of winter ahead, the freight trains withdrawn from the roads, and possible shortage of supplies before freighting would be resumed in the spring. Those who took the trouble to investigate found, however, that the merchants were pretty well stocked with the things most necessary. The immediate community could be supplied, and the only question was as to the number of men who would strike for the central camp from the outlying districts with the coming of winter, with the expectation of procuring all supplies necessary to carry them through.

Miners' wages had been reduced from seven to five dollars per day, but the cost of board and provisions had been correspondingly reduced. With the single exception of the case of "Coal Oil" Johnny Spencer, there was no attempt during the winter to exact unreasonable prices. Business was stabilized; stages were coming and going regularly between Deadwood and Cheyenne and Deadwood and Sidney, with a promise on the part of the management of each line that service would be continued, if possible, without interruption throughout the winter.

Finally a private telegraph line was extended from Fort Laramie and on the first day of December, 1876, the first message was transmitted over it to Cheyenne. The operator was James Halley.[61] The coming of the Cheyenne and Black Hills Telegraph Line was welcomed by everyone and this, with the running of regular coaches, made us feel that we were not altogether out of touch with the outside world.

---

[61] Halley served the public in that capacity until the latter part of '80, when he engaged in the banking business in Rapid City with R. C. Lake, a Deadwood merchant. There he bore an important part for many years in building up one of the strongest financial institutions in the state and the improvement of the city of his choice.

By way of amusements to pass the winter there were always the open saloon and gambling house for those who had the means and inclination to patronize them, but there were also other forms common to less isolated communities.

The most noted caterer to the tastes of the amusement-loving public was Jack Langrishe, well and affectionately known throughout the West, and particularly in the prominent mining camps. A pioneer in Colorado and Montana, Langrishe also became a pioneer of Dakota, entering the Hills in July '76, when he at once set about the erection of a theatre. On July 22, the people of Deadwood were treated to the first presentation of the legitimate drama. Langrishe had brought with him a number of veteran actors; and to those he added from time to time as he could induce talented people to leave the more populous centers and traverse the tedious and none too safe trails to Deadwood. Many noted performances were given in the Langrishe theatre, and those who attended will aver that while the surroundings were not all that might be desired, the talent displayed was beyond criticism. Thus, when "The Two Orphans" was presented by a cast embracing Augusta Chambers and Fannie Price in title roles, and with Martin as Pierre and Gross as Jacques, supported by a well-balanced company, there was little left to desire to make the production worthy the attendance of a metropolitan audience.

DEADWOOD'S GANG OF SHARPERS ACTIVE

During the late fall a man named Spencer, known ever thereafter as "Coal Oil Johnny," quietly bought all the kerosene available in Deadwood. No one suspected his intentions until the community was confronted with a demand for $3.75 per gallon. . . Victims of this holdup indulged in threats but paid the price.

Relief finally came through the arrival from Cheyenne of a big tank of oil, brought to Deadwood by an old freighter with a six-horse team. It was this freighter, however, who fell victim to some of Deadwood's sharpers.

CROOK COMES TO DEADWOOD 153

There was in Deadwood at this time a notorious gang of sharpers. . . . They conducted sure-thing games, used "knockout drops," sandbags, or garroted their victims if they could not otherwise cause them to part with their "rolls." The leader of this gang of thieves and thugs was known as "Ten Die Brown." He was a burly fellow who made no pretense whatever of being any better than he was. He would laugh in the face of a man whom he had victimized and invite him to get redress if he could. He swaggered in the gambling houses and on the streets, and evidently had no fear of any penalty that the court of "Judge" Farnum might seek to exact for his offenses. Another member was a gambler called "Pancake Bill," a sure-thing gambler and capper for a half dozen or more games in which the player had the proverbial chance of winning that the calf has of killing the butcher. He was a soft-voiced fellow, not giving to boasting, as was his leader. But he had the reputation of being a man who would not hesitate at murder, if necessary, to secure booty.

A third member was known as "Kentuck." He was a cripple, and a very important member. He was particularly successful in making approach to intended victims, as he had a manner that suggested diffidence as well as a degree of deference toward those with whom he was attempting to make acquaintance. He probably drew down commissions from a greater number of games than any other capper in Deadwood. The roughneck of the outfit was a fellow known as the "Miner," from the fact that he posed as a hard-working prospector, always trying to enlist capital for the development of a valuable mining property, and always carrying in his pockets samples of rich ore, taken, of course, from other mines of value, but purporting to come from his own.

When the old freighter arrived in Deadwood with his precious cargo of oil, the quartette above described at once marked him as a promising victim. "Kentuck" approached him and in the course of conversation learned that the old man had spent some time in the mining districts of Colorado, and had some knowledge of ores. "Kentuck" said he had a friend who owned a mining claim in which he thought the ore was valuable, and said he would like to have the freighter's opinion of the ore. The "Miner" accordingly was introduced, produced his specimen ore, and the freighter at once saw that it was good.

The "Miner" said he had been trying to have a few tons freighted to Cheyenne for shipment to a Colorado smelter for testing, but that the expense was so great he was unable to do so. He said he could raise money to pay a reduced freight rate on a few tons – in fact, had that much in sight – but feared he would have to wait some time to get the balance necessary. The bait thus thrown out was taken at once. The freighter would be going back to Cheyenne as soon as he obtained the payment for his services in bringing the oil, and he would have no load for his team on the return trip. He could well afford to make a low rate for hauling a few tons of ore and grasped eagerly at the opportunity offered.

After some haggling over the amount to be paid for the hauling, an agreement was reached and the time fixed for loading the next day. A meeting was appointed for that evening to arrange final details. At the hour appointed "Kentuck" and the "Miner" escorted the freighter to a place known as the "Cubbyhole," on Main Street, where they were to take a final drink to bind the bargain.

In this den there was just room for a primitive bar and for customers standing in front of it in single file. When the trio entered, the place was lighted up and "Ten Die Brown" was behind the bar. "Kentuck" introduced the freighter to Brown, told of the deal into which they had entered with him, and said, "Now we'll have a drink on me."

They had the drink, but when "Kentuck" reached for his money to pay for it, the "Miner" insisted it was his treat. Each was insistent; neither would yield to the other, and a quarrel was threatened, when the old freighter said, "Boys, rather than have hard feelings, I'll pay for this," and pulled out the roll of bills he had received an hour or two previously. No sooner had he done so than one of the men grabbed him by the throat, another grabbed the roll, and before he realized what was happening he found himself hustled into the street; instantly the place was dark and locked.

When the victim found an officer and returned to the scene there was nothing in the place to indicate that it ever had been occupied. The bar had disappeared.

The freighter identified Brown as one of the criminal gang and insisted on his arrest. The others had disappeared. An examination was held before Farnum. It was a farce. The log building in which the court held its sitting was packed with thugs and gamblers, friends of Brown and his confederates. Many of the spectators had been partners with them in other equally atrocious crimes. On a bench sat the dejected old freighter. When questioned and badgered by Brown's attorney the old man became confused. His testimony was greeted with jeers and laughter by the crowd, without any attempt on the part of the court to enforce order.

At one end of the bench on which the old man sat was Brown; at the other end was the notorious "Nutshell Bill." Many were the merry jests they passed back and forth for the amusement of the crowd. Finally Bill accosted Brown with, "I say, Brown, hasn't the old man got a pretty good team left?"

To this Brown replied in the affirmative. "Well," said Bill, "I wonder if we couldn't roll him for that."

The old man could get no help from any source and he was glad to accept a pittance given him by one of Brown's friends – probably part of his own money – sufficient to pay his expenses home.

The owners of the big gambling halls, with the faro and roulette dealers and lookouts; the lily-fingered manipulator of the cards over the poker table; the smooth confidence man with a fake mining or gold brick scheme for the undoing of the innocent tenderfoot —those, together with a number of men engaged in more legitimate lines, but who held a precarious footing on the selvage edge of respectability – constituted what might be termed an aristocracy of vice.

They were the main support of the more elaborate mansions of sin whose bejewelled female inmates looked down with scorn upon their sisters in sin upon the lower rounds of iniquity – who found their male companionship in the hurdy-gurdy, and in turn looked down with no less scorn upon the lowest dregs of vice – represented in the brothels and the Chinese harlotry that housed itself in the dens and cubbyholes of lower Main Street.

The reason that Deadwood acquired a worse reputation than any of the surrounding towns and camps was because it was the first established and offered the first field of operations for the vicious; this centering of the worst classes of the population worked to the advantage of other communities nearby in giving them a degree of immunity. Not that other places in and about the Hills were free from such contamination; that could not be expected; but there vice and crime did not flaunt themselves as brazenly as in the metropolis of the Hills, where strength of numbers made the lawless element defiant of restraint. Writers for eastern publications vied with one another in their wild, weird stories of the vice and corruption, and painted the picture in darker colors than even the bad conditions warranted. One writer who contributed to a magazine of large circulation went so far as to declare that Deadwood was "rotten to the core." This was not true. The core was sound and wholesome, composed as it was of fine men and women who stood for personal and civic virtue against the surge of wickedness, and whose influence was the leaven that eventually brought regeneration.

Hunting Expeditions
To Bear Butte and Spearfish

The failure of our placer enterprise had so discouraged our new partners – Wood, Richardson and Westfall – that by early August [1876] they were talking of leaving the country. Smallpox had been quite prevalent in the gulch for some time, and had assumed a virulent form. Deaths from the disease were numerous, as there were no hospital accommodations and many of the patients were housed in a manner offering little protection.

It was decided that before Wood, Richardson and Westfall should start home they would take a short hunting trip; and for this they began preparing. On this trip I was to accompany them.

At that time there were no game laws to interfere with the killing. Fresh meat was a necessity as an antiscorbutic where vegetables were lacking, besides being a welcome variation from the ordinary fare of the camp. There was not the waste of meat killed at this season that might be supposed, for what was not sold to the markets or consumed at once usually was preserved by the process known as "jerking."[62]

On the seventeenth of August, '76 I, with the others named, started out, expecting to find all the game we would want at the head of Whitewood Creek – about twelve miles south. Our route lay up Deadwood to the mouth of Poorman; thence up that gulch to the head and across the divide to the south into the head of Whitetail; thence up Whitetail to the head and

---

[62] "Jerking" was accomplished by stripping the hams in a manner that left a thin membrane covering each piece, and cutting other parts in slices about an inch thick, dipping them for a moment in strong boiling brine, then subjecting them for a brief time to smoke, after which the curing was completed by exposing them to the sun. Those who never have enjoyed a well-cured piece of jerked venison can have little conception of how palatable it is. With a pocket full of this food, a hunter can travel all day without becoming hungry. It is wonderfully sustaining against fatigue. – [HUGHES].

across the divide between that and Whitewood, which was reached by a trail.

On reaching the head of Poorman we stopped to observe a number of men engaged in making a survey[63] on a hill to the northeast... We reached the head of Whitewood in the evening and went into camp. Next morning bright and early we were out hunting, but we found no deer, though we hunted assiduously all day. By evening we found plenty of deer sign and went into camp on the little tributary of Rapid Creek.[64] We now decided to kill enough meat to make good loads for the three pack animals with us. This we did in the two days following. Our packs were made of venison "saddles" only; that is, the hind parts of the animals, cut off just forward of the kidneys, as these sold most readily in the Deadwood market – from which we were now distant twenty-five miles... The forward parts of the animals we roasted for use in camp.

I disposed of the meat we had brought in, taking it with a pack animal from one camp to another, when unable to sell to the butchers. On one of my trips to the Deadwood market I met our old friend "Spike" Tomlins, at the junction of the Blacktail and Deadwood roads. He was driving a team with a tarpaulin-covered wagon. Knowing that he had been engaged in hauling meat for Spaulding, I accosted him, asking him if he was loaded with elk. He stopped and said, "Lift the cover and see."

I did so, and saw in the wagon box the bodies of two men that he was bringing into Deadwood for burial. They had been killed by the Indians at a point near Spearfish, the day previous. One of the men was Brown[65] – one of the locators of the Deadwood townsite. The other was named Holland.[66] Spike had at this time located a ranch on the Belle Fourche, where the settlement named Minnesela was started.

---

[63] And thus saw the very beginnings of Lead City. – [HUGHES].

[64] Named afterward by Joe McKirahan as Irish Gulch, at the mouth of which the town of Rochford is now located. – [HUGHES].

[65] Isaac Brown.

[66] Charles Holland of Sioux City, Iowa.

HUNTING EXPEDITIONS

Early in September, Wood, Richardson and Westfall[67] left us to return to "the States," with regret all around, as they had been good partners and companions.

From the twenty-ninth of August, until the tenth of December 1876, I had worked steadily, usually putting in the first part of the week on job work, and setting the type for the *Weekly Pioneer* from Wednesday morning until the last page was put to press by Joe Kubler on Saturday afternoon. As the paper was merely a small folio sheet, I could do this without difficulty. The printing was done one page at a time on a job press. My prospecting trips before going to work as a printer had a fascination for me, and I longed at times to be out with the other boys – who usually managed to come in and spend the end of the week with me. I could not leave the office, however, without furnishing a substitute; and if there was another printer in the Hills we had not seen him for months. During the summer and early fall there had been an occasional call from an old, itinerant "jour" [journeyman], but with the coming of winter no more came, having departed to regions where newspapers were more numerous and means of transportation more certain.

On the tenth of December, however, a way was opened. On that day there walked into the *Pioneer* office a stranded printer. He told me his hard luck story and I took him to dinner with me. Before he finished he told me he had eaten nothing

---

[67] After leaving the Hills, Westfall was the only one of the trio of whom we ever heard. His fate is an illustration of the old saying that in trying to escape from the frying pan one may land in the fire. On leaving the Hills in mortal dread of the Indians, Westfall proceeded to his home in the Elkhorn Valley of Nebraska. He almost immediately sold his farm and moved with his family, consisting of a wife, son, and daughter, to Kansas where he purchased another farm. In the late spring of '77, a band of Northern Cheyennes that had been moved to the Indian Territory the previous year, broke away from the reservation assigned them and made their way north, intent on reaching their old haunts. On their way they encountered Westfall and his son as they worked in the field, and killed them. Westfall's wife and daughter made a narrow escape by hiding in some brush near the house. It is certain that they, too, would have been killed had the Indians not been fearful of being overtaken by the soldiers, who were even then on their trail. News of the movement of the Cheyennes to the north was sent to every military post convenient to their anticipated route, with the result that they were intercepted, a majority of them killed, and the remnant returned to the reservations. – [HUGHES].

since breakfast on the previous day. He had come into the Hills a week before and had stopped at Custer, finally coming on to Deadwood. At that time he had fifty dollars and a handsome and valuable ivory mounted revolver. This money and gun he was induced to risk in a sure-thing game, and as a result very quickly lost both. If he could only raise "a stake" sufficient to take him back to Fairplay [Colorado]!

I immediately offered to put him on "cases," while I took a "rest." He accepted gladly, and the next morning I accompanied Rochford and Van Fleet to Bear Butte district, where they had been working on a location. Here we spent two days, and incidentally located some lots in a new town to be known as Virginia City – on Bear Butte Creek, about two miles above Galena.[68]

On our second day we were overtaken by two friends from Nebraska, Andrew Farrell and Tim Deegan. They had searched for us first in Deadwood, and then had followed us to Bear Butte Creek. They had two teams of oxen in Deadwood, and as snow had fallen to a depth of a foot or more, it was necessary that the animals be moved to the foothills to obtain forage. Since the snow precluded prospecting, we decided to return to Deadwood to get the cattle and then take a hunting trip out of the Hills toward the Bear Lodge range.

On the thirteenth of December we returned to Deadwood.[69] The snow was deep and soft – as the day was warm – and traveling was difficult and tiresome. At an old tollgate where our trail reached Two Bit Creek, we stopped for a brief rest, and I inquired of a surly individual if we could get something to eat. The keeper of the gate responded in an ungracious tone that he had some biscuits that we could have if we had the

---

[68] As I had made the mistake of neglecting the opportunity to locate town property in Deadwood, I determined I would improve the opportunity here offered, and employed a man with two teams of cattle to haul logs, with which I later constructed several cabins. As Virginia City "died a'bornin'," I, of course, never realized anything from this flyer in real estate. – [HUGHES].

[69] Looking back over the years that have passed, with the experience they have brought, it now seems the height of folly to have contemplated a trip of the kind at that time of year. It can only be said in extenuation that "the hair on the tops of our heads was yet thick." – [HUGHES].

price to pay for them. He was told to produce them, and did so. They were five in number – just one apiece for our party – and not fit to be offered to a self-respecting dog. They were small, had the color of jaundice from an overdose of soda, and rivalled in degree of hardness any of the surrounding rock formations. The price the fellow asked was a dollar and a quarter, twenty-five cents apiece; unfortunately I had paid it before he reached me in the distribution. It simply was an outrage; but the money having been paid, there seemed no recourse. Deegan, always impetuous, was for licking the fellow; but I had made a discovery that seemed to promise something better, and signaled him to be quiet. The gate keeper had taken the biscuits from a box with shelves, nailed to the wall, and in doing so had incautiously exposed a full pan of fresh biscuits which he evidently had taken from the oven just before our entrance. When he stepped outside and engaged in chopping a backlog for the fireplace, I stepped to the primitive cupboard and tossed the fresh biscuits around to the boys, while they lasted. Then we took our departure in better spirits.

Two days were spent in preparation for the hunt. The snow became so deep that it was considered necessary to get the cattle to the foothills where they could feed, as the price of hay in Deadwood was simply prohibitive – not by reason of any corner, but because the supply was practically exhausted. The little hay on hand was of necessity doled out to horses, a number of which it was absolutely necessary to keep, as the only means of transportation. At the last moment it was found that Farrell could not go. He brought a substitute, however, in the person of Charley Miller, who had bought Deegan's cattle, and was anxious to join the party.

Miller proved a very poor companion; he had had no previous experience in living out of doors. He found fault with everything, constantly contrasting this experience with the ease and luxury he had always enjoyed previously. He disliked camp work, and did it awkwardly and with grumbling. He evidently assumed that his companions never had seen life outside of the Hills, and at first was inclined to assume a patronizing air, and to offer instructions and advice. He made a disagreeable and difficult journey even more disagreeable and difficult than it might have been for the others; but certainly it was no picnic for him. All the others accepted what came, as cheerfully as possible, and naturally resented his attitude. Then, added to his troubles, came a fear of Indians – consequent upon learning, on reaching Spearfish,[70] that a band had raided the village earlier in the day. The other members did little, if anything, to minimize the danger.

The reason I did not start with the other boys was that I might be accompanied by another member of the party, Billy Spillner, a Nebraska friend, who decided at the eleventh hour to go. Spillner was the complete antithesis of Miller, above described. He was cheerful under the most depressing circum-

---

[70] Among the most promising towns established in the first year was Spearfish. Beautiful in its location, with the towering mountain background, and with the broad and fertile valley stretching away to the north and the magnificent scenery of the Spearfish Canyon traversed by the loveliest of mountain streams, it has grown to deserve the appellation bestowed upon it at an early day by the eloquent Judge Bradley, of the Queen City. Founded early in '76, by men who appreciated the beauty as well as the material advantages of the location, the town early gave promise of rapid growth, as the lands of the valley became occupied by settlers intent on farming. During the summer, however, this growth was brought to an abrupt stop by the Indians, who found in the nearby rocky and brush-covered hills safe and convenient lurking places from which to sally on their forays of theft and murder, and equally safe and convenient cover in avoiding pursuit. A large stockade was built in the center of town, in which I spent two nights. I would say it occupied about a quarter of a block, the design evidently being to make it large enough to accommodate a large number of horses or cattle, as well as all the people who might resort to it in time of danger. It was built of logs ten or twelve feet in length, with a diameter of a foot. These logs were set on end in a trench two feet deep, and so close together as to make a solid wall through which daylight was admitted only by portholes made at points of advantage in keeping watch of the surrounding country, and in case of necessity of firing upon an approaching enemy. The trench was packed full of dirt to keep the upright logs in place. Almost every day of the summer and fall, Indians could be seen near the town; of almost daily occurrence were the raids upon stock pastured near by. Travel was safe only to those who moved in parties of considerable strength, and on occasion even large trains were held in camp for days by bands of Indians that had concentrated in numbers larger than usual. In several instances young Indians in a spirit of bravado rode the streets, yelling and shooting to stampede the stock. While some of the more timid abandoned their land and the lots they had taken in the town, the majority was not to be driven out, and this post on the frontier was permanently held. – [HUGHES].

stances; always willing to do his full share of the work of the camp or of guard duty in the coldest weather. Among many pioneers with whom I worked and camped and traveled, none excelled Spillner in all those attributes that make a true companion and a friend. Deegan, too, was a man who never grumbled; always had a jest for a bad situation; and was in every respect – save perhaps with too little regard for danger – a model partner.

Rochford, Deegan and Miller started ahead with the wagon to which the four oxen were attached, and expected that Spillner and I would meet them in camp about where the False Bottom enters the prairie. They found the snow deep, but thinning as they neared the foothills. They made camp in the edge of an oak grove where they had abundance of good fuel, and with their shovels they cleared off the snow so that the cattle could reach the nutritious buffalo grass for forage. At noon the next day, they moved on to Spearfish, and camped in the stockade to await our coming. Spillner and I joined them that evening. Here we learned that the Indians were troublesome in the neighborhood, and even had made a raid on a bunch of horses in the village that day. At once it was questioned if it would not be foolhardy for us to go farther out from the settlements.

After leaving Spearfish, we would strike but one ranch on Crow Creek, four miles out. At once Miller was for turning back. The others thought that by keeping on the alert we would not be in much danger.

On the morning of December 19 we pulled out from the stockade and started west, following as nearly as possible the trail made the previous summer by the parties from Montana.[71]

When we kept away from the foothills the snow was not so deep, and we gave the cattle a chance to graze at short intervals.[72] Unfortunately for our expedition the latter half of De-

---

[71] About 0.2 m. from the South Dakota-Wyoming line on US 14 is Montana Lake, named for the Montana Expedition into the Black Hills. Some of the expedition's engineers were attacked here by Indians and forced to abandon their survey. – *Wyoming Guide,* (Oxford University Press, NY, 1941), 373.

[72] To one unfamiliar with the buffalo grass country, it is simply incomprehensible that cattle could live through a cold winter without other food, but through many

cember was a time of unusually heavy snowfall. We made camp on a little stream the first night out from the stockade – about eight miles distant. The weather was not very cold, but some snow fell during the night; in the morning we found our outside tarpaulin covered to a depth of several inches. With the warning we had received at Spearfish, it was deemed necessary to keep guard. The night was divided into five watches for this purpose, so that one man was constantly on guard. Since we were camping in the snow without a tent, we first placed the wagon in the best shelter we could find; then placed a tarpaulin on the windward side of the wagon and fastened to it in a manner to make the best windbreak possible. We uncovered enough ground on the leeward side to make room for our blanket roll, and this we placed on another tarpaulin large enough to double over all – which completely covered us. Experience had taught us that men may sleep with no discomfort in a bed thus prepared, even with a temperature of twenty-five degrees below zero. The worst time was in the morning when it became necessary to roll out of the warm blankets, shake off the snow, and meet the frosty air.

The next morning seemed to bring a promise of clearing skies and, warmed by a good breakfast with unlimited quantities of hot, black coffee, we pushed on. Miller by this time had developed into a veritable grouch, and was making himself exceedingly disagreeable. Rochford finally was delegated to read him a lecture on the behavior necessary to camp life. This, together with the evident distaste for his company or conversation, exhibited by all of the party, did seem for a time to have some effect, and he assumed a more cheerful aspect. It was, however, his nature to find fault with everything that

---

years of cattle growing on these ranges it now has been amply demonstrated that not only is the buffalo grass sufficient to sustain life, but the cattle grazing on it will maintain a good condition throughout. When the snow falls to an unusual depth, then, of course, there is suffering and if it remains long upon the ground it must result in loss, but given just enough snow to ensure moisture and abundance of the nutritive grass and the cattle fare very well. A prolonged period of extremely cold weather causes a shrinkage, but usually an extremely low temperature is of short duration. – [HUGHES].

HUNTING EXPEDITIONS 165

went wrong; and to make an agreeable companion of him manifestly was impossible.

Within two hours of breaking camp we crossed a beautiful stream then generally known as Redwater, though properly named Sand Creek.[73] This beautiful little river – for its volume deserves that name – rises in thousands of fine springs. For a course of a dozen miles it never freezes, even in the coldest weather. We found the stream entirely free from ice on our crossing, and even on our return; after a week of extreme cold, its temperature had not been reduced to the freezing point. Here, too, we saw a bunch of mallard ducks, evidently settled for the winter, and with no intention of migrating to a warmer climate.

Snow continued to fall at intervals, and again we hesitated and debated the question of going farther. We could see, off to the right, the line of the Bear Lodge[74] and occasionally, when the clouds lifted, the top of Warren's Peak was visible. The Bear Lodge had been, in an indefinite way, our objective. Now, with the range looming in view, there developed in all save Miller an intense desire to reach it before turning back. After the crossing Sand Creek we continued on, keeping closer to the foothills than we had expected to do – as we had thought the Montana trail would lead to the right at almost a right an-

---

[73] Even at this day (1930), there is a confusion of those names. The two streams unite, but Sand Creek is far the finer and more important, though below the junction of the stream is known only as Redwater. – [HUGHES].

[74] Bear Lodge is now called Devil's Tower National Monument. In a letter to the President of the Historical Society of Wyoming May 10, 1920, General Hugh L. Scott wrote, "I used to hunt in the Bear Lodge on Upper Belle Fourche and have killed deer and antelope about that rock. I felt outraged that Colonel (R. I.) Dodge should so violate precedent or explorer's ethics as to change the name in 1876 to 'Devil's Tower,' a name without taste, meaning or historical precedent – which received its vogue because there were no white people in the country when Warren and Reynolds made their reports but were coming in when Dodge wrote his work, which was much sought after by newcomers. I had the name 'Bear Lodge' put back on the maps of the Department of Dakota with headquarters in St. Paul in those days and I am writing now to ask you to inform the people of Wyoming of the beautiful Kiowa legend about one of the most remarkable rocks in America and in the hope that good taste and historical precedent will appeal to the people of Wyoming to give its most remarkable rock its own aboriginal name." – First Biennial Report, 1920, *Wyoming Historical Collections,* p. 164.

gle after crossing. This was carrying us farther into Wyoming than we had intended to go. When we camped that night in a dry draw – where we melted snow for our coffee – we discussed the matter and decided that, unless the trail were found to turn to the right soon after leaving camp the next morning, we would abandon it altogether, and strike out on a course of our own, heading toward Warren's Peak. At this camp we found the snow had increased in depth; and more fell during the night. The temperature, too, was falling; we found that it kept all of us busy, to clear grazing ground for the cattle, insure ourselves against frostbite, and prepare and eat three hot meals each day. Miller's complaints, too, did not tend to make matters better. His cattle were the cause of extra trouble, as they were old and not able to forage as well as the other yoke. Under the rather meager fare they received they were visibly weakening, and shortly became a burden rather than an assistance. To crown all, one of the poor brutes found and destroyed about twenty-five pounds of our flour – a real catastrophe. This occurred through Miller's negligence, and did not tend to increase his popularity with the other members of the party. With our supply of flour thus materially reduced it certainly would have been the part of wisdom to have taken the back trail, but we were loath to do so without having reached the Bear Lodge. We debated long and earnestly on the night of the twentieth, and concluded to go on for at least another day.

On the following morning we found, after a few miles of travel, that the trail bore off to the south; more in the direction we wanted to go. For a considerable distance its course lay across a smooth flat plain in which, at about the noon hour, we found a depression with a wonderful spring, or series of springs, from which flowed a stream of water strongly impregnated with sulphur.[75] Here we rested for several hours; since the snow was not as deep as in our camp of the previous night, and there was a good growth of grass, the cattle managed to get a good feed without so much labor on our part in shoveling. The foothills of the Bear Lodge were now close at

---

[75] This place has since become well known as "Medicine Wells."

hand, and after dinner we pushed on. Early in the day we had met a party of three hunters with a wagonload of venison, bound for Deadwood. They had been hunting in the Bear Lodge, and had been camped for a time in an oak grove, from which they now had broken a trail to the point of our meeting. We determined to follow this trail to their abandoned shack, as they told us deer were abundant, and we should have no trouble getting all the meat we wanted. We believed we could get enough meat in two or three days, and get out without serious trouble. We reached the hunters' camp after nightfall, and found it to be a shack with three sides enclosed by brush, and the front open toward the place where the campfire was built. As we went into camp, snow commenced falling, and it continued throughout the night. In the morning the outlook was exceedingly gloomy. There seemed to be no prospect of clearing weather; already the snow was so deep that it was an almost endless task to clear sufficient ground with our shovels to allow the cattle to reach enough forage to sustain life. How we wished for a friendly "Chinook" or even a high wind, that might drift the snow from a hillside so that the cattle could graze. To add to the seriousness of the situation, such exploration as we were able to make indicated that the deer were ranging off toward the foothills, intent on getting out of the deep snow. For three days we spent the time alternately hunting and shoveling snow to allow the cattle to get a little grass but it was not until the 25th – Christmas day – that we got in touch with game and killed two deer. We had had no fresh meat for several days and – as Rochford and Spillner brought in a quarter of venison each, late in the evening – we sat up until midnight in order to have a Christmas roast. In the meantime, the temperature had fallen rapidly, and all members of the party had frosted fingers and toes. The cattle, too, ill nourished, suffered severely from cold. At night, when the blaze of the campfire died down, it was with difficulty they could be prevented from lying down in the live coals.

When I was awakened one night and looked out from my bedding, to see a fiery monster stalking by the camp, I could not imagine myself in a state of sanity, until I realized that it was but one of the poor oxen. Numbed by cold and starvation, it had lain down in the fireplace, until the coals had stuck to his hide, and the burning had forced him to his feet.

We had no thermometer in camp, but we learned afterward that on the night of the 24th, in Deadwood, a temperature of thirty-five below zero had been registered. On the 26th one of Miller's oxen died – the combined effect of starvation and cold. His mate was so far gone that he was a mere encumbrance; on the morning of the 28th we persuaded Miller to kill him – which he did with extreme reluctance. Then we broke camp. Fortunately the air had become somewhat milder. It was with difficulty we broke a road through the deep snow to the foothills. We had abandoned all thoughts of getting game, and were intent only on getting out of our disagreeable situation alive, and with our camp equipage, if possible. Shortly after reaching the foothills we saw a party of three men, with pack horses, entering the hills at a point two or three miles east of the point where we had come out. At the distance we could not determine whether they were whites or Indians. Miller was sure they were Indians and insisted that thereafter greater care be exercised in guard duty. In this, at least, he was right. We learned later that the Indians were still active about the Hills.

Though we had reduced our rations of flour from time to time, we now used the last of our supply in making biscuits for our noon meal. We took the precaution to save one biscuit each, on which we expected to breakfast the next morning. We took a long rest at the big sulphur spring at which we had stopped on the way out and, as this spot had escaped the snows that had overwhelmed us in the hills, it was possible for our remaining team of oxen to secure a better feed than they had had for some days. While resting here we were approached by a party of three hunters, with a team of mules and a wagon. They had been hunting in the Bear Lodge and hauling game to market, and had a camp four miles from that which we had left in the morning. They were now returning from Deadwood for a last load of venison that they had cached at their camp.

When we told them of the depth of the snow in the hills they determined to follow the trail we had broken, as far as our abandoned camp; to leave their wagons there and pack their deer to that point. We tried to procure some flour from them, but they had none to spare; they had not come out expecting to stay, but merely to load their game and return. They told us that the Indians were very troublesome in the Spearfish neighborhood, and cautioned us to keep a good lookout as we approached the Hills. With this advice they went their way, and we took the opposite direction. Our progress was necessarily slow, as our cattle were in no condition to travel.

That night the temperature again fell rapidly, and we camped in a dry draw, in considerable discomfort, due to the fact that we did not wish to make our camp conspicuous by building a big fire – which would have been necessary to ward off the cold. We here ate the last of our venison, excepting enough to eke out a breakfast with our treasured biscuits the next morning; and by dividing the night into five watches, with one man constantly on guard, we slept more soundly than might have been expected under the conditions.

The morning of the twenty-ninth was extremely cold; with a raw wind. We ate the last of our venison and biscuits and, fortifying ourselves as well as possible with copious drafts of hot and strong coffee – of which fortunately we had an abundance – we started out, determined to travel as far as possible that day. Fortunately Rochford killed a deer, and as it was in much better flesh than the venison we had been eating, it proved very palatable, roasted over the coals that evening. As Rochford had killed the deer a long distance from the road he had brought in but a quarter. This just sufficed for supper and a meager breakfast the next morning. The night of the twenty-ninth we camped on a dry ravine, away from the line of travel, and used the same precautions as the night previous regarding camp guard. Now the temperature took a decided change for the better, and indeed the change was welcome. We all felt better with the coming of warmer weather. On this day Spillner and I struck an elk track, and lost several hours and wasted our strength in following it. We did get a shot at the elk, but he jumped up in an unexpected quarter, and we missed him. Spillner, however, did kill a jackrabbit, and this, with plenty of black coffee furnished supper for the outfit.

Shortly after breaking camp on the morning of the thirtieth of December, we were overtaken by the party of three men with the mule team, whom we had met at the sulphur spring on their way in to the Bear Lodge. They had had a thrilling experience. As they told the story – they reached our abandoned camp on the evening of the day we had met them, and had there been attacked by Indians the next morning, while they were preparing breakfast. They stood the Indians off, and even drove them back, until they could hitch up their team. When they started toward the foothills, the enemy followed and kept up a fire at long range. Occasionally when the Indians would close in, the hunters would stop and direct such a rapid and dangerous fire upon them that they would give ground; and the drive would be resumed. Not until the foothills were reached, after a half day of this guerilla warfare, did they shake their pursuers off. As stated heretofore, that morning was exceedingly cold; and one of the hunters had both hands badly frozen. Now, when they passed us on their way to Deadwood, they were hurrying to secure surgical assistance for the injured man, whose sufferings were intense.[76]

With nothing more than a cup of coffee for breakfast we broke camp on the morning of the last day of the year, but had not gone more than a mile or two when a jackrabbit was killed, and we made an early camp for dinner. It made but a scant meal for five hungry men, and we were in hopes that we could make a drive to Spearfish that afternoon. Our team was so nearly exhausted, however, that this attempt was abandoned; we were compelled to camp for the night a short distance after crossing Redwater – or Sand Creek – at a point about a mile and a half west of the South Dakota line.[77]

---

[76] We learned at a later date that it was necessary for him to submit to the amputation of one of his hands. – [HUGHES].

[77] Near the present town of Beulah, Wyoming.

HUNTING EXPEDITIONS

Next morning Spillner and I started on ahead, with the intention of procuring some supplies in Spearfish and returning to meet the others on the road; but our progress was very slow. The insufficiency of the food and the cold we had endured seemed, on this morning, to affect us seriously. For the first two or three miles we found it necessary to lie down to rest at short intervals. We felt too exhausted to carry our guns, so left them behind in the wagon, though we knew there might be some danger from Indians.

We finally reached a ranch near the foot of Crow Creek, where we found three men, and from them obtained a biscuit each, and munching them as we walked, went on. It was wonderful, the change those two biscuits made. We felt strengthened immediately and made our way over the remaining four miles to Spearfish in fairly good time. Equipped with supplies, we took the back track to meet our companions, and intended to have a campfire going when they came up. We had procured some cheese and crackers at the little store, and on these we feasted on our way. On reaching the hill just west of Spearfish Creek crossing we were surprised, and no less pleased, to see our wagon in the distance; the boys had made better time than we thought possible. Spillner and I had been long on the road, owing to our weak condition, so that the cattle traveled almost as fast as we did. On sighting the outfit we immediately retraced our steps to the bank of the creek, built a roaring fire and prepared, so far as we could, for getting quick action in the cooking of a hot and hearty meal.

When the boys reached us, I suggested that a slight dose of whiskey all around might not be amiss; and all partook. As Rochford gasped for breath after swallowing the fiery dose – to which he was altogether unaccustomed – and felt its warming and stimulating influence he said, "I always thought whiskey was altogether bad, but now I believe on an occasion of this kind it strikes the right spot." I believe this was the first drink of whiskey he had ever taken.

To those who never have endured extreme hunger it may be impossible to convey an adequate conception of the pleasure and satisfaction experienced by our party in partaking of the hastily prepared, though abundant, meal that day on the bank of the Spearfish.

While the others of the party lingered, in order to allow the cattle to get what forage they could, Spillner and I again started on. It was the understanding that we would have a campfire built at the point where the False Bottom opens into the prairie, by the time the team should reach it. Before we had left Spearfish a mile behind us, however, a sudden blizzard arose, and increased so rapidly in intensity that, by the time we reached the spot where we intended to camp, it was impossible to see the False Bottom trail. We finally realized that we had passed the place, and concluded that if we attempted to retrace our steps we might miss the wagon altogether. So we decided that there was nothing for us to do but push along the Centennial Valley, hoping to find the Deadwood road where it left the valley for the Hills.

Again the weather became very cold, but with our backs to the wind we walked on without severe discomfort. We disliked the seeming abandonment of the other boys, but consoled ourselves with the knowledge that they at least had ample food and camp equipment with which to make themselves reasonably comfortable. At length we saw a light, and made our way to the cabin from which it shown. Here we found a half-dozen of the toughest looking characters I thought I ever had seen. They were camped in the cabin, and evidently had been there for some time; though for what purpose did not appear. They were not freighters, for they had no freight outfit; they had guns, but no outfit to mark them as hunters. To our request for permission to spend the night in the cabin, not one of them offered an answer. Assuming that silence, if it did not signify consent, at least should not be construed as a refusal, we entered; divesting ourselves of our overcoats, we approached the fireplace, in which there was a roaring fire. It did not occur to us at the time as strange that the occupants of the cabin should be awake and have a big fire at that time of night, for it was then midnight; but we commented on the fact afterward, and indulged in some speculation as to why or for what purpose they were there. That our coming was unwelcome was made very plain, as not a member of the party addressed a word to either of us while we remained. Their conversation among themselves was conducted in a low tone of voice, and it was apparent that a quarrel had been in progress at the time of our entrance. Tired as we were, a bed or even a blanket would have been welcome, but our ungracious reception did not encourage us to ask for such favors. We stretched our tired bodies on the earthen floor, with one deerskin that I found in a corner – on which we placed our shoulders. As the deer from which this hide was taken had been "killed in the red" – that is, out of season when the hair is very thin – the protection afforded us was very slight. Our exhaustion was such that we slept until the fire had died down, and we were awakened by the cold. As soon as daylight appeared we struck the trail for Deadwood, now only seven miles distant. But those seven miles were toilsome and difficult. We were stiff and sore and hungry, and we stopped to rest at short intervals, until, as our stiffened joints loosened up somewhat, we could proceed with less difficulty.

I have mentioned a bottle of whiskey purchased at Spearfish on the previous day. This we had not exhausted. I had placed the bottle in an inside pocket of my overcoat, and now a dram from it proved an acceptable stimulant. As the sun came up the air grew mild and, before we had proceeded half way to Deadwood, it was so warm that we took off our overcoats and carried them on our arms. This was the breakup of the cold weather; nothing so severe as that we had encountered occurred again during the entire winter.

Thus Spillner and I reached Deadwood on the second day of '77. The first place we stopped was a restaurant, at which I had been accustomed to get my meals. When I was paying for the meal, the cashier asked me politely if it would be convenient to pay my bill for the past two weeks. I said I had not been in town during that time. The cashier replied that he was aware of that fact, but added, "This bill was contracted by the man who has been working in your place on the *Pioneer,* and who said you would be good for it." Promising that I would investigate the matter and report later, I went at once to the *Pioneer* office, where I was welcomed. A report had come in that our party had been taken by Indians. I found Loomis, my substitute, still on the job, though anxious to be on his way to Colorado, now that he had earned a sufficient stake to take him home. I asked him how it was that he had presumed to have me charged with his board bill, and he indignantly denied that he had done so. He at once accompanied me to the restaurant; I accosted the cashier with, "This is the man who has been working in my place, and he says he never ate a meal in your place in his life. How about it?"

The cashier at once said, "No, this is not the man I had in mind at all; I do not know that I ever have seen this man before."

The mystery soon was solved. An acquaintance of mine who was somewhat down on his uppers had, on an occasion or two, been invited to take a meal with me at the restaurant. On the day of our departure on the Bear Lodge trip, he presented himself and told the proprietor that he was to act as my substitute during my absence, and that I would pay his board bill. The proprietor, knowing that I was leaving for the trip, and having seen the fellow in my company at the table, cheerfully furnished the meals on which the fellow subsisted until my return. Only once afterward did I get a glimpse of the culprit. As I entered one door he left by way of another, evidently having seen me in time to avoid a meeting.[78]

On the day following my return to Deadwood my substitute on the *Pioneer* "cases" quit work, and I was compelled to re-

---

[78] The individual was one of many bright, educated young men who went wrong in the hurly-burly and temptations of life in mining camps. Unused to hard work, and not finding employment for which his education fitted him, he sought the easy way, finally hanging about gambling halls, subsisting at times by cashing the "sleepers" he could pick up on the faro tables, and sinking so low at last as to use the name and credit of one who had befriended him. This same fellow was the one who gave me the tip on the Polo Gulch stampede. He finally made his way back to his old home in Illinois, where members of his family were politically and socially very prominent. He was killed in a railway accident. – [HUGHES].

sume where I had left off to go on the Bear Lodge expedition. I wished to go out to meet the others of the party, but could not do so.

When at noon of the second day after our arrival, Rochford, Miller and Deegan had not appeared, we became fearful that they had met with some mishap. Spillner started out, and returned that night at midnight, accompanied by Rochford and Deegan. I was rejoiced when awakened by the sound of their voices, and at once got out of bed and prepared supper for them. As they ate with appetites that required no stimulant, they told the story of their experience.

When the blizzard of that evening had struck them they rightly concluded that Spillner and I had missed the grove at which we expected to have a campfire awaiting their coming, and that we had gone on in the direction of Deadwood. They were fortunate in finding some oak timber, and there they went into camp. We learned later that it was just as well that we did not find and direct them into the False Bottom road, as it had been altogether unbroken by teams; it would have been impossible to reach Deadwood with the wagon, over that road, even had the cattle been able to travel.

With plenty of food and fuel they spent the night in comparative comfort, and the morning brought to them, as it had to Spillner and myself, cheerful sunshine and warmer weather. When they started to yoke up the cattle, however, one of them was unable to rise. Realizing that he must be abandoned, they killed him. With the aid of the remaining ox they succeeded in drawing the wagon a little way into the timber, and cached the guns belonging to Spillner and myself, together with other articles impossible to carry. After packing the bedding as best they could on the ox, they started on what they fondly hoped would be the last leg of the journey. Here Miller[79] declared

---

[79] Miller, on his arrival in town, did not come to our camp, and, indeed, I did not again see him until the night of January 1, 1878, just one year from the day I had parted company with him. Our meeting occurred at a dance given on the occasion of the opening of a hotel in Central by Jimmy Van Danniker. When I recognized him, which was difficult, as he was clad in habiliments much different from those in which I had last seen him, I tapped him on the shoulder and said, "Well, old fel-

that he had had enough. Taking his gun and a blanket, he left them; he felt safe enough to make his way alone, the remaining distance; this he did.

Rochford and Deegan made very slow progress, as their pack ox was compelled to lie down at short intervals; they had not made more than five miles when he gave out altogether, and they mercifully put an end to his suffering with a bullet. There was sufficient of value in his pack that they could not leave it behind and they divided it into four smaller bundles. Each of the men would shoulder one of these and after carrying it a mile or two, lay it down. Then they would retrace their steps, take up the remaining bundles, and carry them the same distance. Thus, by relays they made but slow progress; yet they persisted, and that night they camped in the edge of the timber where the Deadwood Road left Centennial Prairie.

In the afternoon of the next day they were glad to see Spillner; and with a new distribution of the loads – after having partaken of a lunch, which Spillner had thoughtfully provided – they again took up the march.

I have stated that during the extremely cold weather all had been more or less frostbitten. Rochford had one foot quite severely frozen, and the rubbing of his boot, as he walked, had aggravated the trouble. Now it was giving him a great deal of pain and necessitated frequent stops to relieve him. When the boys finally reached camp, and the boot was taken from the frozen foot, the injury presented a very angry appearance. It seemed almost impossible that a man could have endured the agony that the long tramp must have caused. Several weeks elapsed before Rochford could walk without a limp. It was some time before we could have the wagon with the other effects brought in. When they finally reached Deadwood we

---

low, the last time I saw you, you were not in the humor of dancing." Miller seemed really pleased to see me and enjoyed going over the story of the dangers we together had encountered, and they were not minimized in the telling for the benefit of some of his friends whom he called upon to listen. Forgotten were his complaints, and forgotten and apparently forgiven the hectoring in which I with the others had sought to repay them. We parted good friends, and he told me he expected soon to return to his beloved New York, where he said a young lady awaited his return to marry him. – [HUGHES].

could call the Bear Lodge adventure closed and were willing to admit that it was an altogether unnecessary and foolhardy undertaking.

Later in the winter of 1876-1877, we unfortunately allowed two fellows into our cabin to bunk with us while they were building a cabin for themselves. Before we dreamed of an infection, our bedding was "seeded" down with disgusting parasites. The fact that Van Fleet was sick with mountain fever at the time made it impossible for us to give the cabin and its contents the thorough renovation necessary to eradicate the pests. Rochford and I did the best we could under the circumstances, but could not see that we made much progress.

Sam Tull once said to me – speaking of a not too clean member of our train – "Any man may become lousy on the road or in camp, but no man need remain in that condition."

Now we simply had to wait with such patience as we could until our partner should again be on his feet so that everything in the way of clothing and bedding could receive the necessary attention.

As soon as Van Fleet was able to remain out of bed there was a general clean-up, and it was most complete. What we couldn't burn, we boiled thoroughly; a good buffalo robe we threw away; and after one or two minor cleanings we felt that we had won the fight, and resumed our self-respect.[80]

---

[80] The experience of this time was exceedingly disgusting, and even now doesn't make pleasant reading, though it may be read with less distaste that before we became familiar with the "cootie" stories that came from the trenches of our boys in the World War [I]. In camps of the early days, where every latch string hung on the outside and every traveler, friend or stranger, was made welcome, there always was a possibility of harboring unclean people, but once they were known to be unclean they were avoided as if they were lepers. – [HUGHES].

Camping Companions
End of Our Partnership

January '77 had been very mild, and the snow had melted everywhere excepting on the north hillsides. The weather was so fine that I was impatient to get out of the office *(Pioneer)*. As soon as I could leave, without inconvenience to my employer, Rochford and I outfitted for the purpose of prospecting the place where I had picked up some "float"[81] quartz, while on a hunting trip in the Silver Creek district of the Central Hills, the previous August. When prospected this quartz disclosed colors.

Intending to stay at least a month we took ample provisions, and started out one day in February. We had two pack mules loaded with our grub, blankets and tools. We made a late start from Deadwood, and when out five or six miles stopped to prepare lunch. There was no snow on the ground, which was unusual at that time of year, and the day was warm and pleasant; so we turned aside from the trail, unpacked the mules and turned them out to graze, while we boiled the water for coffee.

While thus we were engaged, we saw coming along the trail the finest pack outfit I ever have seen. At the head was a giant of a man riding a beautiful chestnut saddle mare, followed by two white mules with packs so perfectly proportioned and adjusted as to mark the packer a past master of the art; as indeed he was. When opposite us the outfit came to a halt, and the man accosted us with, "Hello, boys, don't you want one more for dinner?"

We at once extended a hearty invitation to join us. As we sat at ease, he asked whither we were bound, and when told

---

[81] For the information of those unacquainted with the terms used by prospectors it may be explained that float is rock picked up on the surface of the ground, and taken to indicate the existence of a lead or deposit of the same kind in the vicinity, usually at a higher point. – [HUGHES].

CAMPING COMPANIONS

our destination was Little Rapid Creek, he said, "Well, boys, I've got a cabin at the mouth of Silver Creek, not more than a mile or two from where you're going, and I'd be mighty glad if you'd come and camp with me. There's lots of room, plenty of feed for the mules, and not another man within ten miles that I know of."

The invitation was given with such evident sincerity, and the shelter of a cabin without having to build one so alluring, that it was at once accepted with thanks.

Our host, known in Montana, Idaho and the Black Hills as "Big Louie" Meyer, was almost a giant in stature. He measured six-feet-three-inches in his stockings, and was well proportioned from head to foot, with massive shoulders and a chest that resembled a weather-beaten plank; it was always exposed to the weather, no matter how severe.

"Big Louie" told us he had been wanting someone to talk to for some time, and he figured he would get more out of the arrangement than we could.

Before starting, I had time to size up his outfit. It certainly was such as to delight the eye of anyone who ever had followed the life of a prospector. I have stated that his mare was a beauty, but this does her scant justice. She was one of those rare pieces of horseflesh in which an expert would find neither flaw nor blemish, and she had a disposition so affectionate as to be in keeping with her beautiful exterior. When turned out she did not start grazing until her master had given her a lump of sugar from his pocket. The white mules were no less perfect in their way. They were neither too large nor too small – just the right size to make them perfect for packing. They were pure white, without a spot of another color.

We could have made the twenty miles to the cabin on Spring Creek that night by pushing along rapidly; but the weather was good, and a night in the open, where fuel was plentiful, was not uncomfortable. So we made an early camp on Little Rapid, where the trail left that stream to cross the divide to the head of Silver Creek – at the very draw whence had appeared "Old Rapid," a white horse which my partners and I had captured the previous August. We reached our destination the following day before noon, and went into quarters. I spent a full month with Louie, only half of which time Rochford remained with us. Of all the men with whom I have camped and from whom I have heard stories of the frontier, none were more interesting than Louie.

For a full week following our arrival we prospected faithfully, finding some colors in float here and there, but nothing to cause excitement. On the next Sunday, Rochford killed three deer, or rather killed two and wounded the third so seriously that he knew it could not go far. He was compelled by darkness to leave it and return to camp. In the morning we all started with pack animals to bring in the game. We passed the two deer that had been killed and dressed, and went on to find the third. It had got not farther than a hundred yards from the place where Rochford had turned back the previous evening, and there we found the carcass. One side was badly torn and mangled – evidently the work of a bear or mountain lion. A mountain lion it was; we soon discovered him lying under a fallen spruce tree that was supported on its branches about five feet above the ground. The lion's chin was on his paws as he watched our approach. Seeing himself discovered, the big cat jumped out and ran up a little incline, from the top of which he made a prodigious leap across a gully. As he landed, Rochford fired and broke his neck. He was a fine specimen. In skinning him it was remarked that the meat had a nice, pink color and was in good condition, with not too rank an odor. Someone proposed that we take a piece to camp and try it, to learn if it were edible. In preparing supper that evening, when frying venison, I also prepared a pan of steaks cut from the loin of the lion. We found it slightly tough, somewhat strong, though not altogether unpalatable; a starving man probably would call it good; but with abundance of meat in camp that we knew was good, there was no occasion to use it. When preparing breakfast the next morning I called to the boys, to know if they wanted any more of the lion meat; they agreed they did not; one of them declared that he had dreamed of cats all night, and woke up with a very disagreeable taste in his mouth.

CAMPING COMPANIONS

In the course of the next week another prospector came into the district, and made camp two miles from ours. He was a man who was not popular where known in the Hills, as he was charged with an act of inhospitality which any prospector considered unpardonable. He had refused food to a hungry man because he was not able to pay for it. When Louie learned of the proximity of this man he was very indignant. When later he learned that among his packhorses the man had an old, scrawny, nondescript stallion that he had turned out on the common range, Louie's anger knew no bounds. Danger of contamination of his beautiful mare, "Munch," was to be feared. At once he went to the new camp and notified the owner that if he did not remove the "old man" – the peculiar name given the nondescript – he, Louie, would shoot him; and he made it pretty clear that in shooting he would make little choice between the horse and his owner. The new camper, whose name we will call McKune, gave Louis no satisfaction. Indeed he seemed disposed to treat the matter with levity, which further incensed Meyer; it is probable that his tormenter little realized the danger he courted by his actions.

At this time there occurred an estrangement between my old partner, Rochford, and myself. It began probably in some trivial incident of camp life, for I cannot recall anything serious that could have happened. I only know that the little breach widened instead of healing, and when I found a stake with a location notice on which Rochford's name appeared in partnership with that of the man up the gulch, I felt that I had a real grievance. Never before had either of us staked a claim without placing the name of the other in the location notice. Then and there our partnership was dissolved, each making the necessary transfers to the other to affect the settlement. This estrangement was very painful to me.[82]

---

[82] I had ample assurance afterward that it was equally so to my old partner. I wish to dismiss the subject, as even now when I am an old man, it is not pleasant, but before doing so am glad to record that ere long our old time relations were resumed, and continued until Rochford left the Hills in 1883, and that in the intervening years we were much together to our mutual pleasure, as both became officers of Pennington County, and transacted official business together, before which time we had taken a trip together to our old home in Nebraska, whence we had

With the dissolution of our partnership Rochford returned to Deadwood, while I continued prospecting, sometimes with Louie, sometimes alone, until well along in March.

At night we usually sat up to a late hour – when I would induce my companion to tell of his life in Montana and Idaho – and the stories possessed a deep interest for me.

Louie was present at the hanging of Slade[83] in Virginia City, Montana; when he told of the event and scenes and incidences connected with it he finished with, "It's a damn good thing that the Missus got there ten or fifteen minutes too late, after Jack was dead, or she sure would have raised hell." "What?" I asked, "was Slade's wife there?" to which Louie replied, "Well – his woman."

At this time I suffered an attack of mountain fever. No doctor was available, but the trouble was overcome by the use of alternate strong doses of teas made from the wild sage and the bark of the Oregon grape root.

When the time approached for me to leave, I had contracted a sincere regard for the solitary old prospector, and particularly when I found that he looked forward to our parting with much regret. Every day he would propose some expedition on which we were to be partners, and when I could not conform my plans to suit his he would be much disappointed.

He alluded on several occasions to my misunderstanding with my partner, and invariably insisted on blaming the man up the creek as being the cause of the trouble. Finally, one night, when we had sat up until midnight, I found he was

---

come to the Hills. When men have tramped and worked and hungered and thirsted together; when they have shared a common purse and a common roll of blankets; more than all, when they have stood guard over one-another's slumbers in time of imminent danger, there are forged bonds of affection as those of blood brotherhood. Such had been the experiences through which we passed together, and the strain upon the ties thus formed caused by our estrangement gave both deep grief. When we shook hands and called it settled I know that it brought to both a feeling of great relief. – [HUGHES].

[83] Joseph A. (Jack) Slade, one-time stage superintendent, was a demon and a killer when under the influence of liquor. He was hanged by the Vigilance Committee in Montana in 1863. According to Thomas J. Dimsdale, in *The Vigilantes of Montana* (Norman, University of Oklahoma Press, 1953), 205, "The death of Slade was the protest of society on behalf of social order and the rights of man."

brooding over something. When I tried to rally him, he gave me several short answers, altogether new to my experience as coming from him. I left him to his cogitations and started to prepare for bed. Then Louie asked me to sit down, and said, "I want to tell you something."

I saw that he was in a very sober frame of mind, and sat down. He astounded me by saying, "Dick, I'm going to kill old Mac tomorrow." I was thunderstruck. At first I couldn't believe that I had heard him aright. I gasped, "You're going to – what?"

"Kill old Mac," he repeated. "I've got the place picked out, where the trail crosses the cut bank. I'll just knock him off there, and a little work with a pick will cave the bank and cover him so deep the devil never'll find him."

I was so astonished that for a time I couldn't find words. The man was entirely serious. I felt that he fully intended to do just what he said. I must combat this resolution, but how? The finality of his decision, as manifested in his manner no less than his words, appalled me. My first thought was to attempt to ridicule the determination to take the life of a human being for anything less than a capital offense, but very soon I concluded this was no occasion for ridicule. I asked him seriously to explain to me just what he considered would justify the act he contemplated. He made up the case against his intended victim in a manner that indicated he had given it serious thought, about as follows: First, the general reputation of the man was bad. He had committed the crime of refusing food to a hungry man, though he had plenty of venison in camp. It was clear that in Louie's conception of justice this was sufficient for utter condemnation. Secondly, he had violated the well-known law of the range in allowing such a creature as "Old Man" to run at large; and this with a malicious desire to cause trouble. But the chief indictment he reserved for the last; this was that Mac was the sole cause of the estrangement between my old partner and myself. In making this charge, Louie grew eloquent, and devoted himself to the work of convincing me that he was right in his determination to kill the man whom he held guilty. He said with regard to this, "No, Dick, you know you and your partner were just like brothers; when I saw you together I was glad to see two young boys like you that had been raised together and had always got along fine together and had left home and come together to the Hills, and had prospected and hunted and had good times and bad times together and never had any trouble. That was fine, and I thought of the time when I was a boy, too, and I had a good partner who was just like my brother, and we were just like you and your partner; what he had was mine, and what I had was his; and he died." Here the old man's voice broke. Conquering his emotion, he continued, "Yes, he died on me. We were a long way off from the settlements, and his horse fell with him and broke his leg. God knows I did everything I could for Fred, but I was young and didn't know how to fix him right. . . . Now, Dick, don't you think if any man ever had made trouble 'tween Fred and me that one of us wouldn't have killed him, and serve him right?"

I certainly exhausted all my powers of argument,[84] appeal and persuasion to convince my hearer that though the offenses of which he complained were bad enough, they could not by any means be considered serious enough to warrant the penalty of death; that of the first offense charged we had no proof; as to the presence of the scrub stallion in the district, I would undertake the task of removing him.[85]

At first Louie heard me with manifest impatience, and once became positively angry; he upbraided himself for having been such a damn fool as to have told me of his intention, and said that he couldn't understand the kind of stuff I was made of, that I would stand for such treatment. For a time I well nigh despaired of moving the old man, but finally, when I made him see that an act of revenge might work great injury to innocent children, I was encouraged to think I saw signs of softening, and I persisted. I have few achievements of which to boast in my life, but I feel that one was placed to my credit when fi-

---

[84] To this day I do not know what it was that I was able to say that was effective. – [HUGHES].

[85] Which promise I fulfilled at the first opportunity. – [HUGHES].

CAMPING COMPANIONS 185

nally, just before daylight, I obtained from Big Louie the solemn promise that he would forego his deadly purpose.

A few days later, when I felt sufficiently recovered from the attack of mountain fever to undertake a walk of twenty-five miles, we separated. I returned to Deadwood and Louie, with his pack outfit, started on a trip into Custer County. As I watched them going down along the Rapid Creek trail toward the mouth of Bloody Gulch, up which their route lay to the Castle Creek divide, Big Louie was striding ahead with Munch following, the stirrups of her saddle swinging free, and the two white mules bringing up the rear.[86]

After leaving Big Louie, I fell in with a wagon train. Walking beside one of the wagons was a tall, erect and military-appearing figure. I joined him. He proved to be a Georgian named Rumney – a man far beyond middle age, with white hair and beard, but with a free-swinging stride that denoted

---

[86] I was destined to meet them once again, in September of the same year. One day when I was making some purchases in a Central store, I saw the familiar outfit passing up the street. Louie was riding ahead, with the mules, evidently packed for a long trip, following. I ran out and called. Louie dismounted and greeted me with apparently great pleasure, turned his animals to graze in the mouth of Hidden Treasure Gulch, while we found a convenient seat to have a talk. He told me he was outfitted for a prospecting trip in the Wind River Mountains, where he had found a prospect many years before but from which he had been driven by Indians. He said, "Dick, come along. I've got everything we need, grub, tools and blankets – enough to last two of us for six months. All you need to take is your gun and ammunition and a few clothes. I've got everything but a good partner, and you know we'd get along fine together." I told him I certainly could think of nothing that I would like better than such a trip, but that my plans were such that it would be impossible to join him. . . If ever in the years that have passed since then I have harbored the shadow of a doubt of Big Louie's purpose to kill the man against whom he contracted so violent a hatred, it was utterly dissipated by the news conveyed in an Idaho paper that came into my hands. In this paper was told the story of how "Big Louie" Meyer, who was designated as a prospector well known throughout the Northwest, had killed a man who had jumped one of his claims; had been apprehended and placed in prison awaiting trial; but had overcome his guard and made his escape into the mountains. That he had assistance from outside was apparent from the fact that on the night of his departure, his pack outfit, consisting of a fine saddle mare and two snow-white mules, disappeared from a corral where they had been placed for safe keeping. Between the lines could be read sympathy for the escaped prisoner, and an intimation that he had much provocation for the killing of the jumper, who was not depicted as a very desirable character from which I drew the inference that the search for Big Louie was not likely to be vigorous or long pursued. – [HUGHES].

vigorous health and strength. I learned from him that he had been colonel of a Georgia regiment during the war, but that for some years he had been in the ministry.

The next evening I went down town, and on passing the Melodeon, a noted gambling house, I saw my acquaintance of the previous day. He was standing in the door, accosting those who passed, and notifying them that a religious service would be conducted within. At that time all the games were in progress. At the appointed time the tables were pushed against the walls, all gambling ceased, and the preacher ascended a little platform or stage on which vaudeville performances were given every evening. After a few preliminary remarks, in which he thanked the management for the free use of the building, he offered a prayer, intoned a hymn or two and delivered a very acceptable sermon.

At the conclusion of the service a well-known gambler passed the hat for contributions, and a very satisfactory collection was the result. This was presented to the aged minister, who courteously thanked those assembled, and went out into the night.[87] Then arose the voice of "Nutshell Bill" – well-known sure-thing gambler – with "Now, boys, the old man has been telling you how to save your souls; come this way and I'll show you how to make some money."

Within a few moments all again was activity. The tables were moved out from the wall; again arose the hum of many voices and the sound of the rattle of chips; while above all could be heard the whir of the roulette ball and the exclamations of the man in charge of the game, "Twenty-one in the

---

[87] What effect this experience may have had upon those who attended the service conducted under such unusual conditions is problematical. No doubt there were those who considered it little short of desecration, and yet it may be possible that the serious attention of some was caught and held by the very sharp contrast presented. So far as I know, this was the only religious service ever conducted in the Hills in a similar place or with similar surroundings. The old man Rumney, no doubt, had been a man of note in his younger days, for he bore ineradicable marks of culture and refinement, and spoke often as one who was accustomed to exercise authority. He followed the life of an itinerant preacher for a number of years, but finally his mind became unbalanced. He died at Rochford and his body rests in a neglected grave in the little cemetery at Myersville. – [HUGHES].

red; and around goes the little ball again; get your bets down, gentlemen."

As I have mentioned heretofore, the partnership that had existed between Van Fleet, Rochford and myself was dissolved. This was accomplished without difficulty by the transfer of various interests to one another, without the payment of money, and in a manner satisfactory to all. My share of the common property was made up of our holdings in Bear Butte district. On these I expended some money during the early months of '77, paying a man at the rate of four and a half dollars a day, and board. I could not afford to carry exploration very far at that rate. Since the man whom I employed had faith in the ground and desired to interest a friend with him in the ownership, I sold out to them. I received in payment a lot of provisions and forty cords of wood. This wood was cut and piled between Hidden Treasure and Sawpit Gulches.[88]

After my return to Deadwood from the Central Hills in March '77, I resumed work on the *Pioneer* and disposed of all my mining interests in the northern districts; intent on transferring my activities, when possible, to the district in which I had spent a part of February and March. I was in correspondence with my father, who was to join me later in the season, and I only awaited his coming to make the move.

For a short time that spring, before the freight trains began arriving regularly, prices of all provisions were very high; flour sold for thirty-two dollars per hundred; bacon and sugar, as high as forty-five cents per pound. With the drying of the roads, and consequent free movement of freight, this condition was relieved. Now that danger from Indians was eliminated,[89]

---

[88] When I could get time to try to dispose of it, I found that someone had saved me the trouble. Every cord had been stolen and taken away. – [HUGHES].

[89] Just a word regarding the signing of the relinquishment, in February 1877. I refer to this "cession treaty" not as a treaty of the Indians, but one of the "Chiefs and Head Men." This in truth it was. Those resident in the Black Hills were insistent that outlawry be removed, and that legal, civil government be made possible. So long as the land belonged to the Indians, collisions between them and the whites were certain to occur. The Federal Government could not consistently extend protection to people occupying a district which the government had expressly forbidden them to enter... The animosity engendered by the invasion of the country and the conflicts in the Northwest between the Indians and the soldiers tended to add

there set in a tremendous immigration. From every quarter came wagon trains, and the stages were crowded with passengers.

Deadwood still was the objective point of a great majority of the newcomers, and from there they diverged to the various newer districts, or to the valleys surrounding the Hills, where many settled on the lands, intent on farming.

---

to the disinclination to surrender the most attractive part of their lands... If the signatures of a majority could not be secured, then something less must answer, as the cession was considered of vital necessity. It was decided that the signatures of a majority of the "Chiefs and Head Men" should be deemed sufficient to bind the entire Sioux Nation, and by this means the cession was declared to have been made. Ratification of the relinquishment by Congress assured a cessation of the Indian depredations and marked the beginnings of legally qualified local government and properly constituted courts to deal with the no less troublesome elements of the white population. – [HUGHES].

Father Comes to the Hills

In June '77, I was joined by my father[90] and, with several others who had accompanied him to the country, we moved to the head of North Box Elder, near Custer Peak. There we went into camp and spent several months prospecting for copper;[91] we had found some very good float.

While in this camp game was everywhere abundant, and it was not difficult to keep fresh meat constantly on hand. Bear made almost nightly visits to the camp to pick up such scraps as were thrown out, and frequently could be heard nosing about in the search for food. Learning that several elk had been seen a few miles to the south of our camp, one day – accompanied by Pete Chambers and Abe Reppert, who were camped nearby – I started out in that direction, to try to secure some elk meat by way of variety for our menu.

Crossing the low divide between North and Middle Box Elder we followed up the latter stream to its head; thence crossing the head of Silver Creek; and again across another

---

[90] Michael J. Hughes, born in Dromore, County Tyrone, in the Province of Ulster, Ireland, was brought to the United States at the age of three years. The family settled in Bedford County, Pennsylvania, where he grew to manhood. In 1848, in Shellsburg, PA, he married Mary L. Hite, whose grandfather had been a soldier in the Continental Army for seven years. Mary L. Hite was born in Adams County, PA, October 22, 1822, of German and French parentage. She moved with her husband to Cumberland, Maryland, where they lived from the beginning until almost the close of the War of the Rebellion. Later the family moved to Illinois and in the spring of 1867, went to Antelope County, Nebraska, where they became the first white residents. In the fall of that year they homesteaded opposite the depot at West Point, NE. Mr. and Mrs. Michael J. Hughes were the parents of: Mrs. M. Talt, Albany, Oregon; M. J. Hughes, West Point, NE; R. B. Hughes, Spearfish and Rapid City, SD; and Mrs. W. M. Brayton, Stuart, NE. Michael J. Hughes died Nov. 26, 1897. Mary L. Hite Hughes passed away on Dec. 18, 1900. Both are buried at West Point, NE.

[91] Our prospects did not develop into anything of value and in the fall were altogether abandoned. Later the same kind of rich float rock allured Doc Ammerman, Tom Lapp and others, who did a great deal of work in the effort to find a body of the ore that would be valuable, but without success. – [HUGHES].

low divide to Irish Gulch – which had been named by Joe McKirahan the winter before. We followed down this gulch to the north end of the hill (now known as Montezuma Hill), and here we separated; the plan was to proceed toward Rapid Creek on parallel lines, some three or four hundred feet apart. On Montezuma Hill I had dug a prospect hole the previous March. It extended across the formation about fifteen feet, and was about ten feet deep. As I climbed the hill – the other boys being to my left and out of my sight – I heard a crashing of the brush and just caught sight of a big bull elk as he topped the hill. At this instant Chambers, who had a point of better advantage, cut loose at the elk with a little Henry rifle. Fortunately the bullet struck the animal in a very vulnerable spot – the kidneys – or it might not have stopped him; the Henry rifle, the direct predecessor of the much better Winchester, did not use much lead or powder, and was not considered effective in comparison with the Winchester, Sharps or common needle gun, then much used. As it was, the bullet reached the elk just as he was passing by the prospect hole above mentioned; and into the hole he crashed. He was a magnificent seven-point bull; his horns in the velvet, but about grown; and such was their spread that they caught across the hole and supported the head and fore quarters. Within a few moments Reppert and I joined Chambers, and we attempted to get the carcass from the hole, in which it was tightly wedged. The manner in which it was hung up by the horns made it possible to dress it, and we returned to camp, a distance of eight miles, intending to return for the meat next day, and bring a team for the purpose. This we did. We succeeded in getting the body of the big bull out of the prospect hole and hauled into camp. As the weather was warm it was necessary to take precautions for saving the meat, and this we accomplished by "jerking." Having put up the necessary frame and covered it with boughs, fires were lighted under it and the meat – previously treated to a bath in boiling brine – was placed on it for curing. In this work we remained up until

FATHER COMES TO THE HILLS

a late hour, and when we went to bed we left a good bed of coals under the frame.

I slept in a covered wagon and, as I was tired, slept soundly. Just before sunrise I was awakened by a peculiar noise. On lifting the tarpaulin wagon cover to investigate I was astonished to see four bears busily engaged in devouring the meat. My chagrin may be imagined when I realized that on going to bed I had left my gun in a tent beside the wagon. At a sound of a little noise made by one of the men, the bears scampered into the brush and disappeared. On examination it was found that they had regaled themselves on the choicest portions of the elk, and what they had not eaten of the parts we had cured they had trampled into the ashes and rendered unfit for human consumption. Even the horns had not escaped. As stated, they were a fine pair, and we had brought them with the carcass to camp, where the head was placed on a stump. Being in the velvet, the tips were soft; and these the bears had chewed. Our morning visitors were silver tips – or frequently termed "range grizzlies" – much larger than the black bear, and reaching a weight of six or seven hundred pounds. One of those that destroyed our meat was full grown; probably the mother; another, not so large; and the other two were cubs that would weigh probably a hundred pounds each. They had turned over every article of camp furniture that they found to be movable; and how they could have created all the havoc without arousing anybody seemed a mystery.

A NEAR MINE SALE

Until the close of '77 our camp was in the Box Elder country of the Central Hills. My father remained with me, and we worked and prospected together, taking an occasional hunt, which he greatly enjoyed. During this time we concluded that the copper prospects on which we had done some work did not promise very well, and we made preparations for a change of location farther south to the district in which Rochford and I had spent some time in the previous February and March. During this time I made a trip with Jim and Mike McGuigan into the district and, obtaining some encouraging prospects, located two or three claims. On this trip we found Abe Reppert at work in a prospect hole.[92] He told us that he was about to take down his location notice, as he was unable to get a color from the rock. As we left him he removed his tools and abandoned the location. Jim McGuigan and I went a short distance farther south, where, finding a promising appearing cropping of quartz, we put up notices of two locations; it was our intention to return to do some work upon them at a later time. The locations covered the ground abandoned by Reppert as well as the extension south.[93]

Because of the interest occasioned in the district by the work on the Standby and the location of other more or less promising claims, we concluded to locate a permanent camp; in February '78, we built the first cabin on the ground where the townsite of Rochford was located the following May. While my father remained with me – which was until the fall of '81 – I considered this cabin home. My absences on prospecting trips and at work on the Deadwood papers were frequent, and sometimes of considerable duration but I always was glad to turn my face toward this humble though comfortable abode, where a hearty welcome awaited me.[94]

---

[92] On what afterwards became known as the Standby Mine. – [HUGHES].

[93] Known afterward as the Moro and Como, which with the Standby were relocated later by Rochford and Nyswanger, our right having been allowed to lapse. The new locators found the colors that we failed to find, and made preparations for active work in the spring. The first tunnel in the Standby ground disclosed thirty feet of good ore, and it was considered to guarantee the future of the camp. It may be briefly stated here that Moro and Como were sold for ten thousand dollars, but proved a disappointment to its purchasers. The Standby attracted much attention, and repeated offers were made for its purchase, but the owners were strong in the faith that it would prove of great value, and refused to sell. Finally, on account of some disagreement, Rochford segregated his interest, which was unfortunate for him, as he never realized much from it. . . The late Aaron Nyswanger always maintained that there was good ore in the bottom workings of the mine, though the quality that could reasonably be expected to yield a profit was there confined to a width of about four feet. – [HUGHES].

[94] Never until I had sons of my own had I realized fully the deep pleasure my return always gave my father. When he came to the Hills in the summer of '77, it

FATHER COMES TO THE HILLS

Such prospecting trips as I made at any distance from camp were generally in a southerly direction and thus I became familiar with Castle, Spring and French Creek districts, embracing what I always have considered the most beautiful part of the Hills.

During my time spent in the Central Hills, among the mining claims located was one of unusual promise. This was named the California, and was situated in Smiths' Canyon, about three miles southwest from Rochford. Interested with us in this claim were Archie Seig and Smith Willey. We made the location in August '78, and from the beginning of work upon it found good prospects. We drove a shallow tunnel through it and sank a shaft to a depth of fifty feet. Much "specimen" rock was found; that is, ore in which gold was visible to the naked eye. Experienced mining men know that the existence of such ore is no guarantee of the permanence of a mine, and as a rule they would prefer ore of lower grade and larger quantity. At that time, however, specimen rock created much excitement, and as the samples were exhibited it became the general belief that we had found a bonanza. With depth the free gold diminished in quantity, and day by day we reduced our estimates on the value of the property. Finally we gave an option on the ground, at the price of twenty-five thousand dollars, to two mining men named Brinton and Hoatson from Lake Superior; the latter had been in charge of the Delaware copper mine there.

Two boys to whom our company had given a working interest in the mine were acquainted with the Lake Superior men, and interested them. They examined the property, and had twenty-five tons of ore hauled a distance of six miles to the Enos mill on Silver Creek, and there treated. The ar-

---

was with the purpose of making me a visit, and with no thought of remaining, but he was so delighted with the country, and enjoyed its beauties so intensely, his health also having been benefited by the change, that he at one time contemplated having the remainder of the family join him here to establish a permanent home. This plan, however, was abandoned. He enjoyed his stay in the Hills to the end. – [HUGHES].

rangements for mining and handling the ore and making the mill test were all in the hands of the parties holding the option, and for a time all we could learn as to the result of the test was that it was reasonably satisfactory; while the option still had some time to run, we were pretty well satisfied that the sale would be made. In the meantime my father and I, in company with Gilbert Tower, had engaged in working on some promising prospects eighteen miles farther south. On coming in to our temporary camp from work one evening I found a box, in which our provisions had been packed, set up in a conspicuous position, and on it written with a piece of charcoal from the fireplace the following message, "Be in Rochford in the morning to take Deadwood stage. Money in bank to close deal."

This was signed with the name of Dan Hanley, one of our partners. Dan had found our camp, but not knowing the direction to our place of working, had left the message where he knew we must see it on coming into camp. We took supper and went to bed intending to make a very early start in order to reach Rochford about nine o'clock in the forenoon – the time the stage would pass through. Unfortunately our only timepiece was out of commission, so that we would have to guess at the hour for starting. When awakened I imagined I had slept several hours, and arose and prepared a cup of coffee and some breakfast, Father agreeing with me that when we finished it probably would be time for us to be on our way.

We were camped in dense woods, so that we could not try to determine the time from the location of the stars. There was about an inch of snow on the ground, and this made the trail through the forest clear and as easily followed as in the day. We struck out for our eighteen-mile walk in good spirits, in all confidence of pocketing a good sum of money before night. Surely we did seem to have good reason for confidence. We had been notified by one equally interested with ourselves that the money was in the bank; the deal was made;

FATHER COMES TO THE HILLS 195

and it was only necessary that we be on time to catch the Deadwood stage.

We had not traveled far when, catching a glimpse of the stars, we realized that we had started at a much earlier hour than intended. Now comes in the black cat. As we crossed Slate Creek a black cat came out of a barn by the side of the trail and trotted off ahead of us. For five miles that cat kept us company, occasionally rubbing up against us and purring, and again trotting ahead as if directing our course. Not until we had crossed the divide and reached the old abandoned placer camp of Castleton did our escort leave us. As we passed an old ruined shaft house, he turned off the trail, as silently as he had come; so he abandoned us.

Naturally the old superstition that a black cat invariably brings bad luck occurred to our minds, and was made the subject of jest. Never was there a man less superstitious than my father. Indeed, he was inclined to have little patience with those who professed belief in signs and omens; while I, too, always was inclined to look upon them with ridicule. I believed, in my confidence, that the object of our present journey was practically secure; I even suggested that we consider this a good time and opportunity to test the potency of the nocturnal feline prowler to affect the destiny or affairs of humanity.

We closed our eighteen-mile walk and reached our Rochford cabin a short time after daylight, just as the night shift of the Standby was coming out of the mine. We prepared and ate a hearty breakfast; changed our clothes; shaved and sat down to await the coming of the stage. Within a half-hour of its coming came a man on horseback from Deadwood to notify us to spare ourselves the trip – the deal was off – finally and eternally. I will not attempt here to convey an understanding of this disappointment. I had experienced disappointments before, and have had many since, but this, coming as it did when the consummation of our deal seemed assured, was a very severe blow. My father accepted it more philosophically, and seldom alluded to it afterward.[95]

---

[95] The facts regarding the change of mind on the part of the intending purchaser, as we afterward learned them, were about as follows: Brinton and Hoatson were acting for a mining man of Lake Superior named Center, who was to furnish the money. On the favorable report of his agents he came to the Hills prepared to close the deal, and deposited the money in a Deadwood bank for the purpose. While here Center met an old acquaintance from the copper country named John Casey, who had some mining property at the head of Bobtail, and he induced Center to employ the money in its purchase instead of as originally intended. But what I have wanted someone to tell me is what the black cat had to do with it. Before leaving the subject, I may state that we had the mine patented. I never have had anything from the location save the privilege of paying some taxes, and yet I know there is some mighty good rock in it. Had our sale of the California gone through, as expected, I would have had the pleasure of seeing my father leave the Hills with a comfortable little stake. As it was, he left the country no poorer than he came as we fortunately made an unexpectedly good disposal of some other property, from which we never had the hopes of profit that we entertained regarding the California. – [HUGHES].

MICHAEL J. HUGHES

MARY HITE HUGHES

TOM SWEENEY

Road Agents of the Early Years

With the gradual cessation of the Indian troubles in 1877, travelers to and from the Hills encountered danger from other sources, more frequent in occurrence, and no less disagreeable in character. This was in the attacks by desperate characters – commonly known as road agents – who infested such sections of every highway which traversed districts that offered good hiding places where pursuit would be difficult.

That portion of the Cheyenne road from the Hills to and beyond Hat Creek Station was the chosen hunting ground of several gangs of bandits, and many were the incoming and outgoing coaches held up and the passengers looted during the years 1877 and 1878. The names of Blackburn, Wall and others of the more desperate and daring outlaws became well known. For a long time those leaders and the gang operating with them between the Hills and the Union Pacific railroad pursued their work of plunder with apparent impunity.[96]

During the year 1878, a new gang operated over much the same territory. They finally performed their boldest, cruelest, and financially most successful feat at a station known as Canyon Springs, within the Hills – a short distance from where the stage road crosses the state line into Wyoming.

It was during the earlier activities of Rochford and myself in the Hills that we became acquainted with four of the men who were involved in this most atrocious crime. On our various prospecting trips we had the use of two pack mules belonging to the Geltner brothers, who had a cabin and boarding tent on claim Number Eighteen below Discovery, on Deadwood. There were four of the Geltners, all fine men, whose probity was beyond question. They were glad to give us the use of their mules, as the animals always had abundant forage

---

[96] *See* Agnes Wright Spring, *Cheyenne and Black Hills Stage and Express Routes*, (Glendale, CA; Arthur H. Clark, 1949), 211-12, 219, 220, 227, 229, 230, 235-39, 339.

when out with us. Naturally, when in from a trip, we called at the Geltners' place and frequently dined at their tent. Here we met Charley Carey, Frank McBride, Doug Goodale and Al Spear. We met Carey and McBride frequently; Goodale, less often; and Spear, seldom.

So far as could be seen there was little or nothing to distinguish the quartette from the ordinary, average young men met in knocking about the country. They were accustomed to eating occasional meals at the mess tent; and we understood they were engaged in developing a quartz claim on, or in the neighborhood of, the head of Blacktail – or Sheeptail – Gulch.

As I remember them, Carey seemed the most intelligent and apparently had some education. He talked freely, was a fellow of fine physique and of good general appearance. He was always smoothly shaved when in town. In a general way the others seemed to defer to him. There was nothing so striking in the appearance of the others as in any way to attract attention. It was stated that Carey had come to the Hills with Crook's command in the fall of '76; and I believe I first met him during the winter of that year.

At our first meeting a man who was with him told a story that indicated Carey was a man of nerve. It was related that when with Crook's command Carey had an altercation with a man on horseback. Both began shooting. Carey killed the horse under his antagonist, who dropped to the ground; making a breastwork of the fallen animal, he kept up his fire at Carey from that protection. Carey did not falter. He advanced, laughing and taunting the fellow for poor marksmanship. One or the other would surely have been killed, had not a guard interfered and arrested them.

In the course of time rumors began to circulate that Carey and his friends were implicated in the hold-up of a wagon train from which a lot of provisions and other supplies were taken. It was believed that Carey was the individual who relieved the late S. M. Booth of a pair of new boots, at the time

ROAD AGENTS OF EARLY YEARS 201

remarking that he didn't like to do it, but it was seldom he found a pair to fit him.

Before this time I had bought a horse and saddle from Carey, and had taken the horse to Rochford. It was stolen from there a few days afterward. With the horse I had a bill of sale, which I did not examine carefully until afterward. I found it written in a very good hand and signed "C. G. Carea." Whether this or Carey, as we knew him, was his real name, I do not know. It was intimated to me later that Carey had taken the horse. This I did not believe until developments made it certain that he was a man of most unscrupulous and criminal character.

My first suspicion was strengthened when I learned that the quartette had a rendezvous near the confluence of the two branches of Castle Creek, a few miles southwest of Rochford. Carey never visited our camp in Rochford, but McBride and Goodale stopped with me on several occasions for supper, bed and breakfast. Such accommodations were freely furnished in any prospector's cabin, to all comers.

The stories that one or more of these men had been identified as having taken part in hold-ups naturally were discussed, but did not receive general credence, until the news reached Deadwood of the Canyon Springs hold-up and murder. I was employed on the *Pioneer* at the time; and when I began to write the story, I started it with an interview I had overheard at the door of the office on the evening preceding the tragedy. It is here given substantially as I wrote it then:

It was early lamplight in Deadwood on the evening of September 25, 1878. The boys of the *Pioneer* force had not yet gone to "cases," and the foreman of the office, Dick Burt, was standing in the doorway smoking a last pipe before calling "time." As he turned to go to the composing room he was accosted by "Cap." Smith, one of the "shotgun messengers"[97]

---

[97] The armed guards sent out to guard the treasure coach were called "shotgun messengers," as they carried shotguns. In his script Mr. Hughes referred to these messengers as employees of Wells-Fargo, but records of the company show that it was not until 1887 that Wells-Fargo operated in Deadwood.

[on the Cheyenne and Black Hills stageline] with whom he had had some previous acquaintance in Omaha.

Smith engaged him in conversation on the matter of the frequency of stage hold-ups, and gave the details of one that had recently occurred, as narrated to him by one of the victims. Mentioning the names of several of the most notorious of the road agents, he remarked that there seemed to be a new gang operating north of that part of the road most frequented by Blackburn and Wall – who mainly confined their activities to the stretch between Red Canyon and Hat Creek Station. Smith concluded about as follows:

"You'll notice that while those fellows hold up stages and rob passengers every day or two, they haven't tackled the treasure coach.[98] The boys would find that a different kind of nut to crack, and we would like to have them try it."

Next day the treasure coach was held up. The robbery occurred at Canyon Springs Station; on the west side of the Limestone Range; about thirty miles south of Deadwood; just across the line in Wyoming.

The station was a long building of logs, parallel to the road, with an ell-shaped shed to the north and a corral to the south. The main building was divided into two compartments, in one of which lived the stock tender, the other being used to stable the stock and store feed.

At about two o'clock in the afternoon the station keeper and a special messenger who had been sent out from Deadwood were sitting on a bench outside the station door. The messenger had set his gun inside. They were approached by two men on horseback who asked for a drink of water. The station keeper went into the house to get the water, and when he returned he and the messenger found themselves looking into the muzzles of two Winchesters. They were ordered to put up their hands – which they were not slow in doing. In the meantime the two hold-up men had been joined by three oth-

---

[98] This was a steel-lined coach especially built for the transportation of dust, bullion and other valuables to the railroad, and always guarded by from three to six messengers armed with sawed-off shotguns. – [HUGHES]. See **Agnes Wright Spring,** *op. cit.,* 248-249.

ers, also well armed and mounted. The five proceeded to tie the hands of their prisoners behind their backs and, after inquiring as to the time the coach was expected, locked them in the grain house. They then entered the station and prepared for the attack by knocking the chinking out from between some of the logs on the side toward the road, thus enabling them to fire upon the coach, while protected themselves.

At three o'clock the coach drove up and stopped before the station. On the driver's seat was Gene Barnett – an old-time reinsman – who had, previous to coming to the Hills, driven on various lines owned by Gilmer and Salisbury, in Montana and other parts of the West. By his side was Scott Davis,[99] one of the nerviest and best known shotgun men ever entrusted with the guarding of treasure. In the coach, as messengers, were Gale Hill[100] and "Cap." Smith. There was one passenger, a telegraph operator named Hugh Campbell, in whose favor an exception had been made; it was unusual to allow passengers on the treasure coach. As the horses were brought to a stop Hill opened the coach door and stepped out. Immediately the bandits fired a volley into the coach. Campbell was fatally shot. He died within a few hours. Hill was shot through the body, a second bullet striking one wrist. But he returned the fire, wounding McBride as the bandits had come from their barricade. Shortly after this Hill collapsed.

In the meantime Davis had dropped from the coach on the opposite side of the road, and from the shelter of a pine tree he also kept up a fire. It is believed that Davis killed one of the robbers, of whose identity there is some doubt, and that this man was later buried by his companions.

Carey, the leader, forced Davis to quit firing by marching the driver toward him, thus protecting himself. Davis, forced

---

[99] According to a story written by Scott Davis he said he was inside the coach and that Gale Hill was on the boot. – *Ibid.*, 266-267.

[100] Galen E. Hill, who was so terribly wounded in the fight, and who proved himself on that occasion to be a man of wonderful courage and fortitude, lingered on for a long time between live and death, but finally made a partial recovery. He lived for a number of years but his death at last was the result of injuries he received in the hold-up at Canyon Springs. – [HUGHES].

Mrs. Orson Wilcox, daughter of Galen E. Hill, is a resident of Rapid City, SD.

to abandon the fight, made his way on foot to the next station, where a messenger was dispatched to Deadwood.

But what of "Cap." Smith, the doughty guard who had so boastingly declared that the coach could not be taken? With the first fire Smith groveled on the floor of the coach, crying out that he was killed, though in reality he was not touched. Learning that he was uninjured one of the bandits gave him a kick and cursed him for a coward; then tied him up in the grain house with the others. The driver[101] then was forced to drive into the timber some distance, where he was tied to a wheel, while the treasure box was taken from the coach, broken open with a sledge, and the contents seized. The bandits then took their departure, going in a southeasterly direction.

That four of the attacking party left on horseback, with McBride badly wounded, is certain. That they carried one dead bandit some distance and buried him, is probable. This fifth man evidently was not as well known as the others. . .

When word of the hold-up reached Deadwood posses were organized, and started to scour the country in all directions. First to strike the trail of the fugitives were Captain W. M. Ward – an employee of the company – and Uriah Gillette – a rancher of the Central Hills – who lived not far from where the gang had a rendezvous. This retreat was at or near the foot of Elkhorn Prairie, or, as it often is known, Reynolds' Prairie – between, and not far from the confluence of the two forks of Castle Creek in Pennington County. Ward and Gillette thought it probable that at this point the robbers divided their

---

[101] A fact not generally known is that Gene Barnett, the driver, was suspected by agents of the stage company to have been an accomplice of the hold-up men. It was remembered that Gene had been the driver on various occasions when stages had been held up in Montana. A story has been told of the mysterious disappearance of a load of silver bullion from a coach on which he held the reins, and Gene's declarations that he did not know how or when it disappeared. Scott Davis ridicules the idea of Gene having had anything to do with the plot and says he was a man absolutely honest and should have been considered above suspicion. He was a man of fine appearance and gentlemanly demeanor, and had a host of friends who never would harbor a doubt of his entire trustworthiness. From a somewhat intimate acquaintance with him, I believe his friends were right in their opinion of him. – [HUGHES].

plunder, as from here the trail of only two was found. Those two were Carey and McBride.

It was known that McBride was seriously wounded and it was confidently believed that Carey would be compelled to abandon him or that both would be overtaken. That there was a strong attachment between the two had been apparent to me from my first acquaintance with them, and this was clearly proven in the long flight during which Carey greatly impeded his own progress and imperiled his safety by not abandoning his companion.

The trail taken by Gillette and Ward led still southeastward to Newton's Fork, where it was found that Carey had traded for a light wagon and team; with these he turned to the northeast at, or near, Rockerville. Now, more than ever, were the pursuers confident of overtaking the fugitives. Ward, leaving Rockerville after nightfall, went on to Rapid City, where he was reinforced by John Brennan, agent of the stage company, and a posse composed of Ed Cook, stage superintendent, Bill Steele, Doc Peirce, Frank Moulton, C. B. Stocking, Dr. Whitfield, Howard Worth, Peter Hammerquist, Emmett James and others.

It was learned that a team and light wagon had been seen the previous evening not far from Rockerville, traveling in a course that, if followed, would strike Rapid Creek some miles below Rapid City. Expecting to strike the trail at the crossing of the creek or the main road parallel thereto, this posse moved down Rapid Valley to the confluence of the creek with the Cheyenne River; but found no trace of the fugitives.

It was a certainty that they had not crossed; there were men in the posse well qualified as trailers, and at that time of year a wagon would leave a trail through the curing grass that even a tenderfoot could follow. On returning up the valley next day the posse found the trail. The wagon had crossed the road after the passage of the posse down the valley. Several of the pursuers returned home. The others continued toward the Missouri River, still following the track of the wagon. Not far from where the Pierre road crosses the Cheyenne River the

Rapid City men were joined by Seth Bullock, with a number of men from Deadwood. This outfit had been long in the saddle, and their horses were jaded. Hence, on reaching Mitchell Creek, a majority turned back toward the Hills. A part of the Rapid City posse kept the trail, and one evening the camp of the robbers was discovered. A member of the pursuing party had come upon it while making a reconnaissance. He reported the camp as a short distance off the road in a little ravine, and that it was quiet, with the horses turned out to graze and the occupants, as far as he could judge, entirely unsuspicious of the proximity of their pursuers.

It was decided to surround the camp at daylight. Imagine the surprise of the posse when it closed in, to find that the quarry had escaped. The wagon was there, with some provisions and a little bedding, but the men and horses were gone. It was evident that McBride had so far recovered as to be able to ride a horse; and that the scout of the posse had been discovered on the evening previous. Here the trail was utterly lost. The posse traveled as far east as Fort Pierre without finding a trace; then turned back home. Camping one evening not far from the spot where the robbers had escaped them, Dr. Whitfield, through curiosity, visited the abandoned camp. The wagon was still there. Riding around the head of a little washout nearby, Whitfield noticed a place where the grass had been trampled. On investigation he found a gold bar and retort, that evidently had been hurriedly hidden there before the robbers took flight. This, of course, he salvaged and on the return of the party to Rapid City he was rewarded by the express company in the amount of ten percent of the value of the gold, which was $9,500.

Captain Ward somehow suspected that one of the robbers, at least, had gone down the Missouri River, and finally secured a clue that led him into Iowa. This clue, while it proved illusive as to the man he was after, led to the discovery of one of the robbers whose trail had been altogether lost within a few miles of the spot where the robbery was committed. This was Goodale who, after having made good his escape, perpetrated the folly of going direct to his old home in Atlantic, Iowa. It is impossible to designate his further foolhardiness in placing on exhibition the share of the loot he had secured. Yet this is what he did. Goodale's father was a prominent citizen of the community and a stockholder in one of the banks. In the window of the bank the gold taken in the robbery was displayed. The father proudly related to his friends on the phenomenal success of his boy in his Black Hills mining ventures.

Passing the window in which the display was made, Ward was at once curious. As a result of his investigations he placed Goodale under arrest, and started on the return to Wyoming with his prisoner. On the trip he was accompanied by Goodale's father, and an attorney who had been employed ostensibly to defend the young man. Traveling through Nebraska, while the train on the Union Pacific stopped at an unimportant station, Goodale made his escape. So far as the authorities were concerned he never was heard of afterwards.

Naturally his captor fell under suspicion of collusion in his escape; but this could not be proven, and he suffered no penalty for it, though there is no doubt the company's agents kept him under surveillance for a long time afterward.

Neither Carey nor McBride was ever apprehended. At the time of the robbery McBride had been severely wounded and there were those who believed that he could not long survive. . . That he recovered was afterward made more certain when it was learned that a man who had put up a cash bond of three hundred dollars for his appearance on a charge of horse stealing, before the robbery, was reimbursed from a mysterious source. Spear was caught and sentenced to the penitentiary of Wyoming for life.

The amount of booty in bullion, dust, and other valuables secured by the robbers in this hold-up, has been variously estimated. . . It always has been assumed that the amount was large – never guessed at less than $100,000, and frequently much higher.

ORIGINAL OWNERS OF HOLY TERROR MINE
Left to Right: Tom Blair, Al Amsberry, John Fayel, and William Franklin (the mine was named after his wife)

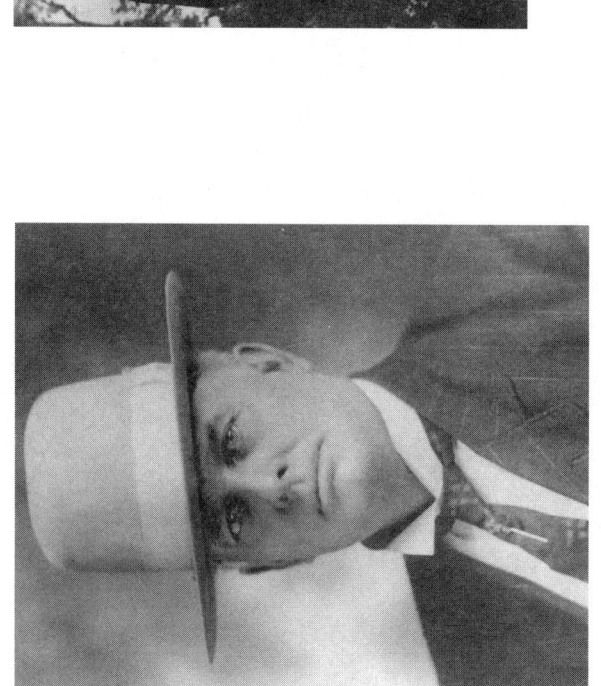

SCOTT DAVIS
Captain of "Shotgun Messengers"

Home from the Hills

In the year '79, I spent two or three months at a time working on the Deadwood papers, and then an equal time in prospecting or working on the development of various locations. Many discoveries of promise were reported from Custer County, and ore of extraordinary richness was taken from a number of locations. Unfortunately none of those flattering prospects developed into mines of permanent value.

In September Rochford came to our cabin one evening and said he intended making a trip to the States to visit his mother and family, and he wanted me to accompany him. My father urged me to go; it had been three and a half years since I had left home, and he knew my mother and sister – who remained on the old homestead – would be rejoiced to see me. Accordingly we took the Sidney stage at Deadwood for the trip over practically the same route by which we had entered the Hills. The only difference in the route was from Deadwood to Buffalo Gap – the road now lying around the foothills by way of Rapid City – whereas on our coming it entered the Hills at Buffalo Gap and passed through Custer.

The coach leaving Deadwood was drawn by six fine, white horses and, with this beautiful team and a skillful reinsman, it made a spectacular exit – as it also made a spectacular entry – each day. This team was taken out at Crook, the first relay station ten or twelve miles out, and returned the next day with the coach from Sidney. Any passenger who imagined the ride through to the railroad would be similar to that to the first relay station, behind this spanking team, was in for a disappointment. Like the big berries on the top of the box, the extra fine outfit was calculated to catch the eye. After reaching Crook the coach proceeded with teams of four, instead of six, horses, and at a much more moderate gait. The service, however, on the whole was good, and passengers were made as comfortable as could reasonably be expected in a ride of three hundred miles, continued night and day; but occasionally one would be found who was inclined to find fault, and make the trip disagreeable not only to himself but to others. We were afflicted with one of this kind. He was a correspondent of an eastern paper who had been sent out to report on the country for the publication he represented; but before we had proceeded far we concluded that he considered it his chief duty to find fault with the country and everything in it. He was nearsighted and wore glasses. He asked innumerable questions, and constantly made notes in a little book. On leaving Deadwood he had secured from the agent of the stage company the privilege of the outside seat with the driver. Before we reached Crook a lady on the coach became ill from the motion, and while the horses were being changed the man on the top was asked to change places with her, that she might get the benefit of the fresh air. This he positively refused to do, insisting that he had bought and paid for that particular seat, and would not give it up to anyone.

At first he was argued with; then it was attempted to shame him into the simple concession that any man should be glad to make for a woman in distress; but to no avail. He had remained in his seat during the stop at the relay station, and obdurately refused to vacate. When the horses had been changed, and the driver had taken the reins, Rochford, speaking for the other passengers as well as himself and me, gave the fellow his choice either to get down voluntarily or be hauled down. He started to demur, but evidently concluded that this was not an idle threat; with much grumbling about a country where a man couldn't have what he paid for, and people who would deprive him of it by force, he took his seat in the stage. Naturally he had incurred the ill will of every other passenger, and all devoted themselves to making his trip as disagreeable for him as possible. If he asked a question he received a curt answer; intent on getting information about the country through which we passed, he invariably was furnished with such misinformation as the ingenuity of the person questioned could suggest. His gullibility was somewhat remarkable, but he was at a disadvantage in being near-sighted; so it was not altogether strange that he should note in his little book the sighting of a band of buffalo when a bunch of cattle was seen on a distant hillside, and one of the passengers was willing to swear they were buffalo.

As nightfall approached, the first day out, we were nearing the scene of a stage hold-up by Lame Bradley and his gang. This occurred only the night before, and the details were given us by the driver of the northbound coach, which we met not far from the place of the hold-up. At that time those attacks on the coaches and looting of passengers were frequent, and anyone traveling the roads, either to Sidney or Cheyenne, took a chance of being interviewed by the so-called "road agents." The last reported encounter with the gang operating on this road naturally furnished the topic of conversation by the passengers, and the correspondent became exceedingly nervous. For his benefit many stories were told of the atrocities committed by the knights of the road; and while the truth was bad enough, it was made ten times worse in the telling. The fellow no longer insisted on his outside seat. The lady for whose benefit he had been forced to give it up had left the coach at Rapid City, but now he seemed to prefer the inside, apparently thinking there might be protection and a greater measure of safety in numbers. If he deserved punishment for his boorishness, he certainly was punished during the hours of darkness between Lame Johnny Creek and the prairie country that opens out before reaching Horsehead Creek. Wherever a dark ravine was crossed some passenger would relate particulars of a hold-up that occurred at that particular spot; and the correspondent spent the night in abject terror.

With the coming of a bright, sunny morning, and a substantial breakfast, his spirits revived, and he resumed his seat on the outside. As we changed drivers, however, on the road through, each new reinsman was told by the man whom he relieved, the character of the companion he was to have on top; and those drivers were adept in the art of making an objectionable passenger uncomfortable. On the last "string" from the North Platte River into Sidney, the driver was Billy Welch – good fellow, fine driver, and popular with all who knew him. But Billy was a most inveterate "josher," and he outdid himself for the benefit of the outside passenger. Objects seen at a distance, and but dimly discerned through the glasses of the passenger, assumed new and wonderful names; a bunch of antelope became blacktail deer; sighting Chimney Rock, the story was told of how at one time it towered a full hundred feet higher in the air until it was shot off by a cannoneer in Custer's command; Court House Rocks became "Bloody Mount," where the last remnant of the Rapidoe tribe, fifteen hundred in number, was surrounded by the Cheyennes and Oglalas, and mercilessly butchered; a lone black yearling was pointed out as a black bear; and all this the correspondent seemed to swallow; but when Billy told him the name of Pumpkin Creek was "Sweetwater," and the reason for so naming it was because there was a sugar spring at the head of it, his credulity was shattered, and he asked for no further enlightenment until Sidney was reached, and we left the coach.

At the sound of the locomotive whistle and the sight of the trains on the tracks of the Union Pacific, we recalled the evening when we had camped at Water Holes, twelve miles out of Sidney, and had witnessed the demonstrations of the returning stampeders when they heard the welcome sound that indicated their proximity to the settlements and a speedy return to their homes. They had been out of sight and sound of the railroads for only a few weeks, whereas we had been away for three and a half years; and we realized fully the feelings that prompted the hearty cheers that arose from the camp of the pilgrims on that April evening, at the first stop we made for the night on our way to the Hills. Since that time we had made our camp in many places, and undergone many interesting experiences, but unlike the boys of the train we met at Water Holes, we were not intent on leaving the Black Hills country for good. We had become sufficiently familiar with it

HOME FROM THE HILLS 213

to know that it was destined to become a great and prosperous country; and with the visit to our home and friends finished, we should be as eager for the return as we were to enter the Hills in the centennial year, when neither of us had reached his majority.

After disembarking from the coach, and having a shave and bath and a change of clothing, we went to call on our old friends, the McDonalds, who had entertained us during our stay in Sidney when on our way to the Hills. At their home I met Mattie A. Lewis,[102] the young lady who was destined a few years later to become my wife. She was a niece of Mr. McDonald, and was spending a week or two in visiting the family. Her home was in Rapid City.

After a very pleasant visit with our Sidney friends, Rochford and I proceeded to the homes we had left as boys. It is unnecessary to dwell on the pleasure of this homecoming; of the welcome we received from mothers, sisters and friends. Such an experience is possible only once in a lifetime. One may always receive a hearty welcome on his return home, but his first homecoming after the breaking of the ties that have bound him to the old homestead must stir his feelings to a depth impossible ever afterward. Hovenden's beautiful and expressive picture, entitled "Breaking Home Ties," should have a companion, possibly to be entitled, "The Wanderer's First Return."

On a visit to Fremont we called at the office of the *Freemont Tribune,* and while there heard the news that Deadwood was burning. We remained until it was reported that the fire had burned itself out, and something like a correct idea was obtained of the extent of the damage. Neither of us suffered

---

[102] Mattie A. Lewis who married me in 1884, was born in Harvard, IL, March 31, 1864. Her girlhood was spent in Canada, Colorado and California. Her father, William Lewis, was in California in 1849. Later he and Mrs. Lewis built the first frame ranch house on Bear Creek, ten miles out of Denver, in 1859. Subsequently they lived in Kansas. In 1877 William Lewis, with his wife and one son and daughter, Mattie, trekked to Rapid City, Dakota Territory, with an ox team. There he built the first frame business house. He took an active part in the growth and improvement of the town until his death in 1896. The Lewis home stood on the lots later occupied by the Schiurring and Dahlin tailor shop. – [HUGHES].

any great loss through the fire – nothing more that a suit of clothes or two left in rooms we had occupied – but we felt deep sympathy for many friends who must have lost everything they possessed. Here, at the beginning of October, with winter close at hand, we feared there must have been much suffering, and no doubt there was; but who ever heard a word of complaint or despondency from Deadwood? Instead, the people went at once to work; there was need of much faith and much mutual forbearance, and these were not lacking. The determination was there to build a better Deadwood.[103]

On my return to the Hills, Rochford did not accompany me. With me, however, came his older brother, John, whom he had delegated to represent his interest, until he should return later.

I certainly found a very unattractive Deadwood. Everywhere was ruin; the streets were filled with the debris of the fire; charred timbers made walking on the streets difficult; and teams, hauling building material and hauling away useless and cumbersome wreckage, had churned the streets into a sea of mud. Several inches of snow covered the ground where it had not been trampled into the mess. The one encouraging feature was the general activity to be noted. Everybody was busy; no one was taking time to grumble about bad conditions; within a few days the streets were comparatively free from obstacles to travel; many of the basements had been cleaned out, and new foundations were being built.

One of my first activities on coming back to Deadwood, after a visit to my father at Rochford, was in the organization of the South Deadwood Hose Company, of which L. F. Whitbeck – then city editor of the *Times* – was elected foreman. I was made secretary. I at once resumed work on the *Pioneer,* and continued throughout the winter [1879-80], with occasional trips to Rochford. Those trips were made on foot, the distance being considered about twenty-five miles. I was a

---

[103] The metropolitan little city of today (1926) well attests how this determination was carried into execution. Deadwood destroyed was a town of wood; it arose from its ashes a city of brick and stone. The great fire was September 25, 1879. – [HUGHES].

HOME FROM THE HILLS

good walker, and a jaunt of this kind was undertaken as any other task of the day would be. Frequently I would not leave Deadwood until ten or eleven o'clock in the day – always apprising my father of the hour at which I expected to start, as invariably he desired to come out some distance to meet me on the way. After spending a day or two with him, I would return to my work at the type case or to do any special job of reporting to which I would be assigned. The latter work was becoming more frequent – not altogether to my satisfaction, as I always was able to set more than an average "string" at the case, and thus made better money.

In the spring of '80, I took a layoff for a prospecting trip that was prolonged well into the summer.

MATTIE LEWIS HUGHES
Wife of Richard B. Hughes
About 1908

WILLIAM LEWIS, 1849
Father in law of Richard B. Hughes

LEWIS HALL
First Commercial Building in Rapid City

RAPID CITY IN 1885

Part III

Rapid City

Home for More Than Forty Years

Becoming An Editor

When I again returned to Deadwood, the red hot political campaign of 1880 was coming on – the hottest that ever has been waged in the Hills up to the present time. The administration of the affairs of Lawrence County had been in the hands of the Democrats, and that some of the officers had been recreant to their trust was notorious. There were many charges of malfeasance and embezzlement; and some of them, at least, were true. Much ill feeling was engendered; and while the Democrats put forth several new candidates for the election, it was plain that they would suffer to some extent from the shortcomings of those whom their party had elected previously.

As the campaign [of 1880] opened I was induced, in company with Tom Ming – the fastest compositor whom I have ever known – to take charge of the *Evening News,* which was a Democratic sheet, with a promise that I would conduct it throughout the campaign. The experiences of that time as a responsible manager – when hitherto I had had little responsibility for what appeared in the paper – were interesting to say the least.

As editor of a partisan paper I found that I was expected to see nothing but good in my party and my party's candidates, and by the same token I was not expected to search out and publish the virtues of the opposition. The party managers gave me less trouble in this matter than came from individuals who had a particular interest in the political fortunes of one or another of the candidates. On one occasion I received an anonymous communication threatening me with dire personal consequences if I did not devote more space and effort on behalf of one of the aspiring politicians, for whom I had little liking, and whose defeat would not have caused me deep grief. The letter was written in a fine feminine hand, and by the merest accident I traced it to the candidate's mother.

Before the nominations were made I was asked to publish an article descriptive of one who would make a first-class treasurer – but without naming him, the object being to allow the public to consider the qualifications enumerated and, if possible, to hit upon the man whom the description fitted – giving the barest hint as a clue to his identity. This I did, and so well did I succeed that I was called upon and thanked profusely by no less than three men for the foundation I had laid, each recognizing in himself the ideal candidate I had attempted to depict.

Before Election Day the indications pointed to a Republican victory, the people being of the opinion that a change all around was desirable. And a Republican victory it proved. There was one exception, and this furnished the great surprise of the contest. The most popular candidate on either ticket was General A. R. Z. Dawson, running as a Republican, for the officer of Register of Deeds. On all hands his election not alone was conceded, but it was expected he would have the largest vote polled.

At breakfast time on the Sunday morning preceding the election, I had seen a bet made in the lobby of the old Keystone Hotel, that Dawson would have 500 majority over Joe Tracy, the Democratic candidate. After breakfast I walked over to the *News* office from the hotel, and on the way met and spoke to Charley McKinnis, so-called Democratic boss, and the man against whom the most violent attacks of the opposition were aimed. I mentioned to him the wager made in the hotel, and he remarked, "That would have been a good bet yesterday; this morning the man who made it has as good as lost his money; not only will Dawson not have 500 majority, but he will be defeated." He enlightened my by saying the deal had been fixed up the night before in Lead City. He proved to have been well informed. Tracy was a popular employee of the Homestake, and the vote of the miners went to him solidly. He was the only Democrat elected.

BECOMING AN EDITOR

One of the considerations that induced me to take charge of the *News* was that, if the Democratic ticket should be successful, the plant was to be moved to Lead City, with Colonel Carmack – a New York gentleman who had come to the Hills as manager of the Cheyenne mine, and a fine editorial writer – as editor, and myself as city editor and business manager. Since the ticket was defeated this plan was dropped; and shortly after the colonel returned to New York. He was one of the most companionable of men, and one of the best-posted on national politics that I ever have met. Looking back over the past I now think that his polished editorials dealing with national and international affairs possessed small interest for the readers of a little afternoon paper published in an isolated community such as this, chiefly interested in its own local affairs.

I turned the *News* back to its owners without regret; the only other incident worthy of mention concerning my management being that my collector absconded with a week's collections – which embraced, among other items, one of $225.00 paid by the Democratic central committee for printing of tickets – leaving me short of funds to pay my help; I was compelled to borrow in order to do so.

I was doing some special work for the *Pioneer*, the editor of which was expecting soon to resign, and who had recommended to the manager that I be offered the position. I was considering the matter when, one Sunday morning – being the twelfth of December (1880) – I received a message that a gentleman who was breakfasting at a restaurant on Main Street, and who was going to Rapid City, desired to see me. I went to the restaurant, and there became acquainted with Mr. and Mrs. H. A. Piper, of Rapid City. I was told by Mr. Piper, he had instructions from Mr. Joseph B. Gossage, of the *Rapid City Journal,* (formerly of the *Sidney Telegraph*), to ask me to return with him. I had previously had several letters from Mr. Gossage offering me a position as editor of the paper – then a weekly – but never had seriously considered the matter. However this was Sunday and a fine day; I thought I might make the trip with little loss of time, and return in a day or two – as I fully expected to do. I therefore rode to Rapid City with no thought of remaining; but the prospect held out – of the easy time on a weekly paper, after the strenuous life on an afternoon daily – proved alluring; and the conditions and surroundings were so congenial that I changed my mind.

On coming to Rapid City I renewed my acquaintance with the young lady mentioned heretofore as a visitor in Sidney, on the occasion of my first trip from the Hills to the States. As a result we were married in March 1884.

For ten years after my arrival in Rapid City I acted as editor of the *Journal* – first the weekly and later the daily – and never in my life did I better enjoy my work. There was for several years enough time for play, and this I chiefly employed in hunting – of which I was very fond – and in the various pleasures enjoyed by the young people of that time. A baseball club, known by the peculiar name of the Eighty-Stamps – in honor of the stamp mills then being erected in the mining districts – was organized; and many trips were made to the towns of the Northern Hills to meet teams of that section.[1]

The Seventh Cavalry, Custer's old regiment, was stationed at Fort Meade, and the Rapid City team usually had a half dozen or more games with the soldier team every season. All such trips were made by team, as there were no railroads or automobiles here.

A dramatic company was organized, and in the various plays given I usually had a part. But the most pleasant memories of the sports of those days cluster around the shoots of the gun club – both on the local grounds and in competition with the Deadwood team – and the many fine hunting trips down the Rapid, Box Elder and Elk Creek valleys, or to the Cheyenne River. Duck and grouse were everywhere abun-

---

[1] In an old file of the (Rapid City) *Journal* we find mention of Richard Hughes making a triple play, unassisted, while playing second base on this team in a game with the Seventh Cavalry. The box score credits him with 1,000 percent batting average for the day.

BECOMING AN EDITOR 225

dant, and as there were no fences in the country, it was possible to drive into every bend of the stream unobstructed.

It is needless to say that such a thing as a "No trespassing" sign was unknown. On many occasions I was accompanied by John R. Brennan, who was one of the founders of the town – a splendid type of the western pioneer, a first-class sportsman, and the most desirable of companions. After the coming of the railroads we frequently extended our hunting trips into the prairie chicken country of Nebraska, and such excursions were thoroughly enjoyed by both.

In the meantime I had been elected as county treasurer, and also the first treasurer of Rapid City, serving one term in each office. The fire department was the most popular organization; and at the meeting to form the first company, I proposed that it be named for Rapid City's most active and prominent merchant, Tom Sweeney. The name was adopted, and by that name the company still (1926) is known. I may say in passing it always has been a credit to Rapid City, and during the days of the popular state tournaments it never failed to gather a good share of the honors. I was honored with an election as foreman, on one occasion, and later filled the office of chief engineer of the fire department; after which I resigned, to allow those less busily engaged to "run with the machine."

The establishment of the daily brought more and harder work and greater responsibility, but I may truthfully say that, taking the good and bad altogether, the years of my connection with the *Journal* were among the best and most satisfactory I have known. This work I discontinued, to take part as a member of the first state legislature in the special session of the fall of '89. The election had been held in November; the territory had been divided; the state of South Dakota admitted; and a session of the newly elected legislature was called at once to elect United States senators and start the machinery of state government. With these purposes accomplished the special session was to be adjourned, the members again to assemble in regular session on the first of January following.

As there was no railroad directly from the Missouri River to this part of the state, the Hills members traveled by the Northwestern. It had reached Rapid City from the south three years previously, running down through Nebraska; thence north through Iowa; thence west through Eastern and Central South Dakota; to reach the capital, Pierre. The distance was approximately a thousand miles; since the mileage allowance was ten cents per mile for travel of the members, each way, and all rode on passes, the four trips – two each way – made the money consideration greater than the salary as legislators.

As it was my first experience of the kind, I was observant of the appearance of those who crowded the train, from the eastern border of the state to Pierre, intent on judging the kind and character of the men who were to constitute the first state legislature. I saw men of many kinds, of course. Those who to me appeared as the brightest and most intelligent I listed mentally as members; others less notable for intelligent appearance or conversation I supposed to be their constituents, intent on visiting the capital to observe how their representatives deported themselves. On the organization of the legislature, I found that I must revise my opinion. Those whom I had classed as not above the average in intelligent appearance were members; those whom I mentally listed as above the average belonged as a rule to the "Third House," with no voice or vote on measures, but no doubt exercising considerable influence upon their farmer friends whom they had elected to represent them. This element seemed vitally interested in the election of the men to represent the new state in the United States Senate. Certainly there were not a few exceptions. There were able men in both houses; several counties and districts had sent entire delegations of admirable quality. The house, with 145 members, was an unwieldy body; the senate, with forty-five, was better. An attempt to cut down the membership of both, on the score of economy, met with scant support, and failed. As a Democrat, I was appointed as the thirteenth member on several committees; every committee was "tailed" with one Democrat, the twelve Republicans on each no doubt being considered a sufficient majority to prevent our doing any harm, had we been so disposed. There were thirteen other Democrats with me in the house, and I presume I should consider it an honor that I received the full vote of my party colleagues for the speakership – though the probability of my election was somewhat remote. The senate had four Democrats, and those, with the fourteen members of the house of the same party, met, organized, and agreed to name a candidate for speaker, and candidates for the two United States senatorships. Of course it amounted to nothing more than a mere matter of form, and furnished no little amusement for our Republican friends, but we decided to let the world know that though the state was overwhelmingly Republican, it possessed a small leavening of militant democracy. Thus, as stated, I was given a complimentary vote for the speakership by my Democratic friends; and when nominations for the senatorships were in order in house and senate, the Democratic contingent placed in nomination Hon. Bartlett Tripp and Hon. Merritt H. Day. Our nominees received the Democratic vote; and thus the record was made.

SENATORSHIP CONTEST – APPROPRIATION FIGHT

South Dakota has had several interesting contests for United States senatorships, but none has been more bitterly waged or aroused greater interest throughout the state than that of the first special session of the legislature in December of '89.

While many prominent men of the new state were nominated as possible or probable candidates, there were three who stood out conspicuously; and it was generally conceded that of those three two would be chosen. R. F. Pettigrew, of Sioux Falls, was admittedly the strongest of the three; and his choice as one senator was practically assured from the time the legislative members were elected in November. The contest developed between Judge Edgerton, of Yankton, and Judge Gideon C. Moody, of Deadwood, for the second position.

The Black Hills members of the legislature were provided with a Pullman sleeper, and this served as sleeping quarters during the special session. Accompanying the members were many friends; and from Lawrence County came representatives of a faction of the Republican Party opposed to Judge Moody's election. The fight between the Republican factions waxed bitter and more bitter, but finally was ended by the offer of the Moody element to support Judge Edgerton for the position of federal judge in consideration of his withdrawal from the senatorial race. Thus Moody and Pettigrew were elected as the first United States senators from the new state. Later the agreement with Judge Edgerton's supporters was carried out, and that gentleman became federal judge.

So jubilant were the supporters of Judge Moody over the result that they could not refrain from celebrating the victory, and a number did so in a very boisterous manner. Headed by a Deadwood saloon keeper named Jim Carney, carrying a torch, and accompanied by a tin pan band, and the tooting of horns, they marched 'round and 'round the Black Hills car, where Dawson lay very ill in his berth, shouting this doggerel:

> Moody runs the engine, Pettigrew rings the bell; The Black Hills kickers are in the soup, and Dawson's gone to hell.

As two senators were elected at the same time, it was necessary for Pettigrew and Moody to determine which should have the long and which the short term, the latter having a tenure of but one year. This determination was made by lot, and Moody drew the short term. By the time the next legislature was called upon to elect a successor to Moody, the wave of Populism was sweeping over the state, and all matters political were in a turmoil. Again the fight against Moody was carried to Pierre and waged with all the intensity characteristic of the first contest.

Dawson was still the leading spirit in the fight, and this time he returned to the Hills victorious. The man elected as Moody's successor was James H. Kyle, a Congregational

BECOMING AN EDITOR 229

minister, who had been elected to the state senate from Brown County. He was little known in the state; was popular with his congregation; and of fair, though not conspicuous, ability. During the progress of the campaign he made a speech that attracted attention and was used by the Populists as a campaign document, as it indicated Kyle's sympathy with various measures of legislation they were demanding. When the senatorial fight became warm – with a half dozen or more candidates in the field, and a long deadlock threatened – the name of the Aberdeen minister was presented as a compromise, and he was elected. From that time to this the western part of the state never has been able to secure a senatorship. During Kyle's first term he gradually drifted around to a more conservative attitude, and at its expiration was elected as a Republican to succeed himself.

During the high tide of Populism, H. L. Loucks was the acknowledged leader of that party in the state, and was a strong contender for the senate; but he failed to attain the honor. He established an office in Huron that became Populist headquarters. While the campaign was on I received a communication from his chief lieutenant, A. B. Cummings, asking if I would accept the nomination of the Populist Party for the office of lieutenant governor. I replied, thanking Mr. Cummings for the compliment implied, but declined to enter the field – considering that I had sufficient experience with state politics to satisfy me. I do not know to the present day if the telegram was sent me with authority of the head of the party or not – as it did not so state; or whether, in friendship for me, the sender did not attempt to test my attitude, with a view to presenting my name to those higher in authority, should I be found a compliant "Barkis."

One of my principal duties during the regular session of the legislature that convened in January, following the special session mentioned, was to secure, if possible, an appropriation for the maintenance of the State School of Mines – then a new institution struggling for existence. The appropriations for all state institutions were to be made for the year only; a new legislature was to be elected before the close of the year, and another session to be held the following January. Unfortunately there was a feeling of hostility to the school in the Northern Hills, where the only mining of consequence was in progress; and at least two employees of the Homestake, in the House, were outspoken in favor of refusing any appropriation.

As a result of the opposition to the school, the appropriations committees of the House and Senate agreed in recommending an appropriation of $2,750.00 for its support for the year. Such an amount would be so totally inadequate that it would mean the closing of the institution; indeed, that was the intention of the committee.

I felt that I must do my best to get an amendment to the report of the House committee, when the appropriation bill should be discussed in the committee of the whole House, but I was much afraid that all I could do might be of little avail. It was fortunate that before my election I had served a term as member and secretary of the board, having especial charge of the interests of the school.

I went first to Sol Star, chairman of the Lawrence County delegation in the House, and told him it would be impossible for the school to remain open with so meagre an appropriation; and that we could not accept it. He told me plainly that we could take that or nothing. I said, "I'll have to take the matter up in committee of the whole," to which he replied, "Do so, and see what you'll get."

I then went to Representative McCormack – whom I learned was to be chairman of the committee of the whole – that afternoon, and told him my dilemma. I told him I should need all the latitude he possibly could give me in presenting my amendment to the committee's report and, if necessary, answering any attacks made upon it. He replied, "Go ahead, and I'll see that you have all the time and opportunity you need." He did. Blessings on his memory! He has been dead many years but I never can forget how he stood my friend that day. The members were restricted to five-minute talks, but he enforced no restrictions on me, nor would he recognize any member who sought to call me down. I gave the history of the school; told of the prominent places occupied by its graduates in the mining and milling world; how one of its professors, in recognition of original work performed in the school, had secured the chair of metallurgy in the Massachusetts Institute of Technology – the greatest school of the kind in the United States, and ranked with the best in the world; named every piece of machinery in the metallurgical building, told of its functions and how they were performed; met the complaint of high per capita cost with comparisons of cost in other schools of like character; and concluded with a showing that the Black Hills had a greater variety of materials than any other country of like area known, and that the work of such a school was absolutely necessary in working out problems of treatment to make them productive.

The story was a new one to a majority of the members, and in a short time I was encouraged to believe that they were finding it interesting. During the last half hour of the ninety minutes I occupied I was not interrupted. My amendment increased the appropriation for the single year to $10,000 – a small amount as appropriations go in these times, but very important in that particular crisis. Two or three of the members spoke in opposition, but the chairman allowed me to answer their objections; Colonel Parker, of Lawrence, and E. B. Cummings, of Butte, supported me, and the amendment passed almost unanimously. It was apparent that much of the opposition to the school was from lack of knowledge as to its merits. Judge Bangs then secured for me a hearing before the committee of the whole Senate, where an identical amendment was agreed to; and on the rising of the committees the amendment was recommended for passage by the two branches in regular session. That was the evening of the session's last day. That night the conference committee, composed of members of the appropriations committees of both branches – after the time limit of the session really had passed – assumed an authority it did not possess. It reduced the amount to $8,000 and gave the $2,000 cut off to another institution. When the report was made to the House at two o'clock in the morning, every member was worn out; the train was made up and waiting on the track for the Black Hills members; so, after consulting some of my friends, I submitted to this petty injustice, knowing that the school would manage at least to live through the single year that should elapse before another appropriation might be secured.

My experience as a member of the legislature I always have considered of value, but I never have cared to attempt to repeat it. I have been offered nominations on various occasions, and in one instance during my absence from home, actually was nominated for the state senate, from Lawrence County. On my return I immediately withdrew my name, as private affairs would not admit of my taking the time necessary for the campaign.

RICHARD B. HUGHES
As First Editor of the Rapid City Daily Journal

SAM SCOTT
Hughes' mining companion, a founder of Rapid City

SIGN AT SOUTH DAKOTA STATE FISH HATCHERY
IN RAPID CITY COMMEMORATING THE FIRST
TROUT PLANTING IN THE BLACK HILLS

Mining Swindles

In every gold mining country, where a valuable mine has been found, many claims have been located close to it; the locators hope perhaps to find upon their ground an extension of the valuable ore body, or, failing in this, at least to give a speculative value to their property by reason of its proximity to something of known worth. It is safe to say that for every valuable claim located, one hundred taken up are of no value whatever, or of so little account as to be impossible to work profitably. This being true, it is not to be wondered that many claims are on the market, and many wiles are used to impress the investor with faith enough in the prospect to effect a sale.

Mining swindles were perpetrated now and then which tended to hurt the reputation of the Black Hills as a mining country, and to discourage investment on the part of those who otherwise would have been disposed to aid in the Hills' development. Outside people sometimes were inclined to blame the residents of the Hills for failure to condemn those practices and expose the swindlers. As a rule, however, the negotiations were conducted so quietly and with such skill that the mischief was accomplished before a warning could be given. As a rule the experts sent out by those contemplating purchase were so confident of their own ability and shrewdness that to offer them advice or to suggest that they exercise caution would be deemed an unwarranted interference.

A good many years ago, before the advent of railways in the Hills, a gentleman styling himself as Professor Underwood and registering from Chicago, came to Rapid City, made his way to *The Journal* office, and stated that he was here for the purpose of examining and reporting upon a mining claim in the Central Hills. It was apparent that he was by no means adverse to acquainting the people, through the press, with the information that Professor Underwood, of Chicago, noted mining expert, was with them; and that it was probable that his coming would prove an important event in the country's development.

One day he told me the location and name of the property he had come to examine. He gave me a copy of a report upon it to read, which had been made by a local expert – well known and not too conscientious. It was the professor's business to examine the property and have a mill test made on the ore; when, if he should find that the very flattering report of the local man was borne out, a sale would practically be assured. It so happened that I was as familiar with the property in question, with the extent of the vein so far developed, and all the working upon it, as anyone aside from the owners themselves. Therefore it was with some interest that I read the report, which was false and misleading in every respect. The extent of the ore body was exaggerated, as was the value of the gold content in the ore. The fact was that the property, while showing a fair prospect on the surface, where ages of erosion had freed the gold and left a local concentration, showed the ore very thin in value, as depth was attained. Mining and milling could not possibly pay a profit.

I not only knew the mine, but I also knew the owners. What to do or say bothered me. The professor was so confident of his ability to guard the interests of his employer that I hesitated, fearing that any advice, or even hint, might be deemed an intrusion. I took a night to study over the matter. In the morning I consulted a friend in whose judgment I placed reliance. We concluded that while it might do no good, a word of warning should be uttered, in order that the professor might not walk blindly into a trap. I approached the subject as carefully as possible, not alluding to his errand in the district, but narrating a few instances in which people had been victimized by owners of worthless ground, while thinking they had taken all due precautions. In conclusion I merely remarked that too much care could not be exercised in transactions involving the transfer of mining property.

MINING SWINDLES

As I spoke I noticed a change in my listener's countenance; instead of taking what I said in the spirit of friendship, the professor became exceedingly angry. He swelled up like a turkey gobbler and informed me that he required advice or suggestion from no one; that he wished to inform me that he was educated as a mining engineer, had examined and reported upon mining properties from the interior of South America to British Columbia. In short, he deemed it little less than an impertinence for any one ever to hint that he could be deceived or hoodwinked by mere prospectors.

He concluded about as follows, "When I have completed the inspection of a mine and made my report upon it, it is final; if I recommend the purchase it is purchased; if I advise against it there is no further consideration of it on the part of those whom I represent."

I could only regret that I had interfered in what I was so plainly told was none of my business. I awaited the outcome. In due course the professor established headquarters at the mine, employed miners to take out twenty tons of ore and engaged teams to deliver the ore at a mill some miles distant. There the ore was crushed, amalgamated, and clean-up made. The professor then took the amalgam to Deadwood, had it retorted, and the resulting gold melted into a bar. He took some satisfaction in showing me this bar as he stopped in Rapid City on his way out of the Hills. He informed me that the ore was found to be a profitable grade and that a sale of the property would result. I was well satisfied that he had been fooled, and so it proved. Ten thousand dollars were paid on the total purchase price of fifty thousand agreed upon; the payment of the balance was to wait upon further development of the mine. This balance was never paid, nor was it ever demanded by the locators of the property – who immediately moved to Montana. After a very little additional work of development the intending purchasers abandoned it. The method of "salting" used in this instance never became generally known; but it was a certainty that the ore was salted – probably by introducing extra gold into the batteries during the mill test.

A man once boasted that when he undertook to sell a mining property he sold it; and if the ore in the mine didn't carry sufficient value it was not difficult to supply the deficiency in the mill. The individual who thus expressed himself on one occasion, visited a location in the Central Hills where two well-known Montana miners were working. He accosted them, inquiring as to their prospects of developing a good mine. A large amount of shaft and tunnel work had been done upon the ground; but though there had been a fair prospect to start with, the developments were not satisfactory. With greater candor than is usual with prospectors, the men admitted this fact and acknowledged that they were somewhat discouraged. Their visitor seemed impressed with the amount of work they had accomplished, and dwelt upon the fact that their various openings indicated that they had been employed there a long time. He made the somewhat peculiar remark that "sometimes a good showing of work is as important as the quality of the ore."

After a pleasant visit he promised to call again. This promise he kept in a shorter time than the miners expected. After some conversation, he asked if they would be willing to give him an option on their ground, to run sixty days, at the price of twenty thousand dollars. He agreed at the end of that time to pay them one-fourth the amount, and the balance in two subsequent payments. As an inducement, he proposed to pay them miners' wages and to furnish necessary tools and powder, if they would continue the development work.

The men were puzzled that their visitor made few tests of the ore. He seemed utterly indifferent as to its value. At the expiration of the time when the first payment was to be made, he gave them a check for the agreed five thousand dollars and paid them for their work. He told them to continue as they were doing. Inquiry at a Deadwood bank disclosed the fact that the check was good. In due time the entire purchase price was paid and the locators of the ground divided the receipts with a silent partner – a well-known gambler who had outfitted them for prospecting – and left the Hills.

MINING SWINDLES

A large amount of money was expended in the introduction of water power and in the building of a stamp mill and other structures. Upon completion of the first mill run, the man who had made the purchase from the prospectors turned the property over to a company – which he had organized in the East – and received a sum of money for it at least four times as large as that he had paid. To accomplish this sale, twenty-dollar gold coins were filed up and the gold from them placed in the mill batteries. This story is well known to a few people still living. Some years ago the man who did the filing told a friend on the Pacific Coast of the part he had played. In this case the chief actor did not scruple to defraud his friends of a large sum of money for the purchase of the ground. He encourage them to spend as much more for machinery, that he knew would never be used for more than a second mill run at that place. A trace of the old water-power ditch and some rotting timbers, and excavations partially filled by caving earth, are all that remain to mark the spot that once was the scene of much activity.

Another mine deal, consummated by the same man who was the principal actor in the story just narrated, required greater precautions to guard against discovery of fraud; the expert sent out by the parties interested in the proposed investment was competent to take his own samples of ore. He was exceedingly careful to keep them where it was difficult for any one so disposed to tamper with them.

The expert, as he secured the samples from the various openings of the mine, placed them in an ore sack, which he kept constantly in his possession. With the aid of confederates, however, the promoter finally outwitted him. A sack was procured, the exact duplicate of the one used by the expert. Two men were dispatched after night to a mine twelve or fifteen miles distant, where they descended a shaft and filled the sack with ore from a small vein of known good values. The pair returned to the camp before daylight, on the day the examiner was to take his samples to the railway for shipment to headquarters where they were to be tested.

On a last visit to various openings of the mine on that day, the expert kept his sack of ore in the vehicle used, carrying it in his hand when necessary to dismount. The sack that the defrauders had hoped to substitute was also in the wagon, covered with a blanket thrown into the wagon box with apparent carelessness. The last round of inspection was made and the party was on the way to camp without an opportunity for the substitution having presented itself, when passing a small opening showing a vein of plumbago, the chief conspirator called on the driver to stop. He exclaimed, "Mr. ____, there is a peculiar formation which seems to resemble black lead. I would much like your opinion on it." For just a moment the man was off his guard. He stepped into the opening, leaving his ore sack in the wagon. In that instant the change was made. All unwittingly he shipped the sack of good ore instead of that which was practically valueless – the ore he had collected. On the results obtained in the test, accompanied by the report of the expert on the work of development, the sale was consummated. The eastern investors were defrauded; a large expenditure was made in the building of a fine mill that was destined after the initial run to fall into idleness. The machinery finally was sold for a trifle of its original cost and transported elsewhere; while the fine buildings were given over to decay.

Another case – the sale of the Greenwood mine – stands out prominently as one of the largest mining swindles perpetrated in the history of the Hills. It involved a large amount of money and was widely advertised, because of the prominence of several of the parties in the transaction. The chief victim was an old gentleman named Laflin, who had been at one time postmaster of Chicago.

The report had become general that developments on the Greenwood were disclosing large bodies of ore of high grade. This report was heard on every hand. There were those who declared that at least a second Homestake had been found. As people are prone to believe that which they wish to believe, throughout the country it became accepted as an established

MINING SWINDLES 241

fact that the Greenwood was a mine of great value. A camp was built containing stores, a school, necessary shops and a sufficient number of houses to accommodate a considerable number of miners and laborers. A splendid mill was built and a day set for beginning the first run of the ore. The chief promoter invited a large number of friends to be present on that occasion. It was rumored, though not generally, that a man sent to examine and report on the property had left his samples for a moment, during which other samples had been substituted; that the change had been effected as the expert stooped to drink at a wayside spring; and that on the test of the substituted samples the determination to build the mill was made.

Laflin had a man on whom it seems he placed implicit reliance. This man was an English preacher named Taylor. While a force of miners was engaged in opening a large cut on the hillside above the millsite, the necessary machinery for a sixty-stamp mill was freighted into the Hills. The erection of the mill building was pushed with all possible dispatch. On the date fixed for the commencement of milling, a large number of visitors reached the new camp, invited by the chief promoter of the enterprise. The writer was among the number and noted with pleasure the beautiful location, the fine stream of water coursing through the little village, the fine equipment of buildings and machinery, and the general air of confidence of the residents, that this day was to mark the beginning of operations of great importance to the entire Black Hills.

At an agreed signal from the mill whistle the steam was turned on, the wheels began to revolve, all the machinery began to function, as the ore was crushed and fed into the batteries through self-feeders. A cheer went up. As a result of that mill test the purchase price was paid. This was generally stated as seventy-five thousand dollars and it is altogether probable that it reached that figure, while the cost of the mill and other equipment and labor was certainly as much more.

While the preliminaries for the starting of the mill were under way, I asked if there would be any objection to my taking a sample of ore across the face of the cut from which the stamps were to be supplied. The foreman in charge said, "Certainly not." He offered to assist me but I declined his assistance with thanks and proceeded to fill two or three small sample sacks with particles broken across the face of the cut.

On my return to town I laid the samples in a drawer of my desk and proceeded to forget them. Nor was I reminded of them until word reached town that the millrun had been extremely satisfactory and that the sale had been made. Then I took the samples to a rear room of the Tom Sweeney hardware store, procured a tub of water, mortar, pestle and pan, and proceeded to test the ore. I was astonished to find that the most careful panning of which I was capable disclosed – scarcely a "color." I crushed and panned again and again. I heated the pan red hot lest some grease might have dropped into it, causing the loss of "flour" gold. Again I made the pan tests. But there was no mistaking the truth; the ore I had taken from the cut was worthless. By the same token the ore that had been milled was worthless, for it had been taken from the same cut. I was astonished, but convinced. Tom Sweeney, the most confirmed optimist ever known in this or any other country, would come from time to time as I panned, and inquire in his cheery way, "Well, old man, how does she pan?"

I offered no information until I had thoroughly satisfied myself that the ore was valueless. Then I called him back and said, "Tom, the stuff that the Greenwood is milling will not go seventy-five cents to the ton."

"What!" roared Tom, unable to believe that he had understood. I repeated. Tom was indignant.

"You don't mean to say that old Bob Flormann and all the others are fooled, do you? You're dead wrong; you didn't get hold of the ore they're working – sure you didn't. You can bet the Greenwood is all right, and the stuff is there."

It was impossible to convince him of the truth. In fact I felt so worked up about it that I only made a half-hearted effort to do so. I said, "Let's wait a little, Tom, and we'll see."

MINING SWINDLES

The second millrun was made, this time under control of the new owners. The mill shut down like grandfather's clock, "never to run again."

The prominence of the parties chiefly concerned, and the large sum of money involved, caused quite a sensation. The victim of the swindle determined that someone should suffer for it. Action was instituted against several of those who were charged with conspiracy in the deal, but the plans had been so skillfully laid that they could not be punished by process of law. Taylor was placed in confinement for a very short time, but his release was obtained as soon as his case came up for hearing. He returned to England, no doubt satisfied that the price he had received for his treachery was a sufficient recompense for a short period of incarceration.

A large portion of the Laflin money was expended in the erection of a large, and for those times, elaborate brick block of three stories, in Rapid City. This block still stands (1926) as a reminder of the incident just related. Although it has changed ownership and an attempt has been made to change its name, old timers still have the habit of designating it as the Flormann Block.

One of the smoothest, most unique, most skillfully planned and executed mining swindles ever perpetrated in the country was in the sale of a mine near Central in the Northern Hills.

An organization of eastern men had become interested in the purchase of the mine. After extended negotiations they paid a small part of the purchase price agreed upon, for a short-time operation, with the understanding that the agents of the organization should have exclusive possession of the property during the life of the option, in order to make thorough tests of the ore in a neighboring stamp mill. Under this agreement possession of the mine and mill was surrendered to the prospective purchasers. Elaborate precautions were taken to safeguard their interests and to insure a complete and reliable determination of ore values. Only miners upon whom the utmost reliance could be placed were employed. These were selected by a foreman whose reputation was a guarantee of sterling honesty in his work. The same care was exercised in the selection of the amalgamator and all the mill hands, who were instructed to exclude all visitors at the mill during the operations. The driver of the team that delivered the ore to the mill, too, was a man of utmost trustworthiness, who also was placed upon his guard against the approach of strangers.

The unloading platform, from which opened the chute leading to the mill crusher, was on a level with the street of Central. The chute was provided with a padlock and the driver of the ore wagon was instructed to lock this carefully on leaving the mill for the mine. Under these precautions against interference or possible fraud, the ore was duly mined and milled; the batteries and plates were scraped; the resulting amalgam was retorted and the gold melted into a bar, which when weighed, was found fully up to the representations of the mine owners. As the whole affair had been carried through to the satisfaction of all, without a breath of suspicion of fraud, there was no quibble over the sale; it ran into many thousands of dollars.

During the progress of the millrun an incident occurred, apparently of so trivial a character as to be unworthy of remark, and yet it proved of the greatest importance later. As the ore shoveler was engaged one day in shoveling a load of ore into the mill chute, there came staggering up the middle of the street an individual, apparently in an advanced stage of intoxication. His face was dirty and his clothing covered with dust. He was having apparent trouble in maintaining his equilibrium. On he came, with difficulty, until he had reached a point just a few feet from the rear of the ore wagon. Here he paused, steadied himself for an instant. Then, taking from an inside pocket of an old overcoat a more than half-filled whisky flask, he proceeded to take a hearty swig of the contents. Then, hiccoughing, he advanced toward the shoveler. With the bottle extended at arm's length he called to him to – "take a-hu-hic-drink with me." He stumbled and fell headlong, the bottle smashing in a hundred pieces in the ore in the chute. Cursing his luck, the fellow with much apparent diffi-

MINING SWINDLES

culty regained his feet and staggered off, muttering imprecations as he went.

This incident furnished amusement to a few bystanders and none enjoyed it more heartily than the man on the wagon. But it did more than furnish amusement; it furnished the wherewithal to make the millrun a pronounced success, for the bottle had contained a sufficient quantity of gold chloride to insure that result. Shortly following the mill test a second one was made – and the mine was abandoned.

Indian Trouble
Battle of Wounded Knee

In the fall of 1890 the various Indian reservations of the Northwest were visited by exhorters, who excited the warriors and induced them to believe that a time was at hand when the country would again be theirs; that the buffalo and all other game would again become plentiful as of yore; and that in some mysterious way the whites would disappear. Dressed in long white shirts, the Indians spent much of their time in dancing and listening to the promises of the "Prophets," until some were brought to a state of frenzy. It was then feared by exposed white settlers that they might be attacked.

It cannot be stated with certainty that such was the intention of the Indians, but their actions caused much apprehension. It was determined to put a stop to their wild demonstrations by apprehending those leaders who were considered most likely to cause trouble. Indian police were sent out to bring in Sitting Bull and it was believed the order was to bring him in dead or alive, with more than a possibility that the authorities would prefer him dead.

Be that as it may, when the police entered the cabin of the old medicine man a fight ensued, in which Sitting Bull and several of the police were killed. Big Foot – one of the chiefs who had taken part in the Custer fight – who was camped not far from Sitting Bull, evidently feared that he would share the fate of his leader if he remained in the neighborhood, and started with his band for the Rosebud and Pine Ridge Reservations, two hundred miles to the south. There is no evidence whatever that this band contemplated mischief; indeed, the fact that it consisted largely of women and children makes it certain that the desire was wholly to escape what they considered threatened danger. As shrewd a judge of Indian character and of the entire situation as Dr. V. T. McGillycuddy stigma-

INDIAN TROUBLE—WOUNDED KNEE

tized the whole affair as an "outbreak" of the whites rather than of the Indians.

Troops were ordered from the nearest military posts to proceed toward the reservations named, in order to hold the young warriors in check should they show a disposition to rise; and particularly to prevent the Big Foot band from reaching its intended destination and to turn it back to the north.

General Nelson A. Miles arrived in Rapid City and took charge of the military movements, making his headquarters at the Harney Hotel. A detachment of the Seventh Cavalry was quartered in Rapid City pending reports from scouts as to the exact route Big Foot was traveling. Settlers along the valleys east of the Hills had become alarmed and a delegation from Spring and Battle Creeks came to obtain arms and ammunition.

In company with Tom Sweeney I waited upon General Miles, and proffered the request of the settlers. We were cordially received, and the general ordered his adjutant to make requisition on Fort Meade for fifty needle guns and 2,500 rounds of ammunition. These came down promptly on the evening train and were delivered to the delegation of settlers. I often have wondered what part of the supplies ever went back to Fort Meade.

As the Seventh was Custer's old regiment, there was a very bitter feeling among officers and men against the bands that took part in the death of their old commander and his men. It was freely predicted that if any detachment of the Seventh should intercept Big Foot, it would be a bad day for the Indians. When orders came for the detachment to move down Rapid Valley and to cross the Cheyenne River to the reservation, a grizzled old major was taking a last drink with friends at the Harney bar. He was accosted with, "Well, Major, I suppose if you find Big Foot and his band you will escort them back to their reservation and Uncle Sam will issue them some extra grub and blankets."

To this the old major replied, "If we can get away from telegraphic communication with headquarters and strike Big Foot, there will be no strings on us."

Not his detachment, but another, also of the Seventh, did find the Indians on Wounded Knee Creek,[2] and surrounded their camp. On the following morning, when the time came for moving camp, a battle was precipitated; practically all the warriors and many of the women and children were killed; the soldiers lost, in killed, thirty-five; among them, Captain George D. Wallace, a very well known and popular officer. Indian survivors declare that the soldiers brought on the fight. It certainly does not seem probable that the Indians would have initiated it, surrounded as they were, with their camp commanded by a machine gun, and with their women and children exposed to annihilation. In the light of all information, and in cool judgment, it must be considered that the Wounded Knee affair was a deplorable and unnecessary sacrifice of life.

Accompanying General Miles during his stay in Rapid City was the celebrated artist, Frederic Remington, whose western pictures – particularly of Indians, cowboys and horses – are acknowledged by some as the truest ever painted. He was an interesting talker, and during a visit to *The Journal* office – where I had the pleasure of meeting him – he told of many incidents of his western trips. He had a great admiration for Lieutenant Casey, the officer who had disciplined, and

---

[2] The Wounded Knee Massacre occurred December 29, 1890, on the Pine Ridge Reservation about seventeen miles from the agency. – James H. McGregor, *The Wounded Knee Massacre* (Minneapolis, The Lund Press, Inc., 1940), 5. In referring to the Wounded Knee Battle, the Commissioner of Indian Affairs said in his 1891 report, (Washington, 1892), 128:

> The next day, December 29th, when ordered to turn in their arms, they (the Indians) surrendered very few. By a search in the tepees sixty guns were obtained. When the military – a detachment of the Seventh Cavalry (Custer's old command) with other troops – began to take the arms from their persons, a shot was fired and carnage ensued. According to the reports of military officers the Indians attacked the troops as soon as the disarmament commenced. The Indians claimed that the first shot was fired by a half-crazed, irresponsible Indian. At any rate, a short, sharp indiscriminate fight immediately followed.

INDIAN TROUBLE—WOUNDED KNEE 249

was at the head of, the efficient Indian police. Remington said, "Casey could make a Sioux Indian herd sheep."

Within a few days after Remington had given utterance to this remark Casey was killed by a young Indian graduate of Carlisle, who shot him as he was riding away from the Indian, entirely unsuspicious of danger. Casey's slayer was apprehended and tried in the civil court of Yankton. Strange as it may seem, he was acquitted; his lawyer advanced the argument that at the time of the killing a state of war existed between the whites and Indians, and as an Indian he was justified in causing the death of an enemy.

On the afternoon that Lieutenant Casey was killed, Dr. V. T. McGillycuddy,[3] former agent at Pine Ridge Agency and well known to all Indians of that reservation – accompanied by Major John R. Brennan and W. J. McFarland, then on *The Journal* staff – rode down Rapid Valley to the Cheyenne River and crossed to the reservation. It was the doctor's desire to meet and talk with any of the Indians who might be in that neighborhood, and to learn from them their attitude. He did not believe that the Indians contemplated an outbreak.

As the party rode eastward from the river, an Indian arose from a place of concealment where he had been observing their approach, and advanced with hand upraised in token of amity. He had recognized the doctor, whom he addressed as "Father," as was the custom of the Sioux in speaking to the Indian Agent. After some parley the Indian asked, "Father, do you know what officer was killed by an Indian near the agency?"

"No," replied the doctor. "There was no officer killed, or we would have heard of it in Rapid City."

---

[3] Dr. Valentine T. McGillycuddy was a member of Professor Walter P. Jenney's Black Hills Expedition in the summer of 1875 and was on French Creek when word was sent to the outside world of the discovery of gold on both Spring and Rapid Creeks. In 1876 the doctor was a member of General Crook's Yellowstone and Big Horn Expedition. From 1879 to 1886, he was Indian Agent at the Pine Ridge Agency, in Dakota Territory. He resigned his position when he became as he said, "tired of what he called 'the buncombe and red tape of the Government'."
See: Julia McGillycuddy, *McGillycuddy Agent* (Palo Alto, CA, Stanford University Press, c. 1941).

"Yes, Father," insisted the Indian, "an officer was killed; an Indian killed him; I know this."

"When did this occur?" asked the doctor.

"Two hours ago," was the answer.

"There must be some mistake," said the doctor. "You could not know of anything that happened near the agency two hours ago, for it is fifty or sixty miles to the agency."

"An officer was killed," the Indian persisted. "An Indian killed him. I know this. I know no more."

Upon the return of the doctor and his companions to Rapid City in the evening they learned of Casey's death, news of which had reached the town by wire in the forenoon. It long has been known that the plains Indians have means of transmitting information over long distances by signals known to all, and here was a practical illustration of their efficacy. Dr. McGillycuddy, from his long experience with the Sioux and familiarity with their customs, knew that scattered bands often were apprised in a mysterious manner of doings at the agency, but was much surprised that the news of Casey's death should have reached members of the tribe at such a distance in advance of transmission to the Hills by wire.

A Pioneer Wins Honors

In 1893 I was invited by the South Dakota World's Fair Commission to make a collection of Black Hills building stone for exhibition, and to help with the mineral exhibit from the Hills at the Fair in Chicago.

During the time I spent at the Fair my name had been mentioned among others in connection with the appointment of surveyor general for the Federal District of South Dakota. In the month of March (1894), I received notice of my appointment by President Cleveland, and of confirmation by the Senate. I was unable to go at once to Huron, where the office was located, because of the serious illness of my little son. I finally received a peremptory summons to appear at the office within a specified time. This notice came from "Governor" Swineford, who had been governor of Alaska during Cleveland's first term, and to whom the gubernatorial title still clung.

As soon as possible I reported to the governor, and was inducted into office. A short time afterwards I was joined by my wife and little son; and I may say that the four years spent in Huron were among the most pleasant of our lives. The work of the office was pleasant and by no means onerous; my associations with my office force were of the most gratifying character; and the acquaintances and friendship of my family and myself with the fine people of Huron, altogether delightful.

I held the position for four years, when a change of national administration brought about a change in all offices of the kind. The position of United States Surveyor General was in many respects a pleasant one, though the salary was not munificent. The occupant of the office is not subject to the beck and call of the general public; and with an efficient corps of clerks, such as I had, the work goes on smoothly with little interference from the higher-ups in Washington.

My office once received a letter signed by the commissioner, criticizing severely an item of fifteen cents that I had allowed in a survey inspector's account; the only thing wrong being that a small pail, for keeping butter in a spring of water, had been designated as "ice pail." This required some extended correspondence before the charge against me of fifteen cents was cancelled. It was clearly due to some over-zealous clerk. Soon afterward, when our office received a warrant from the Indian Department for the sum of $2,111 – for which I had made no requisition and to which I had no right whatever, as the disbursements for Indian surveys for the year had been made and all balances turned back into the treasury – I thought I saw a good opportunity of "getting back" at the Department. I wrote, asking what I was expected to do with $2,111 for which I had made no request. Without any explanation the reply came to return it to the treasury. I soon learned that although a mistake might be made in Washington, it never was so designated; the worst that would be admitted was an "inadvertence."

During my term of office I made numerous trips to the Hills, where we retained property interests; these were chiefly in Rapid City – which we always considered home. On surrendering the office of Surveyor General to my successor, we returned to Rapid City. Here we remained the better part of a year, while I arranged business matters so that I could take charge of the Cleopatra mining property on Squaw Creek, south from Spearfish. A number of Aberdeen and Huron men and I had acquired this property.

James M. Lawson, of Aberdeen, was made president of the company organized to develop the siliceous ore deposits on the ground. I was made secretary and superintendent. The proximity of the mining property to Spearfish made it desirable to make a home at that point; this we did six months after the birth of our second son.

A PIONEER WINS HONORS 253

The development of the Cleopatra mining property was attended with much difficulty and expense, for the country was extremely precipitous. At length, however, roads were constructed, though they were at all times subject to washouts, and entailed almost constant expense in their repairs. After a visit to Mercur, Utah, where the largest mill – and one of the first – for the treatment of ores by cyanide solutions was in operation, and after a study of the methods employed, our officers determined to build a cyanide mill for the treatment of our ores, modeled in various respects on the plan of the Mercur mill. At this early day in the history of treating rebellious gold ores with cyanide, the theory was held that the main part of the values was contained in the cleavages rather than in the close-grained and solid body of the rock; and that coarse crushing – by which the ore would be broken so that the cleavages would be exposed to the action of the solutions – was the best method to be used. It was known that fine crushing created "slimes," and since profitable methods of extracting the gold values from the slimes had not been perfected, the creation of slimes was to be avoided.

For a year and a half after the erection of our mill we worked in development of the mine and in milling operations simultaneously; while much ore milled would have yielded a profit under later methods, it barely served to pay expenses, as treated at that time. The ore bodies proved to be less extensive than we had hoped, and the parties interested felt unable to pay for development of lower levels on which ore might have been found. The result was that with an expenditure of more than $100,000, we recovered not more than $30,000.

I next took charge of the working out of the two lowest levels of the Holy Terror mine, located in the Keystone district of the Southern Hills. It was a small vein of high-grade ore. It was worked to a depth of eleven hundred feet. An excess of water and the consequent heavy expense of operation, to offset which a sufficient tonnage of ore could not be obtained from the small vein, made it impossible to operate the mine to a greater depth at a profit.

The name "Holy Terror" is a strange one to be applied to a mine, and the question frequently has been asked why and how it was so named. The story is this: One of the locators was a rather uncouth Englishman named Franklin, but better known as "Rocky Mountain Frank." While a man of unprepossessing exterior and rough manner, Frank was really not a bad fellow, and was generally liked by those who knew him best. His wife was perfectly suited to him, being a woman of little refinement of manner, though of undoubted kind heart, as could be attested by many a miner and prospector to whom she had ministered in time of sickness. She and Frank usually dwelt in harmony, but there were exceptions. Once in a while Frank would get away to Rapid City or one of the other towns to indulge a taste for strong waters; on such occasions he was prone to forget the flight of time, and remain away from home longer than he should. Finally his wife would go in search of him. Experience had taught her where she might expect to find him, and she seldom, if ever, went wrong in her quest. Usually when discovered he would be more than "half seas over" and engaged in holding forth, to all who would listen, on the wonderful value of his various prospects. Sighting him, his wife would enter the saloon where he was orating, and taking hold of him none too gently, would pour out on his devoted head a torrent of abuse that would astonish all who heard. Frank would take it all without a retort, and with the utmost meekness of spirit. On such an occasion he would merely turn to a bystander and, with a sheepish grin, beg to be informed if she wasn't a "Holy Terror." The name clung to the woman, and as the "Holy Terror" she became generally known in every camp of the Hills. When, in company with two or three others, Franklin found phenomenally rich ore, his partners insisted on naming the mine in honor of his wife, and he assented; and since that time, as the Holy Terror, the mine has been known.

We finally closed down the Holy Terror mine. I immediately engaged, with a number of Spearfish residents, in the organization of a company whose object was the building of a

A PIONEER WINS HONORS

traction line to connect Spearfish, and the valley country adjacent, with the mining districts and markets of the Hills. For the purpose of supplying necessary power, a hydroelectric plant was embraced as a part of the scheme. An appropriation of the waters of the Redwater was made under the state laws, and work on canal excavation commenced as soon as it was possible to secure the necessary concessions from the owners of the lands along the proposed route. The task of securing such right of way was entrusted to Milton Brenn and myself; and when it is considered that the course of the proposed canal lay through alfalfa fields, farm gardens and orchards, it is surprising that it was accomplished with comparative ease, little or no friction, and entirely without a resort to litigation or condemnation proceedings.

The prices asked by the owners of the lands for the right of way were entirely reasonable, and were paid without objection on the part of the corporation, without delay. The power proposition presented the unique feature that the water that would be turned into the canal from the channel of Redwater, fed by large and never-failing springs, was of such a temperature that little or no ice condition would interfere with the flow, even in the coldest weather.

As stated, the company was organized originally as a traction company, in the belief that the building of a traction line to the Hills would prove a great convenience and benefit to the country it would traverse, and be of especial benefit to the town and valley of Spearfish.

Many residents of Deadwood and Lead expressed a determination to make their homes in or near Spearfish, should the project be carried out as outlined, as they would then have reasonably cheap and rapid means of travel to and from their places of business. It was believed that the traction line would be a paying institution to the stockholders. It was found, however, that the owners of the land would not subscribe to the stock. This attitude on their part furnished a reasonable pretext – if one were needed – to the subscribers who invested largely – and without whom the power would not have been developed – to make the project one for the furnishing of electric power to whomsoever was willing to pay for it; thus they insured themselves a certain return on their investments.

Until the right of way was obtained and all contracts for the canal were signed, I acted as vice-president and general manager. With the change from a traction to a power enterprise pure and simple, I resigned. Later, however, I went to Washington and Idaho to expedite the shipment of cedar poles for the transmission line. It was a time when every freight yard and sidetrack in the Northwest was congested with loaded cars. [After exerting considerable ingenuity] I had the poles moving toward the Hills on cars belonging indifferently to both the Great Northern and the Northern Pacific. The poles were set; the transmission wires strung; and the fine power plant on the Redwater was completed. Before the winter set in the current was being delivered in Deadwood for lighting the town and to Lead City for use in the Homestake mills. Those who controlled the stock of the Black Hills Traction Company sold their fine property to the owners of the central system, content with a very reasonable profit. I long regretted the failure of the traction company to carry out the original intention of building a traction line. I believed it would have been a paying investment, as well as a great convenience.

While running the Holy Terror mine, I made an investment in a bunch of cattle and entrusted them to a man who had been some time in my employ, and who took them to the North Grand River country, in the extreme northern part of the state. Here the herd made a nice increase for three years; when I visited the ranch from time to time, it seemed to give promise of making us financially independent. But prosperity spoiled my partner in the enterprise, and he fell into the way of spending his time away from home, in drinking and gambling. In one bad winter storm the profits of three years were swept away, due solely to his neglect; on my visit to the ranch a short time afterward, I saw gulches in the neighborhood packed full of carcasses. As soon as possible I gathered the

A PIONEER WINS HONORS

live remnant of the herd and moved it south to the Hills, and disposed of it, barely getting back the amount of my original investment.

Having disposed of our cattle interests, and stock in the traction company, and closed down work on the mine in which I was interested in the Northern Hills, I found myself for the first time in many years comparatively idle. As there seemed to be no field of activity open to me in Spearfish, I determined to do some prospecting for a location farther west, with a view to moving if I should find a desirable place.

Accordingly I spent some months in California,[4] Idaho, Washington and Oregon, visiting the principal cities and many of the smaller towns. We had previously purchased a residence in Portland, Oregon, and for some time thought of settling there; but after I had spent a week there we abandoned the intention. I heartily enjoyed the trip and met with many old friends in the coast cities as well as in Boise, Twin Falls, Wenatchee and North Yakima, but returned home without finding a country that I could like as well as the Hills.

---

[4] During one of the years of my experience in mining and cattle, accompanied by my wife and two sons, I made a trip to California, where we spent five months pleasantly, moving from place to place. While in the coast area we met many old friends, formerly of the Hills. Among those was Rochford. For nineteen years I had not seen him, and for the greater part of that time I had not even known of his whereabouts. In Los Angeles, I met Rochford's sister by the merest accident, and obtained her brother's address. Only one who has experienced the pleasure of meeting after many long years with one who was the best loved friend, partner and companion of his youth, can appreciate the pleasure with which I sat night after night listening to the well-remembered voice, as he recalled the scenes and incidents of our boyhood, our trip to the Hills together and our life as pioneers. Though Rochford had business of a rather urgent nature elsewhere, he spent a full week with us. During the years that had elapsed since our parting, he had acted in the capacity of mine expert from the interior of Mexico to the interior of Alaska. Nearly all of that time he was in the employ of one large Pacific Coast mining corporation. It was evident that Rochford had the confidence and friendship of the officers of the corporation, as he frequently was entertained at the summer home of the president. It was with great pleasure I noted that he had fulfilled the promise of his young manhood. – [HUGHES].

A letter received at the Hughes home in Rapid City on the day of the death of Richard B. Hughes in 1930, announced Mr. Rochford's intention of making a visit to him that spring.

About this time I received an offer from the *Rapid City Journal* to join the staff of the paper, and almost simultaneously I was offered an investment in the stock of a newly organized bank in the same place, with an active position in the bank. The latter position would not be available until the beginning of the year. As it was then September, I went to work on the paper with the understanding that I would remain only until the first of January.

I found that though I had been out of the newspaper work for a long time, I fell into the old place with little difficulty, and with the pleasant relations that always had existed between the *Journal* and myself now renewed, I took pleasure in the work. While we had been absent from Rapid City for some years, we always had been inclined to think of it as home. Here we had been married; here our four children had been born; and here two who died in infancy[5] had been buried. With the growth of the town in the early years I had been closely identified through my newspaper work and as an active member of the so-called Board of Trade, trying to keep the name of the town before the public; working to secure railway communication with the outside world; or any other material benefit that should aid in making the town a city of importance.

Thus, in coming back to Rapid City, we came among many old friends and associates. Another and potent reason for the return was that through the years of our absence we had retained property interests in Rapid City; these, though unproductive of anything but taxes, now, with a strongly accelerated growth of the town, began to give promise of value. My wife had inherited from her parents one-sixth interest in a subdivision of the Boulevard addition. This consisted of one hundred and sixty lots and some acreage, desirably located, as the town had now grown to the line of the property. Difficulty was experienced in securing the various other interests in the property; two of the other sixths had been divided into

---

[5] Mary Edna Hughes was born July 14, 1885 and died October 20, 1885; and Edith Alice Hughes was born February 21, 1887 and died August 8, 1887.

A PIONEER WINS HONORS

twelfths and several former owners had died, while others had scattered from New York to Seattle. Before our return to Rapid City I had secured all but one-sixth, title to which had passed to my friend, George Hunt, who was engaged in the real estate business. To him I sold an additional one-sixth. With this accomplished, the property was ready for market and found prompt sale. As I write (1926) this subdivision is practically all occupied with residences.

We also prepared at once to build three stores on Main Street property. One-half of this my wife had inherited; the other half was left to her brother, from whom we purchased it before building.

On the first of the year following our return to Rapid City, I took a position in the bank, where I remained until a rheumatic affliction forced me to discontinue work and seek relief. As the years have passed I have grown to love this beautiful country as I know I never could love another. I am rejoiced that I have lived to see its beauties everywhere acknowledged; that I have witnessed its development from a state of nature to the possession of all the things that exalt and embellish civilized life; that I have witnessed its towns grow to the proportions of fine little cities, with fine churches, schools and every refining and educational influence possessed by the older communities of the East; that in this growth and development it has permitted me to bear at least a small part. Finally, as I take what ease I may in a comfortable home with my dear wife and with our two sons[6] and two

---

[6] Richard B. Hughes had two sons. The older, Richard Lewis, married Mabel Wilson of Greeley, CO, the daughter of Mr. and Mrs. T. T. Wilson of that city. Mr. Wilson was a pioneer newspaperman of Greeley and a Collector of U. S. Customs in Denver on a presidential appointment. The family resided in Rapid City until 1924 at which time they moved to Denver, CO. Richard Lewis died in 1942 and Mabel in 1974. Richard and Mabel had a daughter, Dorothy Mae Hughes, who married Herbert T. Johnson and resides in Denver, and a son, Richard Wilson Hughes, who married Helen Putman, and are the parents of Richard Putman Hughes and Kathryn (Kate) Elizabeth Hughes, married to John Christian. Richard Wilson's family also resided in Denver; he died in 1971. Richard B. Hughes' younger son, Clarence William, married Newell Chase, youngest daughter of the well-known pioneer merchant, Isaac H. Chase – who came to Deadwood in 1877 and owned stores in several Black Hills towns. Clarence and Newell had two chil-

grandchildren and their own dear mother close at hand, I feel that I have much for which to be thankful; and among the privileges I have enjoyed, I hold none higher than that of having been a Black Hills Pioneer.

At the time of the death of Richard B. Hughes in 1930, there remained as pioneers in Rapid City only his lifelong friend, Jacob Morris – who opened a store in Custer about the time of the author's arrival there – and Mrs. Charles Haxby – who was a small girl in Rapid City in 1876. A corporal's guard of the old timers remained in the Northern Hills through the years. They braved a March blizzard to follow the remains of Mr. Hughes to Mountain View Cemetery in Rapid City, where they conducted the customary ritual of the Society of Black Hills Pioneers.

In triangular Halley Park, at West Bouldvard, Main and St. Joseph Streets in Rapid City, stands the Pioneer Cabin, sponsored by the Fortnightly Club and Ladies' Group of Rapid City. It is now a part of the city park system. To the right of the doorway is a marble slab upon which is inscribed a poem written by Richard B. Hughes, which reads:

> I was built in the olden, golden days,
> When this was an unknown land;
> My timbers were hewn by a pioneer
> With a rifle near at hand.
>
> I stand as a relic of 'seventy-six,
> Our Nation's centennial year;
> That all may see as they enter the Hills,
> The home of a pioneer.
>
> R. B. H.

---

dren. A daughter, Helen Stevens Hughes, married (1) William C. Burns and (2) Philip Bagwell. She had three children, Candace Stevens Burns, William Robert Burns and John Michael Burns. Mrs. Bagwell lives in Douglas, AZ. A son, William Lewis Hughes, married Stella Marie Platt of a pioneer Rapid City family. They had four children, Elizabeth Helen Hughes (Holderman), James Edward Hughes, Judith Lee Hughes (Cockrell), and Michael George Hughes.

CLEOPATRA MINE ON SQUAW CREEK

FAMILY OF R. B. HUGHES ABOUT 1902

Appendices

Appendix A

DIARY OF RICHARD B. HUGHES[*]
1876-1877

1876 (West Point, Nebraska)
JANUARY, SATURDAY, 1. Around with M. Rochford. Arranged with him to go to Black Hills in April. About home all day...
FRIDAY, 7. Taught. B. Hills fever...
SATURDAY, 22. B.H. Fever raging. Guess if nothing happens will make a "go" of it...
SUNDAY, 30. Went with Bob Hall to see M. Rochford. Arranged with them and Briggs to start on or about Apr. 1st.
FEBRUARY, TUESDAY, 1. Coldest day so far this winter. Taught to six pupils.
FRIDAY, 4. Taught. Wanted to teach five Saturdays, in order to get through by the first of April. Old Lacey won't allow it...
THURSDAY, 10. Taught. Old Lacey refused to allow me to teach a week of Saturdays...
THURSDAY, 17. Taught. Saw Rysong about teaching on Saturdays. He's willing.
FRIDAY, 18. Saw Bolt in morning. Went to Lacey's at noon. H's got to give in about teaching on Saturdays. Taught. Went to Spelling Skule.
MARCH, SUNDAY, 19. Had B.H. meeeting. Didn't amount to much. Mike and I conclude to go *via* Cheyenne. Very stormy. Back to West Pt. Through storm with Jay, Hunlock & Wheeler...
APRIL, SATURDAY, 1. Delivered my pony to Kyler and rec'd $40.00 cash for her...
THURSDAY, 6. Out hunting a little. Shot 4 chickens and one duck. Rec'd a letter from M. Rochford.
MONDAY, 10. Down river with Mr. Zehrung. Shot 5 ducks and 2 chickens, one muskrat and two quails...
THURSDAY, 13. Rec'd a letter from M. Rochford to send down money for gun, as he cannot sell it in Scribner. Will send in morning.
FRIDAY, 14. Sent down to Scribner for gun, but Mike has sold it. Van Fleet says he will be ready to go with us.
SATURDAY, 15. Packing up. Pa says he will be packing up by the 27th of May. Ready for Monday.

---

[*] Entries which have been omitted pertained to small daily occurrences, the weather, visiting neighbors, teaching, or attending social affairs. – A. W. S.

SUNDAY, 16. Easter. Up at O'Sullivans took dinner. Home rest of day. Gahagan down to see me off.
MONDAY, 17. Started for Fremont. Down to Fremont. Have to go to Omaha for tickets. Down to Omaha. Got tickets and back to Fremont. M. Rochford and Wm. Van Fleet with me. Met McGavock at depot.
TUESDAY, 18. Traveling. Passed Kearney, and N. Platte. Fear of pickpockets. Watched up all night.
WEDNESDAY, 19. Got into Sidney at day-light. Stopped at McDonald's. Don't know whether will go on to Cheyenne or not. Mike went to Cheyenne.
THURSDAY, 20. Down with Mr. McD. to Lodge Pole, 25 miles. Stop over night at ranch.
FRIDAY, 21. Got back to Sidney. Looked around. Went fishing and caught nothing. Saw Black Hillers about hauling goods.
SATURDAY, 22. About Sidney all day.
SUNDAY, 23. Got everything ready to start. Will start in the morning.
MONDAY, 24. Started for the Hills. 34 men in the outfit. Camped at Water Hole. Elected Burns Capt'n. Met Black Hills party coming back.
TUESDAY, 25. Camped at noon at Greenwood. At night at Court House Rocks. Went up to see Rocks. Shot jack rabbit with n. gun.
WEDNESDAY, 26. From Court House Rocks to N. Platte Crossing. Stopped. Water high. Can't cross. Laid over.
THURSDAY, 27. Waiting at river. Expect to cross to-morrow.
FRIDAY, 28. Got across river at noon. Started again and camped for night at "Red Willow."
SATURDAY, 29. Away in morning. Got to Snake Creek at noon. Left Snake Creek and made a dry camp.
SUNDAY, 30. Drove til 2 0'clock and camped at Running Water. Rained.
MAY, MONDAY, 1. Moved on to within 8 miles of Agency, where we camped. Stood guard. Heard Indians drumming all night.
TUESDAY, 2. Moved on 12 miles. Passed through Red Cloud Agency.
WEDNESDAY, 3. Traveled on and camped. Left Burn's party, and go on from here with 20 men.
THURSDAY, 4. Reached Horse Creek, 8 miles from Cheyenne River. Camped with a party of returned Black Hillers. They tell a bad story. Nearly shot for an Indian.
FRIDAY, 5. Moved on to Cheyenne River through the rain. Camped. Stood guard.
SATURDAY, 6. From Cheyenne River to mouth of "Buffalo Gap" that dreaded abode of Sioux. Burn's camp ½ mile below.
SUNDAY, 7. Started on thro' "Buffalo Gap," Saw a man that had been killed by Sioux. Traveled entirely through Buffalo Canyon and reached Custer at 11 o'clock. Camped.

APPENDIX—DIARY

MONDAY, 8. Looked around Custer City and found quite a town. News from above good. Man shot by Indians at the edge of town.

TUESDAY, 9. Burns' party in. Made arrangements to go to Deadwood in the morning.

WEDNESDAY, 10. Started for Deadwood. Reached Spring Creek, 2 miles from Hills, where we camped.

THURSDAY, 11. Traveled. Camped early on Spring Creek, and prospected. Saw a nugget worth $38.00.

FRIDAY, 12. Traveled. Camped on Spring Creek.

SATURDAY, 13. Hunted nearly all day. Got lost in hills. Had to travel 12 miles to catch the train. Camped on a small creek 10 miles from Deadwood.

SUNDAY, 14. Traveled. Reached Whitewood. Hunted nearly all day.

MONDAY, 15. Laid around Deadwood. Rained all day. Prospected. Intend to start prospecting in the morning.

TUESDAY, 16. Started for Spearfish. Some of the boys killed a bear and I ate bear for dinner and supper. Camped on top of a mountain peak nearly up among the clouds. Melted snow for coffee.

WEDNESDAY, 17. Traveled all day and camped on Spearfish. Living on wild game. Never had such an appetite in my life.

THURSDAY, 18. Traveled a while. Camped on Potato Creek. Prospected.

FRIDAY, 19. Camped on Potato Creek. Some of the boys took claims.

SATURDAY, 20. Off for camp on Deadwood again. Camped with the rest of the boys on Spearfish. Started with Jim and Red Cloud for home. Got in at sundown.

SUNDAY, 21. Off with Mike and W. Lemon. Prospected all day. Got no good prospects.

MONDAY, 22. . . Down Whitewood. No luck.

TUESDAY, 23. Up Whitewood prospecting.

WEDNESDAY, 24. Prospected a gulch running into Deadwood. Pretty fair prospects. Intend going back in morning.

THURSDAY, 25 through MONDAY, 29. (Prospected. Cold and rainy.)

MAY, TUESDAY, 30. Prospected Over on Spruce Creek.

WEDNESDAY, 31. Prospected "Charley's Gulch." Good prospects.

JUNE, THURSDAY, 1. Snow. All went and prospected the lower gulch. Guess we will work it. Snowed all day. POCKET.

MONDAY, 5. Will and I worked on upper Gulch all day. Got good prospects. Got back in evening and heard that Elkhorn train was in. Met C.F.D.S. "Col. M" in Deadwood. "You shall pack tomorrow."

TUESDAY, 6. Out around with Steve. Met Charley Bender.

WEDNESDAY, 7. Rained all day. Around camp. "Steve" and F. Kettle with us.

THURSDAY, 8. "Steve" and F. Kettle left in morning. Fine weather again.

FRIDAY, 9. Prospected.
SATURDAY, 10. Down to see the printers. Did not do much. Steve came back. Visited *Pioneer.*
MONDAY, 12. Represented lower gulch. Found fair prospects. B. Street came up. Steve came up.
TUESDAY, 13. Street, Will, Rich and I prospected "M.G." Gulch. Good prospects.
WEDNESDAY, 14. Street started back for Custer. Will came back and worked M.G. Gulch. Prospected claims on Whitewood. Will not take it.
THURSDAY, 15. Up at quartz lead.
FRIDAY, 16. Rained. Did not do much. Someone jumped "M.G." Gulch.
SATURDAY, 17. Rained. In tent all day. Read.
SUNDAY, 18. About home. Prospected lower gulch a little with Graham. Arranged to go up toward the head of Spearfish tomorrow.
MONDAY, 19. Started with Graham and Jim Vanderberger to False Bottom. G. lost his gun. All along creek.
TUESDAY, 20. Up False Bottom. Prospected a gulch and over home. Not much of an opinion of False Bottom. False Bottom Stampede.
WEDNESDAY, 21. About camp. Wrote a letter for Graham to *Republican.* Street came up.
THURSDAY, 22. Moved up to "M.G." gulch. Rich and I over to tributary of "False Bottom." Prospected. Found what we believe to be a silver lode.
JUNE, FRIDAY, 23. Took some specimens of quartz to camp. Pronounced good. Back again with "Dick." Worked on lead.
SUNDAY, 25. Hunted in forenoon. Lay around camp. Mike came out with Rich and Wood. . .
THURSDAY, 29. Woods says lead is worth $150,000.00. Hope it may prove so. Rained all day hard. At camp.
FRIDAY, 30. Rained. "Steve" wants me to go on stampede to "Polo." Will go.
JULY 1876, SATURDAY, 1. Over to "Polo" with Steve. Got claim. We prospected. No colors. Back to camp.
SUNDAY, 2. Lay around camp all day.
MONDAY, 3. Worked at Prospect hole in "M.G." Gulch. Got Bed rock. No prospects.
TUESDAY, 4. Went down to Deadwood. Nothing going on. Stayed all night with Sam.
WEDNESDAY, 5. Rocked out some dirt in gulch. Prospects not good.
THURSDAY, 6. About the cabin all day.
FRIDAY, 7. Over to lead with Harry. Stayed all day. Home after dark.
SATURDAY, 8. Around camp all day. Down to Deadwood.
SUNDAY, 9. . . . Got some specimens and wrote a letter and sent home by Mr. Wise, of Scribner.

APPENDIX—DIARY

MONDAY, 10 through FRIDAY, 21. [Short entries "About Camp" and "Worked on ditch."]
SATURDAY, 22. Worked on ditch. Down town in evening. Got two *Republicans* containing my letter and poetry about the "G's." Stayed with Sam.
SUNDAY, 23. Got letter from home.
MONDAY, 24. Went over to "False Bottom."
TUESDAY, 25 through SATURDAY, 29. Worked on ditch.
SUNDAY, 30. Wrote three letters. Down to Deadwood and posted them.
MONDAY, 31. Dug prospect hole in "Ring Tail" gulch.
AUGUST, TUESDAY, 1. Down to Carty's trial.
WEDNESDAY, 2. Worked on ditch. Wild Bill killed.
THURSDAY, 3 through SATURDAY, 5. Worked on ditch.
SUNDAY, 6. Hunted all day. Down to Deadwood in evening.
MONDAY, 7. Worked on ditch. Finished it but water would not run.
TUESDAY, 8. Tinkered around on ditch. Water very low in Deadwood.
WEDNESDAY, 9. Dug out some dirt and fixed up sluice boxes.
THURSDAY, 10. Working around at everything in general. Smallpox in Deadwood.
FRIDAY, 11. Fixed up ditch some.
SATURDAY, 12. Hauled down 7 loads of dirt and sluiced it out. Didn't pay very well. Got $3.55.
SUNDAY, 13. Lay around camp.
MONDAY, 14. Not feeling very well.
TUESDAY, 15. Went after Rich's mules.
WEDNESDAY, 16. Lay around camp.
THURSDAY, 17. Down to 17 and borrowed 2 saddles. Went out hunting with Rich Wood and Ferdinand. Camped on the head of Whitewood. Very pretty country.
FRIDAY, 18. Moved camp over on to head of Rapid Creek. Very little game. Out of grub. Shot squirrels for supper.
SUNDAY, 20. Up early and out. Shot my first deer a white-tail. Have got nearly a load.
MONDAY, 21. Hunted. Ferdinand and I started in. Got off the trail in storm and had to camp in the woods. Rained all night.
AUGUST, TUESDAY, 22. Up and got into camp early. Having lived on "venison straight" for five days I "went for" the bread. Returned the saddles to Will Schafer. Not very well. 5 men killed by Indians two miles from town.
WEDNESDAY, 23. Back to camp. Got there at 3 o'clock. Boys glad to see bread coming. Have got 8 deer already.
THURSDAY, 24. Big Frost. Out in the morning. Shot a black-tail. Hunted all day. Wood and I had a "serious time" packing the deer into camp.

FRIDAY, 25. Indian signs. All started into town after catching "old Rapid." Night caught us at the herd ranche but we kept on and reached camp at 10 o'clock, passing over the worst trail I ever saw.
SATURDAY, 26. My feet very sore. Lay around camp all day. Loaded shells.
SUNDAY, 27. Boys all left. Went down to Deadwood to see about a job in printing office. Told to call on Tuesday.
AUGUST, MONDAY 28. About camp all day and "represented."
TUESDAY, 29. Down to Deadwood and met "Joe" on the road coming up after me. Went to work in printing office. Up to camp in evening.
WEDNESDAY, 30. Worked in office. Boys not in yet.
THURSDAY, 31. Worked at job-work. Boys not back yet.
SEPTEMBER, FRIDAY, 1. Worked in office. Don't know what can be keeping the boys.
SATURDAY, 2. Tom Carr. Worked in office. Got $5.00 from Merrick. He offered me $15.00 per week if I'll stay until spring. Boys not in yet. 2 men caved under a shaft.
SUNDAY, 3. Down and saw a man taken out of a shaft. Lay around camp. Bought a hat. Wonder what keeps the boys.
MONDAY, 4. Agree to work for Mr. M. until spring at $15.00 per week. Worked in office. Boys got in from hunt.
TUESDAY, 5. Worked in office. Boys moved down. Wood, Rich and Ferdinand to leave in morning for the States. Danced schottische with Rich before we went to bed.
WEDNESDAY, 6 through SATURDAY, 9. Worked in office. . .
SUNDAY, 10. About town all day.
MONDAY, 11. News in that Crook is only 20 miles out and has whipped the Indians. Worked in office.
MONDAY, 18 through SATURDAY, 23. Worked in office.
SUNDAY, 24. About the house all day.
MONDAY, 25. Worked in office. Mike went to Bear Butte prospecting.
TUESDAY, 26 through SATURDAY, 30. Worked in office.
OCTOBER, SUNDAY, 1. Lay around the house. Mike got in from Bear Butte. Thinks he has "struck it."
MONDAY, 2 through TUESDAY, 10. Worked in office. Sick. Lay around camp.
THURSDAY, 12. Feeling better. Boys in from Bare Butte. Say prospects are good.
FRIDAY, 13. Helped Mike on fireplace. . .
SUNDAY, 15. Went down to office. Helped get the paper up.
MONDAY, 16. Down to office. Merrick would like me to go to work again. Recd. $15.00 from M.
TUESDAY, 17. M. sent up for me. Went with Mike up to claims.
WEDNESDAY, 18. Went to work in office again at $3.00 per day. . .
SUNDAY, 22. Lay around cabin.

APPENDIX—DIARY

MONDAY, 23. Around town. Recd. $10.00 from M.
OCTOBER, TUESDAY, 24. Around camp.
WEDNESDAY, 25. At work. Worked in forenoon. Boys from West Point got in. Down to their camp in evening. Mike got in. Boys stopped all night.
THURSDAY, 26 through SATURDAY, 28. Worked in office.
SUNDAY, 29. Lay around camp.
MONDAY, 30. Around prospecting.
TUESDAY, 31. Lay around camp.
NOVEMBER, WEDNESDAY, 1. Worked in office.
THURSDAY, 2. In office.
FRIDAY, 3. In office. Mike and Abe started for the "Wolf Mountain stampede."
SATURDAY, 4. No paper in so I did not work. Lay around camp.
SUNDAY, 5. About cabin all day. J. McKeegan and T. Deegan in.
MONDAY, 6. Tomorrow is election day. People generally don't think there's much chance for Tilden. Lay around camp. (Tilden Hayes.)
TUESDAY, 7. Down town in forenoon. Out to Bare Butte in afternoon, with Tom, Bill, Joe, McK, and Joe McDonald. Camped 1 mile below Bare Butte Ranche.
WEDNESDAY, 8. Down to where Cumming Country boys are camped. Worked with Tom on "Mountain Tiger" lode.
THURSDAY, 9. Up with Tom and staked the "Mountain Tiger." Started with Joe McDonald and walked into town. Rec'd 2 letters, and a paper from West Point.
FRIDAY, 10. Worked in office. Joe off on stampede. Worked until 11 at night.
SATURDAY, 11. Worked in office til 11 at night.
SUNDAY, 12. Worked in office till 1 o'clock. Lay about camp. Went to Varieties in the evening.
MONDAY, 13. Went hunting with "Andy" Farrel over to False Bottom. Got nothing. Back after night.
TUESDAY, 14. Worked in forenoon. Lay around in afternoon.
WEDNESDAY, 15. Cut my thumb so could not work.
THURSDAY, 16 through THURSDAY 30. (Worked in office.)
DECEMBER, FRIDAY, 1. Worked in office. Extra 2 ½.
SATURDAY, 2. Worked in office Extra 5 hours.
SUNDAY, 3. Lay around camp.
MONDAY, 4. Got a letter from Annie [his sister]. Staid around camp.
TUESDAY, 5. Hunting with "Ab." All day. Got nothing.
WEDNESDAY, 6. Didn't work. Went up the gulch.
THURSDAY, 7 through SATURDAY, 9. Worked in office.
SUNDAY, 10. Got ready to go to Bare Butte in morning.
MONDAY, 11. Went over to BB with Mike. Got there at dark. Had dispute with 5 Englishmen.

TUESDAY, 12. Looked around leads. Tim [Deegan] and Andy [Farrell] over.

WEDNESDAY, 13. Back to Deadwood. Stopped for "biscuits" at toll gate.

THURSDAY, 14. Didn't go to work till afternoon.

FRIDAY, 15. – SATURDAY, 16. Worked in office.

SUNDAY, 17. Intended to go out with Andy and Tim, but weather bad, so lay around home all day. Snowed 15 inches.

MONDAY, 18. Andy came at 10 o'clock and wanted Mike and me to go with Tim. Started expecting to find Tim on Blacktail. But he was gone. Walked over to Spearfish and overtook Tim, Charley, and Bill Camp.

TUESDAY, 19. Traveled on and camped on a little creek three miles from Redwater. Snowing all night.

WEDNESDAY, 20. Crossed Redwater. Traveled on and camped in a canon. No water. Used snow to make coffee. Snowed all night.

THURSDAY, 21. Traveled on. Took dinner at Sulphur springs. Reached camping ground at Oak Spring away after night. Deep snow. Snowed on us all night.

FRIDAY, 22. Hunted all day through snow and very cold weather. Saw about 5 or six deer. Got nothing. Snowing. Snow three feet deep.

SATURDAY, 23. Hunted all day. Very cold. Saw 30 or 40 deer but got nothing. Snowed all night.

SUNDAY, 24. Hunted all day. Very cold. Christmas eve. I am thinking of home. Snowing. Mercury down to 35° below.

MONDAY, 25. Christmas. No venison. Had biscuits straight!! Suppose folks at home are thinking how I am spending Christmas. Don't suppose they think I am out in the Bear Lodge. Mike and Bill got a deer apiece at dark. Stayed up til 1 o'clock at night to have a Christmas roast. Had it too.

TUESDAY, 26. Hunted a little. Got nothin. Very cold weather. Went and helped carry in rest of deer. One of Charley's oxen died. Snow about 3 ft. deep.

WEDNESDAY, 27. Pulled out from "Oak Spring" after Charley shot his last ox "to save its life." Reached "Sulphur springs" and stopped to let the cattle eat. Saw a party of Indians or hunters off to the left, going to Bear Lodge. Moved on and made a dry camp in Dry Creek. Charley very much afraid of Indians. Stood guard until 12 o'clock and slept with his boots on til morning.

THURSDAY, 28, 1876. Moved on and camped at head of "Elk Canon." Met party of hunters going to Bear Lodge.

FRIDAY, 29. "Billy" and I went down canon. Struck an elk and got shots at him but did not get him. Crossed Redwater and camped for dinner. Moved on and made a dry camp at about 12 o'clock. Told us that Indians run off stock from Spearfish.

APPENDIX—DIARY

SATURDAY, DEC. 30, 1876. Nothing to eat since yesterday at noon. "Billy" and I started on ahead nearly played out. Had to lie down at about every 300 yds. Till we reached ranch at the foot of "Crow Canon." Got a biscuit apiece and went on to Spearfish. Got something to eat and drink for ourselves and the boys and had them ready when they got in. Went on, intending to camp at "Oak Draw" but snow was drifting bad and we got off on the Centennial road. Tramped on til 12 or 1 o'clock and got to lie on a cabin floor till morning.

SUNDAY, DEC. 31. Started at daylight on empty stomachs and walked into Deadwood, about 8 miles. Nearly worn out. Ate something. Rec'd $5.00 from Merrick. Went up to Blacktail to meet boys but they did not get in. Guess they are on the other road. Met Steve at Charley Benders. He run out as soon as I entered.

MONDAY, JAN. 1. 1877. "Boys," – Mike and Tim got in at about 2 o'clock. Got up and got supper for them. They had to leave all the things on the road. Find that the Indians were close after us after all. The party we met at Bear Lodge were run 30 miles. Lost all their game. We lost all our cattle.

JANUARY, 2. Intended to go out to Centennial for guns &c but waited till too late. Lay about cabin.

WEDNESDAY, JAN. 3, 1877. Worked in office. Bill went to Centennial and brought in the things.

THURSDAY, 4th. Worked in office. Not well all night.

FRIDAY, 5th. Did not go to work in forenoon. Was not well. Worked in afternoon and night.

SATURDAY, 6th, '77. Worked in office till 11 at night. Got paper up. Gardner wants claims.

SUNDAY, 7th. Lay about cabin. Went up to the "boys" cabin in the evening. Burns wants two lower claims.

JANUARY, MONDAY, 8th, 1877. Done some washing. Guess won't sell to Gardner.

TUESDAY 9. Up to Burns' and talked trade to him.

WEDNESDAY, 10th through SATURDAY, 13. Lay around. Worked in office.

SUNDAY, 14. About cabin. MONDAY 15. About cabin.

TUESDAY, 16. Up the gulch and saw-pit.

WED. 17th. Over to Lead City. Dined at Vans.

THURS. 18 through SAT. 20. Worked in office.

SUN. 21st. About cabin.

MONDAY, 22nd. Went with Mike to Saw-pit, and made contract with Taylor, Hornley and Pinney to drain Hidden Treasure claims.

TUESDAY 23rd and WEDNES. 24th. Lay around camp.

THURSDAY 25th through SAT. 27. Worked in office.

SUN. 28th. Lay around camp.

MON. 29th through WED. FEB. 7th. Tanning some deer hides. Working in office.
SUN. 11th. Fixed some buckskin. Down to Sam's in evening.
MONDAY, FEB. 12 through SAT 17. In office.
SUN. FEB. 18. Down to Sam's.
MON. 19. Up the gulch to claims.
TUES. 20. Simonton. Up to the head of Iron Creek, thence to Sand Creek, thence to Red Water, following this to the head. Bald Mountain to the right. Follow the divide to the right up 18 or so miles; cross the divide striking one of 3 gulches which leads into the main gulch.

NOTICE

We, the undersigned claim 1500 feet on this lode, lead or ledge, running (750) seven hundred and fifty feet in an easterly direction and (750) seven hundred and fifty feet in a westerly direction and 150 feet on each side for milling purposes.
M. D. Rochford, Wm. Van Fleet, James Vanderburger
This lode shall be know as the Mountain Tiger!

Two letters by R. B. Hughes to the Editor of *West Point* (NE) *Republican* and published in that paper.

Deadwood City, Black Hills June 1, 1876
Ed *Republican:* Knowing that many of your readers are anxiously looking for news from the Black Hills, I take the present opportunity of giving them, through the columns of the *Republican,* the facts, as nearly as possible, concerning this much-talked-of land of gold.

We left West Point on the morning of the 17th of April, and arrived in Sidney on the morning of the 19th, where we were hospitably entertained by Mr. McDonald, formerly of West Point, during the time we stopped in town. Here we concluded to outfit, and the morning of the 24th of the same month found us fairly on the road to Custar City via Red Cloud Agency.

Along the roads we passed many objects of interest. Among those most worthy of note are the famous "Court House Rocks," about 30 miles out.

As seen from a distance of 15 miles, they reminded one forcibly of the old castles of feudal times with their towers and battlements. Here we found that appearances are certainly deceitful, for at this distance we would imagine them to be but about two miles away, at most, while one of our party contended that they were no more than one mile distant, and wished to push on and camp for dinner at their base. It was then 11 o'clock in the forenoon. By traveling steadily we reached Pumpkin Creek that evening at 6 o'clock; and when the sun was about a half hour high, two others and myself started to walk to the rocks, supposing them to be at the most 600 yards distant. Here we were again deceived, for it was only after traveling until after dusk that we reached their base, and it was 11 o'clock at night before we again reached camp. The next morning we took a view of the rocks by sunrise, and it amply repaid us for our trouble. We found them to consist of solid sandstone, with here and there a layer of cement-like whiteness through it. The winds and rain of centuries beating upon it have carved and chiseled it into many fantastic shapes. Climbing the rocks, we found the names of hundreds of travelers carved in the sandstone, and we added ours to the list. The large rocks are perhaps 350 feet in height, and three sides of the larger one are nearly perpendicular. The distance around the base of this rock is perhaps a half mile.

Leaving Court House Rocks behind us, we reached North Platte River crossing at noon. Here we were delayed two days by high water. We crossed on the 28th, and on the 2nd day of May we reached Red Cloud Agency. Here we were reinforced, so that on leaving our party numbered 80 men. On May 4th, owing to some misunderstanding, our party divided, and we pushed on with 19 men, crossed the Cheyenne River on the 6th, and camped at the mouth of "Buffalo Gap." From this point to Custar City is considered the most dangerous part of the road. On the morning of the 8th we started early, and reached Custar City at 11 o'clock that night. We passed over the whole route without seeing a hostile Indian. All along the road we met stampeded parties en-route for the States. We were told by them that the Black Hills excitement was the greatest fraud ever perpetrated upon the people, and that it was impossible to travel through the Black Hills with any degree of safety on account of the Indians. Some of those parties, we afterward learned, had arrived in Custar one day and left for the States the next, so that their Black Hills experience did not amount to much.

CUSTAR

On looking about on the morning of the 9th, we found curiosities in the midst of a town consisting of about 500 houses, situated in a natural park, and containing 800 to 1000 souls. A great number of the property holders were out north prospecting, which accounted for the small population in town. Some mining is now being done on French Creek both above and below town. Some little attention is being paid to farming and grading in the neighborhood of Custar, but the country is not so well adapted to agricultural pursuits, as we had been led to believe, before we came to the Hills.

At Custar we heard reports of the great wealth of the northern part of the Hills, and on Wednesday, May 10th, we found ourselves again on the road, bound for Deadwood. We examined the creeks and gulches along the route, and found very fair prospects; especially on Spring Creek and in Parmer's Gulch. The latter is a gulch heading at the base of Harney's Peak. I saw a nugget worth $38 taken out of the diggings in this gulch while we stopped here. Claims along this gulch pay $10 to $15 per day per man. Leaving here, we arrived at Deadwood on the 4 [14]th. Here we find ourselves in the heart of the mining country. On all sides we see the work going on. We are surrounded by a perfect network of ditches, drains and flumes, and the satisfied looks of the miners show that they are all well paid for their work. Whitewood, and its tributary, Deadwood, are probably the best paying creeks yet discovered in the Hills. Claims here on Deadwood are paying from $100 to as high as $2000 (two thousand) per day. Wages paid here are $4 to $5.50 per day, and men are plenty at that. New discoveries are being made further on, and prospecting parties are leaving every day. Some good diggings are found on Iron, Potato, Bear and Sound Creeks, and those are being rapidly opened up.

A large party left for the Powder River, and the Big Horn country, about three weeks ago, and I will report to you when they return what prospects they find. Another party is fitting up to start to the Big Horn on the first of July.

We have now been in the Hills a month, and have found that there is gold here. We have also found that it takes work to get it. We have been duly laughed at by "old residents," and have come to almost look upon ourselves as experienced miners. We think ourselves privileged to stand with our hands in our pockets and laugh at awkward attempts of those unhappy individuals known as "tenderfeet." Up to last Monday we had met no acquaintances in the Hills, but on coming into town on that evening, we learned that a train from the Elkhorn had arrived, and upon entering the "bank" I saw a form and face which struck me as being familiar, although upon the latter "the beard had been growin'" for many a day" and upon closer scouting, I recognized C. G. D. Stevenson, of West Point. I walked up to him, and laying my hand on his shoulder, said, "You shall pack tomorrow." A heartier greeting I have never had, and we adjourned to camp, where we sat by the fire until morning, talking of things and people of West Point, and of the Mulligan guards in particular, and wished we might have a meeting here as we had it at Headquarters in West Point. "Celso" remained with us until this morning, when he left for Custar. He likes the Hills very much, and is determined to try his fortunes here for the summer at least.

And now a few words about the country in general: That there is gold here in paying quantities is a fact closely demonstrated. Claims on Deadwood that were opened early in the spring have already a large amount of gold, and new claims are being opened every day on streams lately discovered. Miners of experience say that not one tittle of the wealth of the country has been developed. Rich quartz leads have been discovered and are being opened up as fast as circumstances will permit. A scarcity of water has interfered with mining on French Creek for the past two weeks, but the miners are contriving ways and means to get the water into the diggings. The depth of bed-rock from the surface on Spring Creek has retarded the development of the mines on that stream, but as rich prospects are being continually found there, that country will undoubtedly be under the pick and shovel before fall. The claims now opened there are paying well. Plenty of water and a shallow bed-rock, present facilities for the opening of the mines this far north, that the miners quickly appreciate, consequently Deadwood is the best developed in the Hills.

The timber throughout is very fine, and good lumber can be bought at $35 to $40 per M.

Such game as bear, deer and elk is plenty. Trains loaded with provisions arrive every day, so that prices are coming down, and flour and bacon can soon be bought at very reasonable rates.

The Indians are quiet, except in the Red Canyon on the Cheyenne route, where they trouble freighters considerably.

Custar will soon become a military post and then Uncle Sam will protect people passing in and out.

Will write again when the Big Horn party comes in.

Yours truly, Barney.

Deadwood, July 23, 1876
Ed *Republican:* Since writing my communication of June 1 to the *Republican,* surprising changes have been going on throughout this country. Custar City is no longer the metropolis of the Black Hills, but has given place to towns of later birth. The growing popularity of the Ft. Pierre route from the Missouri River to the Hills has cut off a great deal of travel from Custar, and the new towns have sprung up as if by magic in this portion of the Hills. Deadwood City, at the mouth of Deadwood creek, has a present population of perhaps 2,500 souls and many new comers arrive every day. Building is going on continually, and every business house is crowded. The class of buildings is very good. Deadwood is at present the largest and most populous town in the Hills, and will probably remain so for some time.

On Whitewood creek several towns have sprung up in the last two months. Of these, Centennial and Montana are rapidly building up. Crook City, on the Ft. Pierre route, near the foot Hills, is growing fast, and promises to become a large town. Gayville, two miles above Deadwood

Gulch, is a thriving village, containing about six hundred inhabitants, and presents a very lively appearance.

A gambling house in Gayville was the scene of a shocking murder on the night of the 19th inst. The victim was a man named Hinch, formerly a resident of Pioche, Nevada, where he left a wife and family. Hinch had been engaged in gambling with two men named McCarty and in the course of the game a dispute arose. Hinch had won some money from the others, and one of them demanded its return. H. refused to return the money, but the quarrel was finally amicably settled as everybody supposed. About 12 o'clock that night, Hinch was sleeping on a table in the saloon, when the McCartys entered, and waking him asked him to drink. He walked with them to the bar, when one of them drawing a knife plunged it into his back, while the other made incision into his abdomen, almost disemboweling him. The murderers then mounted their horses and rode off. Hinch lived until 9 o'clock next morning. A party started in pursuit of the murderers and traced them out by Crook City toward Ft. Pierre. It is supposed that if caught, the McCartys will not get a jury trial.

New Quartz leads are being continually discovered, and returns coming in from specimens assayed, show some of them to be very rich. It is believed that mills will be brought in this fall, when the ore can be thoroughly tested.

Claims on Deadwood, Gold Run, Black Tail and Bob Tail still continue to pay well, and those who pretend to know say that times will undoubtedly be better here next year than the present. The champion claim on Deadwood is No. 16 below discovery, out of which $3,000 was taken in a run of fifteen hours.

The Big Horn party, on their return, report no paying digging found, but indications favorable. They could not prospect thoroughly on account of high water, and scarcity of provisions. They left 36 of their men in the mountains, and we have since heard they have joined Crook's command for protection.

Bad reports reach us from the Bighorn country, and we understand that Sitting Bull contemplates putting the whites on a reservation.

Will write when anything of interest transpires.

Yours truly,   Barney

April, Friday, 21. 1876.
Got back to Sidney.
Looked around.
Went fishing & caught nothing.
Saw Black Hillers about hauling goods.

Saturday, 22
About Sidney all day

Sunday, 23
Got everything ready to start. Will start in the morning

April, Monday, 24. 1876.
Started for the Hills 34 men in the outfit. Camped at Water Hole. Elected Burns Capt'n. Met Black Hills party coming back.

Tuesday, 25
Camped at noon at Greenwood. At night at Court House Rocks. Went up to see Rocks. Shot Jack rabbit with'n Run

Wednesday, 26
From Court House Rocks to N Platte Crossing. Stopped Water high. Capt Cross Laid over a d.

April, Thursday, 27. 1876.
Waiting at river. Cap'd to cross to-morrow.

Friday, 28
Got across river at noon. Started again, & camped for night at "Red Willow".

Saturday, 29
Away in morning. Got to Snake Creek at noon. Left Snake creek, n made a dry camp

April, Sunday, 30. 1876.
Drove till 9 o'clock & camped with some Black Hillers, at Running Water. Rained

May, Monday, 1
Moved on to within 8 miles of Agency, where we camp. Stood guard. Heard Indians drumming all night.

Tuesday, 2
y 12 m moved on 12 miles. Passed through Red Cloud Agency

AUGUST, MONDAY, 7. 1876.

Worked on ditch
Finished it but water
would not run.

TUESDAY, 8

Tinkered around on ditch
Water very low in Dead-
wood

WEDNESDAY, 9

Dug out some dirt &
fixed up sluice boxes.

AUGUST, THURSDAY, 10. 1876.

Working around at
everything in general
Smallpox in Deadwood

FRIDAY, 11

Fixed up ditch some

SATURDAY, 12

Hauled down loads of
dirt & sluiced it out
Didn't pay very well
Got $3.55

AUGUST, FRIDAY, 25. 1876.

Indian signs
All started into town
after watching. "Old Rapid"
night caught us at the
ferd ranche but we
kept on & reached camp
at 11 o'clock, passing over
the worst trail I ever saw

SATURDAY, 26

My feet very sore. Lay around
camp all day. Loaded shell
was brought in from
Spearfish dead, killed
by Indians

SUNDAY, 27

Boys all left. Went down
to Deadwood & see about
a job in printing office
"Voto" to call on Tues-
day.

AUGUST, MONDAY, 28. 1876.

About camp all day
& represented.

TUESDAY, 29

Down to Deadwood
& met "Joe" on the road
coming up after me
Went to work in print-
ing office.
Left camp in evening

WEDNESDAY, 30

Worked in office
Boys not in yet.

Appendix B

SAM TULL

Sam Tull died a few years ago, well along toward his eighty-fourth year, surrounded by the love and affection of all who knew him. His partners in the mine remained in the Hills a short time, when they, too, retired and settled down in their old Kansas homes.

It was my good fortune to meet Tull on two occasions after he left the Hills in '77. The first was thirty years later, when he visited my family and myself at our home in Spearfish. He had come back to travel over some of his old trails. Of the party that had entered the Hills with him in the spring of '76, there were left only two – Jim Sheppard, of Slate Springs, and myself.

In memory of old times we went up to our summer home on Spearfish Canyon, and there spent one of the most delightful weeks of my life in camp. It gave me deep pleasure to see the old man take my two boys into his affections as he had taken me when we first met on the Sidney trail. I had in response to the eager inquiries of youth told them of the interesting occurrences of the early days, and while I am confident they never doubted, it seemed a satisfaction to them to have them repeated or corroborated by my old captain. As for Tull, he gave himself up to the pleasures and duties of camp life with all the zest of a boy. Always he had been a fine cook, and he insisted on acting in this capacity during his visit.

He taught the boys many of the simple things that make such a life delightful, and the experiences of that week and the kindly manner in which the lessons were imparted, they never can forget. When the time came for Sam to go, all were loath to say farewell, for it seemed not probable that we should meet again.

The Burden (Kansas) *Times* of July 11, 1907, carried the following item from *The Spearfish* (South Dakota) *Enterprise:*

> R. B. Hughes was pleasantly surprised last evening by a visit from an old and valued friend, in the person of Captain Sam Tull, of Burden, Kansas. Mr. Tull was captain of a company of which Mr. Hughes and M. D. Rochford were members, and which arrived in Deadwood gulch on the twelfth of May, 1876. From that time until the fall of 1879 he prospected over the Northern Hills, hunting occasionally for game for the Deadwood market. He was fortunate enough to locate the Sam's mine on Bobtail Gulch, at the present site of Terraville. This property he sold for a good stake, returning to southern Kansas, where he has since made his home,

though in the meantime he had done some mining in Colorado, and other parts of the west. When it is considered that Captain Tull is a veteran of the Civil War and a pioneer of half a dozen western states, one can but wonder that his seventy-two years sit so lightly upon his shoulders. His form is erect, his eye bright and he still enjoys a hunting trip as of yore, and takes an extended outing every year. It is a great pleasure to him to talk of the early days of the Hills, of the friends and companions of the camp fire, the nights in the old Spearfish stockade and all the scenes and incidents that lent charm to the pioneer's existence. Friends of Captain Tull will be glad to know that he is prosperous and able to enjoy a green old age in plenty of comfort. He will be the guest of Mr. and Mrs. Hughes while in the city.

Fate had, however, in store for me another meeting with my old captain a short time before his death. On my way to the Gulf Coast to spend the winter in 1918, accompanied by my wife, I stopped for a time at Excelsior Springs, Missouri. From that point I wrote to Tull, telling him that if possible I hoped to make a detour on our way north in the spring to pay him a visit. Realizing that his vitality was fast weakening, and afraid that if he waited for spring we never might meet, he summoned a mutual Black Hills friend, John Stout, from his home in a neighboring county, and together they surprised me by a visit at the Springs.

Between Stout and Sam there was a remarkably strong bond of affection. He was a veteran of the Civil War on the Confederate side, but the fact that he and Tull had stood in opposing ranks during the war, never for an instant affected their friendship and esteem. Stout had been with us in the Hills from the first, and frequently we had been companions on hunting and prospecting expeditions, and a more congenial friend or partner one could not wish. This was our first meeting since the days of our pioneering, and that he could accompany Sam on his visit was a great pleasure. Sam was cheerful, and his eyes held the same kindly light as of yore, as he said, "When I got your letter I thought John and I shouldn't take any chances on what might happen before spring; I was determined to see 'my boy' once more, now that he was within my reach, and so here we are."

While the visit gave us great pleasure, it was of necessity shortened by Sam's weakened condition, and saddened by the knowledge that his end must be close at hand, but it was evident that he would meet death with the same spirit of equanimity that he had summoned in meeting the various trials of life. A few months later, I received a letter from Stout telling me that our old friend had passed from earth calmly and peacefully. – [HUGHES].

Appendix C

SIDNEY, NEBRASKA TO HARNEY'S PEAK, 1875[*]

Sidney to Springs – plenty of wood, water and grass, 14 miles. Springs to Omaha Creek, plenty of wood, water and grass, 14 miles. Omaha Creek to North Platte River, driftwood, water and grass, 14 miles. North Platte River to Willow Springs, no wood, water and grass, 11 miles. Willow Springs to Snake Creek, no wood, water and grass, 15 miles. Snake Creek to Running Water, very little wood, water and grass, 20 miles. Running Water to Prairie Springs, very little wood, water and grass, 10 miles. Prairie Springs to Spotted Tail Agency and Camp Sheridan, wood and water, but no grass, 15 miles. Spotted Tail Agency to White River, wood, water and grass, 10 miles; White River to Thin Butte Creek, wood, water and grass, 7 miles; Thin Butte Creek to Springs and creek, wood, water and grass 12 miles; Springs and creek to Cheyenne River, foot of Black Hills, wood and best of grass, 20 miles; Cheyenne River to Harney's Peak, or Custer's Park, 20 miles. From Sidney to Harney's Peak, 202 miles. The nearest and most practicable route from the railroad.

---

[*] The *Rocky Mountain News,* May 1, 1875.

FROM CUSTER CITY TO SIDNEY VIA HOMAN'S CUT-OFF

In 1876, Both's Hotel at Custer Ave., between 6th and 7th Streets, Custer City, Dakota Territory, published a card for its patrons which gave the mileages on the route from Custer City to Sidney, Nebraska, via Homan's Cut-Off as follows:

Point of Rocks	10	
Cheyenne River	17	27
Junction	16	43
Big Cottonwood	6	49
Little Cottonwood	8	57
Red Cloud Agency	6	63
White Clay Creek	6	69
Running Water	10	79
Pott's Ranche	14	93
Snake River	12	105
Red Willow	12	117
Platte River Bridge	10	127
Court House Rock	8	135
Greenwood	8	143
Water Hole Ranche	12	155
Sidney	12	167

Sidney Stage Office   One Door West of Cheyenne Stage and Telegraph Office.

Appendix D

THE MONTANA MEN IN THE HILLS

In 1877, immediately upon completion of the cession of the Hills by the Indians, Seth Bullock – who had come in from Montana – was appointed sheriff by the governor of the territory of Lawrence County, then just organized. He later opened up and operated a large ranch under irrigation in the Belle Fourche Valley, where he did much to call attention of the country to the great value of alfalfa as a forage crop. In later years he became a friend of Theodore Roosevelt, by whom he was frequently entertained at the White House after Roosevelt became President, and at whose hands he received two important appointments, first as Forest Supervisor, and later as United States Marshal for South Dakota. It is well known that at the time these appointments were made the President offered as alternatives the governorship of Alaska and the commissionership of the General Land Office, but such was Seth's love for his Black Hills home that he did not desire a position that would require him to live elsewhere. When the Spanish-American war broke out Bullock organized a company of his friends, called the Black Hills Rough Riders; was commissioned captain; and was stationed in the South where, much to his disgust and that of his men, the company was kept until the trouble was over, without an opportunity to go either to Cuba or Manila. To the duties of Forest Supervisor and those of Marshal he brought the energy and strong common sense that characterized him, and while in the forest service was not such an idealist as his superior officer, Gifford Pinchot. He was familiar with local conditions, and not expecting impossibilities from his rangers, was able to get efficient service; as he did from his deputies when Marshal. He was a man who loved his friends – and did not love his enemies. That he fully reciprocated the affection of Roosevelt was certain; and it was due to his efforts that one of the lofty elevations of the Hills bears the name of Mount Roosevelt; and that a monument has been erected upon it in memory of the late President, who preceded Seth to the grave by only a few years.

One day when Seth was paying a visit to the President in Washington, Roosevelt turned toward him while they were taking a stroll in one of the parks, and in the well-known impulsive Rooseveltian manner said, "Seth, I'd like to have you down here with me in Washington. How would the commissionership of the General Land Office or of Indian Affairs suit you?"

Those who knew Theodore Roosevelt will realize how well he relished Seth's answer. "Mr. President," he said, "there is just one position in Washington that I would accept, and you are filling that in a perfectly satisfactory manner."

Bullock, known ever after the Spanish war as "Captain," possessed a fund of dry humor that made him a delightful companion, and many anecdotes are told of him by his friends. While acting as Forest Supervisor, Seth had an experience with one of his rangers which he enjoyed narrating. This particular ranger had not been selected because of possession of a college degree, but because of an intimate knowledge of the country, its timber resources, and general fitness to get over the trails quickly in case of the emergencies caused by forest fires. It was one of his duties to assist in adjusting differences between settlers that sometimes arose over the location of line fences. It fell to his lot to intervene in a case in which the two parties had become bitter enemies. Neighbors of the two had made many complaints to the supervisor's office, setting forth that unless the matters were adjusted serious results might be expected; such complaints were called to the attention of the ranger by letters from the Supervisor instructing him to investigate, and make a report. To the first and second letters no response was made, and as complaints continued to come to the office, Seth wrote a third letter couched in the most peremptory language, ordering the ranger to send in a report at once, on pain of dismissal from the service, should he neglect to do so. This brought a letter from the ranger, in which he apologized for failure to reply to the former communications, but in extenuation submitted that it was because of his expectation that he would be able before this to report the settlement of the affair without necessity of official interference, as "both parties to the dispute are carrying guns, and one will surely kill the other if allowed to settle it between themselves."

Among the men from Montana who had also been pioneers in California and Idaho was Bart Henderson. He had also spent some years in the various mining districts of British Columbia, and was a member of the first prospecting party to enter the Boise Basin. During a lifetime spent almost wholly on the frontiers of civilization he had taken part in many interesting events well worthy of appearing in printed history. He had hunted Indians; had hunted with them and been hunted by them. He had penetrated to remote districts in his search for placers, and when he chose to tell of his varied experiences he never failed of having interested listeners. It is not to be wondered at if, stimulated by urgent and credulous hearers, an old timer would on occasion "draw the long bow," and thus acquire a reputation for an active imagination rather than for strict adherence to facts. Some of Bart's tales of adventure were of a character to tax the credulity of the average hearer, and thus it came to be believed that he dealt largely in fiction.

APPENDIX—MONTANA MEN

How Bart once confounded his unbelieving partners is told thus: He, with several others, had located some salt springs on the west foothills of the Hills, where they put in a system of evaporating pans and for a time produced salt for market. One of the duties that devolved upon Bart was to keep the camp supplied with meat, which he was well qualified to do, as he was a splendid hunter. On his return from a hunt one day he said to his companions, "Boys, I saw a deer today as white as snow."

"Sure," said one of his partners. "You said it was as white as snow."

"Yes," chipped in another, "that's the kind of deer they have in these parts."

A third said, "Of course, we know you saw a deer as white as snow. You might tell that to people who don't know you and they might think it was a mistake; but we know you, and we know that what you say goes, even to a white deer."

Thus they chaffed Bart, and kept it up until it became tiresome. Merely muttering, "I'll show you smart Alecks," he prepared some grub, took his packhorse, rifle and blankets and struck off into the woods. It was evening of the second day before he returned to camp, and loaded on his pony was a deer. And it was white as snow, as could be attested by many people who saw it, for the hide was mounted by Doc. Ammerman of Rochford, and the rare specimen stood for a year or more in the lobby of the old American House in Rapid City, until taken by Frank Noble to his home in Boston.

Three of the Montanians who have been named herein were the Argue brothers – John and George – and Con Stapleton; the last named being made the first marshal of Deadwood upon the establishment of a provisional government. Those three men, some years before coming to the Hills, had taken part in an Indian fight a short distance north of the International Boundary, that threatened for a time to involve our government in difficulties with that of the British possessions.

John Belding was a well-known Montanian, friend and deputy of Bullock during the latter's term as United States Marshal; but older than Bullock by several years. His time on the frontier dated back to the days of Jim Bridger – with whom he was well acquainted, and of whom he could tell many interesting stories. Of all the men who had a reputation for the telling of extravagant yarns Bridger easily was chief. Yet, as Belding remarked, every story had a foundation in fact. His sense of direction and memory of remote places once visited were the most remarkable attributes of this remarkable frontiersman. Belding told of one occasion when Bridger was guiding a train guarded by a military escort through a stretch of very dry country. The party had traveled far without water, and teams and men were suffering. Bridger promised the commander that within a certain number of miles he would lead them to a spring, though he had been in that vicinity only once, and that many years before. Finally the thirst of the outfit became almost unendurable. It was thought the distance to the water estimated by the guide had been traversed, and yet no water had been seen. Questioned as to whether he might not have lost his reckoning, Bridger replied, "When we reach that divide just ahead if you look off a half mile to the left you will see a ravine and in it a single cottonwood tree; twenty feet from the foot of that tree is water."

Cheered by the confident prediction of the old guide the outfit hurried on, and when the top of the divide was reached all eyes turned anxiously in the direction he had indicated. Here was bitter disappointment. There was a small ravine, but neither tree nor shrub in sight. Clearly, for once in his life the memory of the old man was at fault. But, remarkable as it seemed, he was entirely cheerful under the reproachful glances of his companions. Merely saying, "Come," he led the way into the ravine, proceeded a distance of a half mile, and told the commander to have a hole dug at a spot indicated. Water was found in abundance within a few feet of the surface. The remains of the cottonwood tree, too, were found where the tree had blown down and had been partially destroyed by fire. The spring had been drifted over with sand, evidently during one of the sandstorms not uncommon in that region. – [HUGHES].

Appendix E

SOME MINES IN THE HILLS

On the west side of Deadwood Creek in Hidden Treasure and Blacktail Gulches discoveries were made of a conglomerate, composed of quartz gravel, schist and various kinds of wash cemented together with a kind of binder resembling iron oxide in colors, and some of this was extremely rich. The pay in this was found in streaks similar to the gravel in a placer claim. The first machinery for the reduction of ores was introduced by Captain C. V. Gardner, and was known as a Bolthoff Ball Pulverizer. It consisted of a revolving hollow cylinder in which were steel balls, intended to crush the ore introduced with them as they tumbled from side to side with the cylinder's revolutions. This machine was not a success in its operation on the ore of the Hidden Treasure, where it was introduced, and soon gave way to a ten-stamp mill – also introduced by Captain Gardner and his partners, who owned the mine named.

During the year 1876, several other stamp mills were brought in, the heavy machinery being transported from Cheyenne by bull and mule trains; and before the opening of winter quartz mining and milling had become a very important industry of the Hills. During this winter discoveries of large bodies of ores containing good values in gold were made in the Bald Mountain country at the head of Deadwood Creek. So refractory, however, were the ores in character that the values could not be extracted by stamping and amalgamation, the process used in treating what were known as the free-milling ores; and until a smelter was introduced and later the chlorination and cyanide processes for treatment of the siliceous ores were perfected, little gold was obtained from them.

With the improvement of those processes the mines of the Bald Mountain district and those of like character in the Ruby Basin district began to add appreciably to the gold output, and since have swelled the aggregate by many millions.

In the Bear Butte district, eight miles east of Deadwood, galena ores were found, some of which were rich in silver; from two or three of the mines some shipments were made to Colorado smelters, but the total product never was important; and with the decline in the price of silver, work on the mines practically ceased. The town of Galena was organized and at a later date another, named Virginia City, was laid out on Bear Butte Creek in the hope that development of the silver mines might warrant growth; but this hope never was realized and Galena is now nothing more than a post office, while the name Virginia City never more is heard.

In Rochford district in the Central Hills the Standby mine was located in '78 by Rochford, Nyswanger and others, and seemed to give promise of developing into a really valuable mine. It was sold to a company and a sixty-stamp mill erected and operated for a time, but without profit; though quite a town grew up in the hope of becoming the center of a great mining district, this hope was not realized. The district and camp were named for my friend and partner.

The Uncle Sam mine, located on Elk Creek about fifteen miles from Deadwood, promised well for a time, and turned out some very good ore. An excess of water made it impossible to operate it at a profit to any considerable depth.

In the Carbonate district, ten miles west of Deadwood, the Iron Hill mine created great excitement for a time. It yielded quite an amount of very rich ore, the principal values of which were in silver; and a silver mill and smelter were introduced for their treatment. Soon a boom camp grew up; and largely because of the belief that a veritable bonanza had been found, a mining exchange was organized in Deadwood —where were daily enacted scenes rivaling those of the New York Stock Exchange or the Chicago Wheat Pit. The working out of the richer ores of the Iron Hill and the decline in the value of silver caused a drop in the price of the stock from a maximum of nine dollars to a few cents per share; and the spree was over. It is estimated that during the time of its operation the Iron Hill yielded approximately one million dollars.

The Wasp mine, the Cleopatra and several others, the ores of which were treated with cyanide, yielded amounts of bullion important in the aggregate; but as they were horizontal deposits of no great thickness, a few years at most sufficed to work them out.

Second only to the great Homestake in importance have been the properties of the Golden Reward, Horseshoe, Trojan and Portland companies in the Ruby Basin and Bald and Green Mountain districts; they have yielded many millions in gold and enriched the men who had the faith and perseverance to develop them through many difficulties and discouragements. Vast bodies of siliceous ores still lie undeveloped in the district adjoining on the west, but of a character so rebellious that it still remains for science to devise a process by which they may be profitably treated.

The great Homestake, now developed to a depth of more than two thousand feet, and apparently of undiminished width and value, remains as it has been for forty years or more – the backbone of the Black Hills mining industry – and certainly among the greatest, if not the very greatest, of the gold mines of the world. – [HUGHES].

Appendix F

ANCESTRY OF RICHARD B. HUGHES

The oldest ancestor of Richard Brown Hughes, of whom there is any record but whose name is uncertain, was his great grandfather, born in Ireland about 1730. The family had lived for several generations in the parish of Errigal-Truagh in the county of Armagh; but in the middle of the eighteenth century, this ancestor and his brother left their unproductive farm in search of a better livelihood. The ancestor settled in Trough in the county of Monaghan and married a McKenna.[1] One son of this union, Patrick, was born in Cavan-Montray, County Monaghan, the other, Michael, perhaps born there also, was the grandfather of Richard B. Hughes. There were also four sisters.

The two brothers, Patrick and Michael, rented farms together in Armagh and later in Annaloghan in County Tyrone. They left Ireland and came together to Pennsylvania about 1818 or 1819.

Patrick Hughes was born about 1761 and died 11 April 1837 in Chambersburg, Pennsylvania. He married Margaret McKenna in Ireland. She was born there about 1766 and died in Chambersburg, Pennsylvania, 30 September 1830. He settled in Chambersburg where the family owned and operated a brewery until it was closed at the advent of Prohibition.

Patrick and Margaret had seven children, all born in County Tyrone, Ireland. Two children, Mary and Peter, were born and died in Ireland; two older sons were named Michael and Patrick; and the third son, John Joseph (1797-1864), entered the priesthood and was ordained in Pennsylvania in 1826.[2] He became the first Archbishop of New York and founder of St. Patrick's Cathedral. A sister, Ellen (1806-1866), entered the Sisters of Charity in 1825, receiving the name of Sister Mary Angela. She founded New York's first mission and the city's first Catholic hospital, St. Vincent's. In 1885 she was elected mother general.[3] Another sister, Margaret, married William Rodrique.

Michael Joseph Hughes was born 1772 in County Tyrone, Ireland and died 10 August 1862 in Juniata Township, Bedford County, Pennsylvania. He married (1) in Ireland a woman whose name is not known. They had five children, Nancy, Mary, James, Sarah, and Susan. He married (2) Mar-

---

[1] John R. G. Hassard, *Life of The Most Reverend John Hughes, D. D., First Archbishop of New York*, (New York: D. Appleton and Company, 1866), 11.
[2] "Notable Irish-Americans" in *The Irish-American Almanac & Green Pages*, 69-70.
[3] New Catholic Encyclopedia.

garet Mary McGirr (called Mary), who was born 1791 in Ireland and died 11 May 1888 in Pennsylvania.

Michael was a prosperous farmer in Ireland, but a large part of his prosperity was due to proceeds from his business of "moonshining."[4] Michael probably came to Pennsylvania about 1819, then returned to Ireland for a time, finally immigrating with his family in 1826. They went first to Chambersburg before settling in New Baltimore, Somerset County, Pennsylvania, where some of Mary McGirr's relatives were already established.

As in Ireland, Michael was soon operating a still, and the family continued to do so for two more generations.[5] Michael first purchased land near New Baltimore, and later 260 acres in Napier Township, Bedford County.

Michael and Mary had eight children, the first four born in Ireland: Catherine T. (1817-1888), Margaret (1819-1902), Rosanna (1823-1896), Michael J. (1823-1897), Philip (d.y.), John Joseph (1829-1905), Francis Patrick (1831-1904) and Theresa (1834-1907).

Michael J. Hughes, son of Michael Joseph Hughes and father of Richard Brown Hughes, was born 18 September 1823 in Dromore, Ulster, County Tyrone, Ireland and died 26 November 1897 in West Point, Nebraska. He married Mary Lucille Hite, of German and French descent, the daughter of John Hite, who fought in the Revolution, and Maria Magdalina Lang.

In 1851 Michael Joseph gave his son, Michael J., 85 acres of land, perhaps to encourage him to settle nearby, as family tradition described Michael Jr. as being somewhat "adventurous." But by 1857 he had sold this property to his brother John and moved to Somerset County; from there the family went to Cumberland, Maryland, where they kept a hotel until 1864; then lived in Dixon and Peoria, Illinois; and they finally settled in West Point, Nebraska.[6] Adventurous he must have been to have journeyed from Nebraska to the Black Hills in 1877 to join his son and to prospect there for several years.

Michael J. Hughes and Mary Lucille Hite had seven children. Mary Euphrasie (1848-1850); Anna (Annie) Catherine Marie (1850-1918), married John Henry Talt; Michael Joseph (1853-1910), married Mary Elizabeth Gahagan; Richard Brown (1856-1930), married Martha Agnes Lewis; Mary (Mollie) Theresa (1858-1941), married Ward N. Brayton; Margaret Jane (b.&d. 1861); and Ellen Jane (1862-1864).

Martha Agnes Lewis, wife of R. B. Hughes, was born 31 March, 1864, in Harvard, Illinois and died 4 July, 1933 in Rapid City, South Dakota. Her parents were William Lewis, born 10 November, 1828 in Edwardsburg, Ontario, Canada, and Mary Ann McDonald, born 1829 in Crysler, Ontario, Canada, and died 22 February, 1902, in Spearfish, South Dakota.

---

[4] Daniel Talt, *Michael Joseph Hughes; 1772-1862*, 1984, 2. Mr. Talt, of Freemont, CA, is the great-great grandson of Michael Joseph Hughes.
[5] *Ibid*, 3.
[6] Doane Robinson, *History of South Dakota* (B. F. Bowen & Co., 1904).

Index

Index

ALLEN, W: 115
American Horse, Chief: fatally wounded, McGillycuddy operates on, 144
Ammerman, Doc: 287
Amusements: *see* Deadwood
Anchor (Dak.): 81
Annaloghan: county of Tyrone in Ireland, 291
Annie Creek: 65
Antelope: in great numbers, 28
Argue Brothers (John & George): 85, 287
Armagh: county in Ireland, 291
Ashton, George: 134
Atlantic (IA): 207
Ayres, George V: diary, 118

BABBIT: ambushed by Indians, 38
Bald Mountain: 63-65, 95, 289, 290
Bangs, Judge: 231
Barnett, Gene: driver of treasure coach, 204
Bartholomew, J. S.: publisher of *Central Herald*, 86
Bear Butte Creek: 58, 137, 160, 187, 289
Bear Lodge: 100; hunting trip, 160-73
Bears: grizzly in Deadwood, 64, 68; disrupt camp, 191
Beaver Creek: 64; camp, 67
Bedford County (PA): 292
Belcher: claim, 92
Belding, John: 85; knew Bridger, 287
Belle Fourche River: 106; valley, 285
Bennett, Granville G.: federal judge, 87
Beulah (WY): 171
Big Foot: *see* Indians
Bismarck Tribune: quoted, 124

Black cat: 195
Black Hillers: leaving Hills, 13-14, 29, 151; going north, 47
Black Hills: described, xii-xiii; gold in, xiii, 2; whites forbidden, 2; tickets to, 4; loom in sight, 35; in general, 276-77; timber in, 277
Black Hills expeditions: Custer's, 2; "Gordon Party," 2; Jenney, 3, 249; Kansas men, 9; wagon train, 13-14; returning to States, 19-20; warned against going in, 23; from Sioux City, 32; from Powder River and Big Horn country, 276-77; Big Horn party, 278; Montana men, 285-88
Black Hills Pioneer: 118
Black Hills Pioneers: 260; cabin, 260
Blacktail Gulch: 79, 96, 158, 200, 278
Blanchard, A. S: discovery of gold in Deadwood, 75
Blodgett, Samuel: 75
"Bloody Dick:" *see* Dick Seymour
Bobtail Creek: 75, 77, 79, 93
Boland, John A.: 134
Booth, S. M: 200
Box Elder Creek: 57, 224
Brenn, Milton: 255
Brennan, John R.: 114-15, 134; stage agent, 205; a founder of Rapid City, 225
Bridger, Jim: 287-88
Briggs, Rachel: killed by Indians, 6
Brinton and Hoatson: 193, 196
Broughiers (John and Charles): 123
Brown, Dick ("Banjo Dick"): 82
Brown, Isaac: killed by Indians, 158
Brown, "Ten Die": 153-55

Bruguier, Theophile: 123
Bryant, Frank: explores Hills, 75
Buffalo Gap (Dak.): camp at, 36, 116; 209, 275
Buffalo hunters: 16
Bullock, Seth: 85; joins posse, 206; 285-86, 287
Bullwhackers: 18
Buntline, Ned: *see* E. Z. C. Judson
Burden (KS) *Times*: carries story of Tull, 281-82
Burke, Martha Jane Canary (Calamity Jane): 122, 123
Burns: captain of wagon train, 14, 19; makes flour deal, 23, 45; arrives in Custer, 45
Burns, Mrs.: in wagon train, 13
Burt, Dick: 201
Burt, Major: speaks for Crook, 148

CALAMITY JANE: *see* Burke
Caldwell, Cal: 85
California Joe: *see* Milner
Camp Crook: *see* Crook City, Pactola
Camp Robinson (NE): 22
Campbell, Hugh: killed, 203
Canary, Martha Jane: *see* Burke
Canyon Springs (WY): 199; holdup, 201-08
Carbonate district (Dak.): 290
Carea, C. G. *see* Charley Carey
Carey: lawyer, 88
Carey, Charley: 200-01, 203-07
Carmack, Colonel: 87, 223
Carney, James: 115
Carr, Tommy: in tunnel accident, 106-108; death, 108-09; recorder, 110
Carrigan, Dennis: owner of dog, 139
Carty, John R: trial, 116-121
Casey, Lieut: killed by Indian, 248-50

Castle Creek: 55, 193
Castleton: abandoned camp, 195
Caulfield: lawyer, 88
Cavan-Montray: county of Monaghan in Ireland, 291
Centennial Prairie: 116
Centennial Valley: 172
Central (Dak.): 81
Chambers, Pete: 189-90
Chambersburg, PA: 291
Chapline, A. B.: 105, 120
Cheyenne and Black Hills: stage line, 202; telegraph line, 151
Cheyenne *Democratic Leader*: quoted, 124
Cheyenne River: camp, 33, midnight alarm, 33-34; 55; 205; 224; 247; 249; 275
(Chicago) Northwestern (railroad): 226
Chimney Rock (NE): 15
City Creek (Deadwood, Dak.): brush shack on, 63; 74, 136
Claggett: companion of Twain, 87
Clemens, Samuel L. (Mark Twain): 87
Cleveland, Pres. Grover: 251
Coleman: locator of DeSmet lode, 92
Collins, Charley: founded *The Champion*, 85
"Colorado Charley": *see* Utter
Cook, Ed: stage superintendent, 205
Corson: first chief justice, 87
Court House Buttes (NE): 15, 274-75
Crawford, Capt. Jack: head of Custer Minute Men, 43, 50
Crazy Horse: epitaph, 136
Crime: murders in Black Hills, 114, 115; trial of Carty, 116, 121; trial of McCall, 121-27; murder of Hickok, 121-27; Indians murder men at Rapid

INDEX 297

City, 134; sharpers in Deadwood, 152-56; mining swindles, 235-45; road agents rob stagecoaches, 199-208; horse stolen, 201; stage hold-up by Bradley, 261

Crook, Gen. George: calls miners' meeting at Custer Park, 41; camp named for, 55, 123, 143; comes to Deadwood, 143-50; ordered to leave Black Hills, 150; Carey with, 200, men join command, 277, 278

Crook City (Pactola, Dak.): 55, 99, 143, 209, 278

Crow Creek: 163

Cummings, A. B.: 229

Cummings, E. B.: 231

Custer, Gen. George A.: *Life on the Plains*, 122; massacre, 105, old regiment at Fort Meade, 224; Seventh, 247

Custer (Custar, Dak.): 19, 22; train arrives, 41; townsite company organized, 41, 42; first town in Hills, 42-47; Indian troubles, 115-16; first church service, 118; store in, 260; 275-76

Custer (Dak.) *Chronicle:* 133

Custer Minute Men: 43-45

Custer Peak: 189

DAVIS, Dep.-Marshal I. C. (Jack): 116-121

Davis, Scott: shotgun messenger, 203-04

Dawson, A. R. Z.: 105, 222, 228

Day, Hon. Merritt H.: 227

Deadwood (Dak.): 58-60; build shack in, 63; named, 67; 70; townsite laid out, 78; growth, 78-79; 81; amusements, 82-84; newspapers, 85-87; lawyers, 87-88; Fourth of July celebration, 103-105; gambling house "Number Ten," 124; described by Finerty, 145-46; receives Crook and his men, 148; in touch with Crook, 149; Langrishe theatre, 152; dens of vice, 153-56; market for game, 158; 187-88, 199, 201; destroyed by fire, 213-14; South Deadwood Hose Company, 214; 255, 276, 277

Deadwood Creek: 75, 77, 78, 91, 112

Deadwood Gulch (Dak.): gold discovered, 3; exploration, 75-76; discoverers of, 81

Deadwood stage line: 195

Decker, Gene: journalist, 87

Deegan, Tim: 160-61

Denver Brand Book: quoted, 144-46

DeSmet, Father: xiii; mining claim named for, 92; 93, 117

Devil's Tower National Monument: 165

Dietrich, Charles H.: 109-11

Dimsdale, Thomas J.: author of *Vigilantes of Montana,* 182

Dodge, Col. R. I.: named Devil's Tower, 165

Dog: Snoozer, 137-139

Donan, Col. Pete ("Pat"): 86

EDGERTON, Judge: 227-28

Elizabethtown (Dak.): 59, 81, 105

Elk: killed, 66

Elk Creek: camp, 58; valley 224; Uncle Sam mine, 290

Elkhorn (NE): 276

Elkhorn Prairie: *see* Reynolds' Prairie

Engh, Alex: partner of Manuel brothers, 91

Englesby, Joe: 3

Enos mill: 193

Erquot, John: 134

Errigal-Truagh: parish in County Armagh, Ireland: 291

FALSE ALARM: 33-35
False Bottom: *see* stampedes
Farnum, Judge: of Deadwood court, 128, 129-32, 153
Farrell, Andy: 160-61
Finerty, John (Long): writes of Crook's visit, 145
Firearms: frontier, 1, 8, 44; Maynard rifle, 69
Fish: in streams, 55
Flaherty, John: locator of DeSmet lode, 92, 117
Flormann, Bob: 242
Flour: prices, 187
Flynn: founder of *The News,* 85
Food: prices high, 187
Fort Laramie (WY Terr.): 120
Fort Meade: 247
Fort Pierre (Dak.): 206. 277
Fountain City (Dak.): 81, 105
Fourth of July: celebration, 103-05
Franklin (Rocky Mountain Frank): 254
Frawley: lawyer, 88
French Creek: 48, 193, 275, 277

GALENA (Dak.): 289
Gambler: 80, 121-22; Melodeon gambling house, 186
Game: wildlife, 68, 277
Gardner, Capt. C. V.: 133-34; introduced Bolthoff Ball Pulverizer, 289
Garretson, Fannie: 83-84
Gay, Alfred: 3, 75, 81
Gay, William (Bill): 3, 81
Gayville (Dak.): 81; mine accident, 106-08; crime in, 116-17; murder in, 278
Geltner, "Ad": 51
Geltner brothers: 199-200
Giant: 91

Gillette, Uriah: 204
Gilmer and Salisbury: 203
Gold mining: methods, 48-50; yield, 52; in Deadwood Gulch, 75-77; nuggets found, 76; $35 nugget, 267
Gold Run: 75, 76-77, 79, 81
Golden Gate: 81, 92
Golden Star: 91
Golden Terra: 93
Goodale, Doug: 200, 206-07
Gooding: lawyer, 88
Gordon, Mrs. Ralph: 134
Gordon party: 2
Gossage, Joseph B.: 133, 223
Gough, Andy "Red Cloud": 64-67, 70
Graham: lawyer, 88
Great Northern Railroad: 256
Gregg, Harry: 85
Green Mountain: 65, 290
Greenwood mine: swindle, 240-43
Gruard (Frank): scout for Crook, 143, 147

HAGGARD: 3
Hall, Jesse: 16; 69
Halley, James: telegrapher, 151
Hammerquist, Peter: 205
Hanley, Dan: partner of Hughes, 194
Hansen, George; 75
Harney Peak: 48, 276
Hassler, George: court treatment, 129-32
Hat Creek Station (WY): 127, 199, 202
Hawley, N. H.: 134
Haxby, Mrs. Charles: pioneer, 260
Hay: price, 64, 161
Henderson, Bart: 85, 286-87
Hickok, J. B. ("Wild Bill"): murdered, 121-22
Hicks, James: 3

INDEX

Hidden Treasure Gulch: 74, 109, 111, 185, 187
Hill, Galen (Gale): 203
Hill, Ruth Brennan (Mrs. Web Hill): 134
Hill City (Dak.): deserted, 51-52
Hinch, Jack: murdered, 116-21
Hoatson: *see* Brinton and Hoatson
Holland, Charles: killed, 158
Hollis: Carty's lawyer, 120
Horsehead Creek: 29, 211
Hughes, Clarence W: poem by, xiv; family, 134
Hughes, John Joseph: first Archbishop of New York, 291
Hughes, Sr. Mary Angela: founder of St. Vincent's Hospital in New York, 291
Hughes, Mary L. Hite (Mrs. Michael J.): 189
Hughes, Michael Joseph: grandfather of R. B. Hughes: 291; family, 291-92
Hughes, Michael J: comes to Hills, 189; family, 189; 192, 192-93, 194-96
Hughes, Patrick: 291
Hughes, Richard B: teacher, 1; bound for Black Hills, 1-5; does camp cooking, 13; diary, 265-74; party leaves train, 27-32; arrives Custer, 42; from Custer to Deadwood, 48-56; panning, 52; in danger, 53-55; plants trout, 55; camp at City Creek, 63-64; prospecting, 64-70; moves to Pocket Gulch, 74; conflict over claim, 92-93; interest in Justice claim, 92; sold interest to Nichols, 93; ore tested, 95; prospecting, 103; helps build ditch, 111-12; interviews Merrick of *Pioneer*, 113; covers Carty trial, 116-21; writes story of Brant Street, 126; gets Hassler out of jail, 131-32; newspaper reporter in Black Hills, 133-37; camp at City Creek, 136; makes buckskin suit, 139-40; hunting trip, 157-58; to Bear Butte, 160; to Bear Lodge, 163-73; returns to *Pioneer,* 173; cabin clean-up, 177; prospecting Central Hills, 178-88; prevents murder, 182-85; mountain fever, 182-85 return to Deadwood, 182-85; partnership dissolved, 181-82; Bear Butte prospect, 187; moves with father to North Boxelder, 189; hunting trip, 189-91; near mine sale, 193-96; reports holdup for *Pioneer,* 201; home for visit, 209-14; back to Deadwood, 214; editor of *Evening News,* 221-23; marriage, 224; editor of *Rapid City Journal,* 223-24; activities, 223-25; elected to legislature, 225-32; appropriation for School of Mines, 229-32; worthless ore samples, 242; World's Fair collection, 251; appointed Surveyor General, 251-52; runs Cleopatra, 252-53; in charge of "Holy Terror," 253-54; organizes traction company, 254-56; invested in cattle, 256-57; to Pacific Coast, 257; returns to Rapid City, 258-60; death and burial, 260; family, 260; poem by, 260; letters to *West Point* (NE) *Republican,* 274-78; visit from Tull, 281-82; ancestors, 291-92
Hughes, Mrs. Richard B.: 213; owns property, 258; family, 219
Hughes, Richard L.: introduction by; xii-xiii; family, 259

Hunters: professional, 167, 170
Hunting expeditions: 157-173

INDIAN COMMISSION: at Spotted Tail Agency, 148-49
Indians: friendly chiefs, 7; depredations, 13-14; boys expert with bows and arrows, 20; dancing, 21; visit camp, 28-29; kill men on Red Canyon trail, 30; attacked trains, 30; kill Wood and attack train, 37-38; shoot oxen, 40-41; wound "Smoky" Jones, 42-43; 44; tracks, 53; Crow Agency, 101; Custer battle, 105-06; murder men near Rapid City, 134-35; attacked by Crook's men near Slim Buttes, 143; troubles with, 149-150; 158; 169; sign "cession treaty," 187-88; 199; Battle of Wounded Knee, 246-250
Ingalls: promoter of Pony Express, 80
Irion, Jimmy: 44, 50, 137
Irish Gulch: named, 158
Iron Creek: 64, 67

JAMES, EMMETT: 205
Jones, G. W.: 135
Jones, "Gassy:" 4
Jones, "Smoky:" wounded, 42-43
Judson, E. Z. C. (Ned Buntline): 122

KANSAS: party from Cowley County, 9
Kelley, Bill: 9
"Kentuck:" a sharper, 153-54
Keystone District: 253
Kingsley: Lawyer, 88
Koenigsberg Brothers: 85
Kubler, Carol: 133
Kubler, Joe: 133, 159

Kubler, Joe Jr.: 133
Kubler, William: 133
Kuykendall, Judge (William): 105
Kyle, James H: 228-29

LAFLIN: 240-41
Lake, R. C: 151
Lame Johnnie Creek: 211
Langrishe, Jack: writes poem, 101; on *Pioneer*, 135, 152
Lardner, William: recorder of Lost Mining District, 76, 92
Lawrence County (So. Dak.): 230
Lawson, James M: 252
Lawyers: *see* Deadwood
Lead (Dak.): 75, 158, 223, 255-56
Leedy, Carl: 134
Lemmon, George: 51
LeRoy, Kitty: 84
Lewis, Mattie A: see Mrs. Richard B. Hughes
Lewis, William: 213
Little Spearfish: 67
Livermore, L. S: 134-35
Livestock: buffalo grass, 165
Lodge Pole Creek (NE): 8
Loomis: tramp printer, 174
Lost Mining District (Dak.): 76
Loucks, H. L.: populist, 229
Lowe, Richard: 75

MAGUIRE, Judge H. N: names Pactola, 55
Mail: distribution, 80-81
Manuel, Fred: 91
Manuel, Moses: 91
Martin, Eben W: 88
Martin, W. P: names Rapid City, 115
Mason: lawyer, 88
Massey, Capt. Bill: carries ball that killed Wild Bill, 124
May, Ernest: 85
McBride, Frank: outlaw, 200, 203-04, 207

INDEX   301

Mc Call, Jack: 121, 124-25
McCandless (McCanles): affair in Nebraska, 121
McCarthy (McCarty): 116, 278
McClintock, John S: *Pioneer Days in the Black Hills*, 75
McCormack, Representative: 230
McDonald, Mr: of Sidney (NE), 6; of West Point (NE), 274
McGillycuddy, Dr. V. T: notebook quoted, 144, 246, 249-50
McGregor, James H: author, 248
McGirr, Margaret Mary: grandmother of R. B. Hughes, 291-92
McGuigan, Jim: 192
McKay, Ed: 3, 75
McKenna, Margaret: 291
McKinney, Doctor: 105
McKinnis, Charley: 222
McKirahan, Joe: 158
"McKune:" an undesirable character, 181-84
McLaughlin, Judge: 87
Medicine Wells: 166
Mercur (UT): mill, 253
Merrick, A. W: 133
Metz, Mr. and Mrs. Charles: killed by Indians, 6
Mexican: decapitates dead Indian, 143
Meyer, "Big Louie:" known in Montana, Idaho and the Black Hills, 178-85
Meyer, C. W: on *Pioneer*, 135
Miles, Gen. Nelson A: arrives in Rapid City, 247-48
Miller: founder of *The News*, 85
Miller, Charley: as hunter, 161-76
Miller, J. K. P: 85
Miller, Judge: 105
Mills, Capt: 147
Milner, Moses E. (California Joe): 123, 134

Miners: supplies, 7-8; parlance, 48; claims, 76; wages, 79, 151; equipment, 79; courts, 128-29
Ming, Tom: 221
Mining Claims: Homestake, 75, 91, 93, 222, 240, 290; Old Abe, 91; Standby, 192; Montezuma Hill, 190; Moro and Como, 192; the California, 193-96; Number 18 below Discovery, 199; Cleopatra on Squaw Creek, 252-53; "Holy Terror," 253-54; Mountain Tiger, 274; Hidden Treasure, 289; Uncle Sam, 290; Iron Hill, 290; Wasp, 290; Golden Reward, 290; Horseshoe, Trojan, and Portland, 290; others, 77; on Deadwood, Gold Run, Blacktail, and Bobtail, 77; swindles, 235-45
Mining Machinery: 289
Minnilusa Historical Association: 134
Mitchell Creek: 206
Montana: mining districts, 101
Montana Lake (Dak.-WY): 163
Montana men: mining camps, 76; come to Dakota, 84-85, 238, 285-88
Moody, Charley: 85-88
Moody, Judge Gideon C.: 227-28
Moody, Jim: 9, 115
Moon, Thomas: 75
Morris, Jacob: 260
Moulton, Frank: 205
Mountain City (Fountain, Dak.): 105
Mountain Lion: steak, 180
"Munch:" mare, 179-80, 181, 185
Murkle, Dan: 3

NEGRO: woman killed by Indians, 6
Nelson, John: 56, 98

New Denver (Dak.): 115; *see also* Rapid City
Newspapers: Deadwood, 85-87
Newton's Fork: 205
Nicholson, O: 135
Noble, Frank: of Boston, 287
North Grand River: Cattle Ranch on, 256
North Platte (NE): 5
North Platte River: 212, 275
Northern Pacific Railroad: 256
"Nutshell Bill:" 186
Nyswanger, Aaron: 85, 192

OLSON, James C: *History of Nebraska*, 111
O'Neill: locator of DeSmet lode, 92
O'Sullivan, Pete: 85
Outlaws: 199, 201
Overman, A. M: 105

PACTOLA (Dak.): 55
Palmetto-American Flag: 91
"Pancake Bill:" a sharper, 152-55
Parker: lawyer, 88
Parmer's Gulch: 276
Patterson, J. W: 135
Pearson, J. B: 3
Pearson, John: 75-76
Peierman, James: 75
Peirce, Ellis T. (Doc): 45, 205
Pendleton, Thomas: 135
Pennington, Governor John L: 150
Pennington County (Dak.): 204
Pettigrew, R. F: 228
Pickens: ambushed by Indians, 38
Pinchot, Gifford: 285
Pine Ridge Agency (Dak.): 249
Pine Ridge Reservation: 248
Pioneer, (Deadwood): 135, 136, 145
Piper, Mr. and Mrs. H. A: 223
Plowman: lawyer, 88

Pocket Gulch: 74; cabin built in, 74; 106, 111, 136
Political campaign of 1880 (Dak.): 221-22
Pollock, Capt. Edwin: in Hills, 2
Polo Gulch: 99
Poorman Gulch: 157
Potato Gulch; prospecting trip to, 64-72; 102
Pratt, J. G: freighter, cattleman, 17
Pratt and Ferris: 17
"Preacher Smith:" *see* Rev. Henry Watson Smith
Prospecting trips: to Potato Gulch and Nigger Gulch, 64-72; dry gulches, 73-76; nuggets found, 76
Pumpkin Creek (NE) : 212, 275

RAPID CITY (Dak.): Indian raid, 114; townsite laid out, 114-15; 134, 151, 255, 259; fire department, 225; railroad reaches, 226; home of Hughes family, 252, 258, 259; Pioneer Cabin, 260; Fortnightly Club and Ladies Group, 260; American House in, 287
Rapid City Journal: first issue, 87; 133, 224-25, 248-49
Rapid Creek: 53, 55-56, 59, 158, 205
Red Canyon: 30, 32, 116, 202
"Red Cloud:" see Gough, Andy
Red Cloud Indian Agency (NE): 17, 20, 23, 143, 274, 275
Red Water: *see* Sand Creek
Red Willow camp: 18
Religion: first church service in Custer City, 118
Remington, Frederic: accompanies Gen. Miles, 248
Remington rifle: 127
Reppert, Abe: 189, 192
Reynolds' Prairie: 204

Richardson, Foster: 111, 157-59
Rochford, John: 214
Rochford, Michael D. (Mike): to Black Hills, 1-5; 7, 10, 21, 31, 33-35; in Custer, 42; 53, 63, 70; on Wolf Mountain stampede, 99-01; 92; sinking shaft, 109-10; 136; on hunting trip, 163-76; tries whisky, 169; partner of "McKune," 181; partnership with Hughes dissolved, 181; 187; home to Nebraska, 209-13; in California, 257
Rochford (Dak.): first cabin, 192; 193,195,214
Rockerville (Dak.): 205
"Rocky Mountain Frank:" see Franklin
Rocky Mountain News (Denver, Colo.): quoted, 118, 122; story of Crook's Deadwood visit, 145
Roosevelt, Pres. Theodore: 286
Route: Sidney, 6-7, 10, 284; Red Canyon and Buffalo Gap trails, 13, 116; difficult, Custer to Deadwood, 48-56; Ft. Pierre stage route, 143, 277; Cheyenne to Deadwood, 199; Deadwood to Sidney, 209-213; Red Canyon to Cheyenne, 277
Ruby Basin: 289-90
Rumney, Colonel: preaches in Melodeon (Deadwood), 185-86; buried at Myersville, 186
Running Water camp: 19

SAINT CLAIR, "Ponca George:" 4
"Salting:" 98
Sam's mine: 93
Sand Creek (Dak.-WY): 165, 255
Sawpit Gulch: 187
Schafer, Bill: 51
Scott, Dan: reporter, 87

Scott, Gen. Hugh L.: opposes name of Devil's Tower, 165
Scott, Samuel (Sam): 134-35; plants trout, 55; lays out Rapid City townsite, 115
Seig, Archie: 193
Seymour, Dick ("Bloody Dick"): Pony Express man, 80; 122
Shaughnessey, Ed: killed, 83
Sheeptail gulch: 200
Sheppard, Jim: 9, 64, 115
Sheridan (SD): 52
Sherman, General: transmits instructions from President to Crook, 150
Sidney (NE): 6-10, 12, 209
Silver Creek district (Dak.): 178, 189, 193
Simmons, A. J.: 85
Simonton, A. H: elected judge, 119
Sitting Bull: 106
Slade, Joseph A. (Jack): 84, 182
Slate Creek: 55
Slim Buttes: Sioux village attacked, 144; 147
Smith, "Cap.": shotgun messenger, 201, 202-04
Smith, "Buckskin" Frank: 44, 50
Smith, Rev. Henry Watson (Preacher Smith): 118-19
Smith's Canyon: 193
Snake Creek camp: 19
Snider, Major W. R: editorial writer, 86
Snoozer: dog, 137-39
Songs: 82-83
South Bend (Dak.): 81
South Dakota: politics, 225-32; School of Mines, 229-32
Spaulding, John T. (Buckskin Johnnie): 16, 38, 45, 64-70
Spear, Al: 200; caught and sentenced, 207

Spearfish (Dak.); 110, 162-63, 252, 255
Spearfish Canyon: 64-66; "deadening" in, 67; camp in, 70
Spearfish Creek: 66, 172
Spencer, Johnny ("Coal Oil"): 151-52
Spillner, Billy: on hunting trip to Bear Lodge, 162-73
Spring, Agnes Wright, v, vi, ix, 80, 199, 202
Spring Creek: camp, 48-51, 52, 53; 193, 276, 277
Stagecoach: passenger, 209-12; drivers, 210, 212
Stage line (Sidney): 121, 209-10
Stampedes: Hughes and partners "represent" on, 64; of '76, 94-96; to Polo Creek, 96-99; to Wolf Mountains, 99-102; False Bottom, 127-29
Stapleton, Con: 85, 287
Star, Sol: 85
Strahorn, Robert E: accompanies Crook, 145
Steel: lawyer, 87
Steele, Bill: in posse, 205
Stevens, John: 9, 42
Stevenson, C. G. D: of West Point, 276
Stocking, C. B: joins posse, 205
Stokes, George W: on *Pioneer*, 134
Stout, John: friend of Sam Tull, 282
Street, Brant: 126-27
Street, Dick: 126
Sweeney, Tom: 225, 242; waited on Gen. Miles, 247
"Sweetwater:" *see* Pumpkin Creek
Swineford, "Governor": 251

TALLENT, Annie D: 75-76, 97
Tallent, David G: 97
Tanning: deer hide, 139-40

Theater: *see* Deadwood
Thomas: lawyer, 87
Thompson, Alex: 41
Tomlins, W. C. (Spike): 16, 69, 158
Tower, Gilbert: owns ranch, 57; working on prospects, 194
Tracy, Joe: 222
Trainor, Bill: 117
Treasure: coach, 202, 203
Treaty: signed, February, 1877, 187
Tripp, Hon. Bartlett: 227
Trough: county of Monaghan in Ireland, 291
Tull, Sam: 9-10, 20; good shot, 21; 27; elected captain, 28; 31, 40, 64, 69; Sam's mine, 93; 177, 281-82
Twain, Mark: *see* Clemens
Two Bit Creek: 58; toll gate, 160

UNDERWOOD, Prof: mining expert, 235-36
Union Pacific Railroad: 4, 199, 212
Utter, Charlie: pony express carrier, 16, 122-23, 126
Utter, Steve: 122-23

VAN CISE: lawyer, 87
Van Fleet, William: goes to Black Hills, 1-5; 13, 63, 70, 109; prospecting, 136, 160; 177; partnership dissolved, 187
Vanderberg, Jim: 64
Vanderburger, James: 274
Virginia City, (Dak.): 160
Von Leuwitz, Lt. A. H: wounded, 144; leg amputated, 144

WALLACE, Capt. George D: 248
Ward, Capt. W. M: 204; arrests Goodale, 207
Warner, Porter: founded *Times*, 85

INDEX

Warren's Peak: 165
Water-holes: 13, 212
Weather: disagreeable, 73; heavy snows, 164-70; 176
Webster: founded *Enterprise*, 85
Weekly Pioneer (Deadwood): 133
Welch, Billy: stage driver, 212
Wells-Fargo: 201
West Point (NE) *Republican:* 1; publishes Hughes' letters, 276-80
Westfall, Ferdinand: 111, 157-59; death, 159
Whitbeck, L. F: newspaperman, 86; foreman of hose company, 214
White, "Pony": 123, 145
Whitehead, Charles: 43
Whitetail: 157
Whitewood Creek: vii, viii, 59, 75-76, 77, 79, 81, 105, 143, 158, 277-78
Whitfield, Dr: joins posse, 205; finds stolen bullion, 206
Whitton, J. M.: 87
Wilcox, Mrs. Orson: 203
"Wild Bill" Hickock: *see* Hickock
Willey, Smith: 193
Wilson: lawyer, 88
Wolf Mountains: *see* stampedes
Wood, W. H: 41
Wood, W. W: from Colorado, 111, 157
Worth, Howard: 205
Wounded Knee Battle: 246-50
Wyoming Historical Collections: quoted, 165

YANKTON (Dak.): 116, 120, 126, 249